Soul-psychic Sleuthing

Soul-psychic Sleuthing
Techinques of
Telepathy, Clairvoyance and Psychometry

Nandlal Vanvari
M.Sc.; M.Tech.; Ph.D.
Former Senior Member of IEEE

DK
PRINTWORLD
Publishers of Indian Traditions

Cataloging in Publication Data — DK
[Courtesy: D.K. Agencies (P) Ltd. <docinfo@dkagencies.com>]

Vanvari, Nandlal, 1940-
Soul-psychic sleuthing : techniques of telepathy, clairvoyance and psychometry / Nandlal Vanvari.
p. cm.
Includes bibliographical references (p.).
ISBN 9788124606506

1. Telepathy. 2. Clairvoyance. 3. Psychometry (Parapsychology) 4. Psychic ability. 5. Soul. I. Title.

DDC 133.8 23

ISBN: 978-81-246-0650-6 (HB) ISBN:81-246-0650-1
ISBN: 978-81-246-0651-3 (PB) ISBN:81-246-0651-X

First published in India in 2013

Printed and published by:
D.K. Printworld (P) Ltd.
Regd. Office : '*Vedaśrī*', F-395, Sudarshan Park
(Metro Station: Ramesh Nagar)
New Delhi – 110 015
Phones: (011) 2545 3975; 2546 6019; *Fax*: (011) 2546 5926
e-mail: indology@dkprintworld.com
Website: www.dkprintworld.com

Dedicated to

all those Mystics and Scientists

who unveil

The Beauty and Harmony

of

The Eternal on the Earth

Preface

In the 'New Age', soul-psychic sleuthing assumes a place of significance. The sleuthing, an integrated theme of this book, is the search for a method of assessment and study of human problems and their solutions.

Some people, being tormented by the sufferings of the world, are pining for mental peace, while others want to know how to solve the problems that arise in their daily lives. Some seek advice on worldly problems, while still others want guidance in their personal life.

Our universe is a sphere of activity. This activity to be creative demands the fine art of intelligence gathering, processing and its application. However, the state of the highest knowledge is so sublime and mysterious that it is difficult to reach it without the aid of self-sleuthing.

Soul-psychic sleuthing is a complicated subject having vivid scope for discourse and elucidation. Blaise Pascal said: "Since we cannot know all that is to be known of everything, we ought to know a little about everything." Presented here is that little.

> Camerado, this is no book,
> Who touches it, touches a Man . . .
> — *Walt Whitman*

Having touched the man, the text goes on discussing the three sleuthing techniques, viz. telepathy, clairvoyance and psychometry, in detail.

The sleuthing is also to achieve staggering powers, used down through the ages by the strong-willed and powerful men on the earth, to bend, control, command, rule people with the mighty powers of telepathy, clairvoyance, psychometry and magic (mass hypnotic spell).

However, "If one expects accurate information from clairvoyants, psychometrists, dream interpreters and seers, always, one might as well expect the Moon to be green cheese", said an unsung philosopher, "as a word of caution."

Learn that which is useful for your growth, and start practising it, and that which is beyond your grasp and interest, leave it for now.

I have gathered whatever information this book contains from, I may say, the four corners of the earth, and in presenting this information to those who desire to develop, I do so with the knowledge that I have understood to be desired part of this book. I earnestly request the reader for its conscientious study and application.

I have tried to avoid sexist language, either by using inclusive language, or else when appropriate by using he and she interchangably.

If the work is received with anything like favour, I shall be constantly on the watch to improve it, and honest criticism will be welcomed and carefully considered.

Contents

Preface vii

1. Sleuthing Circle 1
   - 1.1 Sleuthing Centre 6
   - 1.2 Sleuthing 11
   - 1.3 Sleuthing Techniques 29
   - 1.4 Sleuthing Sojourn 36
   - 1.5 Sleuthing Scope 49
2. Our Sleuths 55
   - 2.1 Carnal Eyes 59
   - 2.2 Mind's Eye 64
   - 2.3 Eye of Soul 77
   - 2.4 Hands 84
   - 2.5 Consultants 86
3. Telepathy 91
   - 3.1 Intuition 96
   - 3.2 ESP 98
   - 3.3 Thought Waves 103
   - 3.4 Telepathic Nervous System 115
   - 3.5 Development of Telepathic Faculty 121
   - 3.6 Telepathists 128

3.7	Trance-mediumship	128
3.8	Psychotronics	133
3.9	Psychokinesis	135
3.10	Telekinesis and Teleportation	139
3.11	Tulpa	140
3.12	Thoughtography	144
3.13	U.F.O.	145
3.14	Telepathic Voices of Dead	147
3.15	Telepathy of Rebirth	149
3.16	Telepathic Networks	152
3.17	Telepathic Sense	153
3.18	Telepathy's Truths	156
4.	Clairvoyance	165
4.1	Types and Order of Clairvoyance	168
4.2	Mystic Clairvoyance	173
4.3	Clairvoyance Development Techniques	174
4.4	Clairvoyants	183
4.5	Clairaudience	185
4.6	Clairsentience	187
4.7	Crystal-gazing and Clairvoyance	190
4.8	Dream Clairvoyance	192
4.9	Witchcraft Clairvoyance	199
4.10	Dzogchen	200
4.11	Seers and Mystics	201
4.12	Seen	207

5. Psychometry 209

5.1 Psychometry Talent Development 212

5.2 Investigation Technique 218

5.3 Predictive Psychometry 221

5.4 Telegnosis 222

5.5 Psychic Readings 224

5.6 Psychic Tracking 229

6. Sleuthing Oracle 239

Bibliography 267

Index 269

1

Sleuthing Circle

NATURE is so beautiful, so lovely . . . . There are animals and ants; there are birds and bees, bright stars, Sun, Moon, . . . milkyways. Should we activate our 'eye of the mind' we could explore beyond . . . touch and taste the fruits grown in the gardens of Heaven, and experience ecstasy! The whole universe outside us dwells in our innerness — the macrocosm in the microcosm (man). This is the activity sphere.

The activity sphere in the two dimensions represents the sleuthing circle. This circle having the same centre as our activity sphere will bisect in the activity sphere in the two hemispheres of good and bad, love and hate, hot and cold. . . .

At present, our sphere has gone topsy-turvy, life is in scurry, troubles and tensions, strife and worry are always shadowing us. Pollution gives problems, sewage water stinks, the green has gone and the sky is not blue, politicians keep lying and apathy hits us; is this the master plan that God drew? In these troubled times, life's ebbs and flows can be understood, seen from a larger perspective, accepted and acted upon to develop a healthy attitude for our overall growth and evolution.

Most people want to find a "magic key" or Aladdin's lamp that will grant all our wishes. We want to think that there's "some secret of life" that, could we but discover it, would instantly solve all our problems. Is soul-psychic sleuthing a solution?

The prevalence of paranormal faculties in human beings has been a marked feature of civilization from its earliest beginnings. The very fact that, notwithstanding the blasting tirades of sceptical writers during recent times and the chilling attitude of science, popular interest in the supernormal and the occult, instead of dying down, has augured upwards in an unprecedented spurt and even the erstwhile incredulous scientists and thinkers are being carried away by the wave, is proof enough to show that we are dealing here with a basic impulse in the human psyche, which modern knowledge mistakenly chose to ignore so far. The recrudescence of popular interest in the paranormal even in Russia should be enough to open our eyes to the fact that the lure of the supernatural and the numinous in the human mind is irresistible.

We have entered New Age. The 'New Age' is an adjective used for seekers of spiritual alternatives, they include mystics, occultists, psychologists, parapsychologists, ecologists and herbalists.

The seekers of one country and one faith no longer hesitate to learn the doctrines and texts of other faiths and to give trial to their methods and disciplines as they do to their own.

However, paranormal faculties are not the exclusive property of mediums, seekers and sensitives alone. They are not exhibited only in science chambers or in the presence of accredited mediums and psychics. Millions of people, in all walks of life all over the Earth, possess them in more or less degree. There are crowds of people who, at one time or the other, have premonitory dreams, myriads who have clairvoyant perception of other places or events, myriads who have unforgettable moments of lucidity and illumination.

We have the ability to discover an unlimited intelligence within ourselves when we choose to ponder over what Nature is, rather than always thinking of what comes to us by means of our senses — that is, what we see, hear, smell, taste and touch.

We need to stop and look inward and listen for instant. And behold, what marvellous things flow into our souls! What beauties flood our minds! What sweet harmonies of nature fill our ears! A moment ago we did not hear the music of birds, or the sweet soughing of the wind in treetops; we did not see the waving of the grass in the meadows; we were not conscious of the wondrous beauties all around us. For a moment we seem to be in another world, a world of unsurpassed loveliness, of sweetness, of harmony, a world free from care or jar or fret of any kind. Our thought world transforms the outer world to its likeness.

> The more faithfully you listen to the voice within you the better you will hear what is sounding outside. And only he who listens can speak.
> — Dag Hammerskjold

The inward-looking, watching, behaving, managing and living are to be developed into a system of soul-psychic sleuthing. The soul-psychic sleuthing is just a concept, an idea. In yoga traditions there is a concept of "*Brahman*". The soul-psychic sleuthing concept is the beginning of metaphysical realm having causation beyond physical, whereas realizing the concept of *Brahman* is the highest achievement. It is of very little use to have a concept, until it is transformed into a living experience. And, when the concept of *Brahman* is transformed to living experience, the vibrations committed by the person can alter everything with which they come in contact.

There is a story[1] about a swami that illustrates this point. When this swami first came to the *ashram* he was very much taken by the idea of *Brahman Om* — omnipotent, ominpresent, omniscient — the trascendental reality — God. He thought it was something one could realize instantaneously. So he asked Paramahamsaji how he could evolve quickly to the state of spiritual experience where he could realize *Brahman*. Paramahamsaji told him to begin with the simple idea of *Aham Brahmasmi*, 'I am *Brahman*'. He told the swami to practise this for at least one year in order to develop this idea with total intensity. The swami began the practice and towards the end of the year he came to Paramahamsaji and said, "I think I have grasped the idea. I am *Brahman*, you are *Brahman*, this *ashram* is *Brahman*, the person sitting beside you is *Brahman*. My whole perception has changed, all I can see is *Brahman* everywhere."

1. Swami Nirajananda Saraswati, *Yoga Darshan, Vision of the Yoga Upanishads*, Yoga Publication Trust, Munger, Bihar, India, 2002, p. 194.

Paramahamsaji said, "That is very interesting. Now go to the market to buy some vegetables." So the swami went to the market and he came very near to it, where he saw a very large number of people running in all directions. On asking, a man replied, "There is a mad elephant. Run!" Swami thought over it and said to himself, "Mad elephant, well I am also a mad swami. Let us see who wins. Perhaps my vibrations can alter the mood of the mad elephant." With this thought he sat down in the middle of the road and waited. He explained to himself very rationally that if you pour a glass of water into a bucket of water, the water from the glass will merge with the water in the bucket, and since he was a *Brahman* and the mad elephant was also *Brahman*, what would happen if two *Brahman*(s) clashed with each other? Nothing. One *Brahman* would merge with the other. So the elephant, which was not in a philosophical or spiritual mood, picked up the swami with its trunk and threw him as far as it could. A couple of days later, when swamiji returned from the hospital, Paramahamsaji said, "You forgot one thing, the man who told you to get out of the way was also *Brahman*, so you should have listened to him."

What this story conveys is that the idea of *Aham Brahmasmi* has to be converted into a force which emanates from the personality. In places where there is a high, vibrant spiritual energy, the attitude and behaviour of opposite forces are changed. A goat and a lion can drink from the same waterhole, forgetting their animosity towards each other. That is the transformation of an idea. We all live within the limits or dimensions of ideas, but are unable to convert these ideas into a living force. That requires 'harmonious control', where everything moves according to the laws of nature and the divine, where there is no control of human being, of the mind or of the desires. Everything is just the spontaneous, harmonious expression of higher force.

In order to come to this stage, where harmony is experienced at all levels of our personality, different ideas have to evolve further from the main concept of *Brahman*. Those ideas evolve in four dimensions: gross, subtle, causal, and transcendental; or physical, mental, psychic, and spiritual. These four areas or dimensions of human experience have to be integrated so that the physical energy and action is in harmony with the mental energy and movement, the mental expression is in harmony with the psychic investigations and experiences the spiritual or transcendental state of being: "I am what I am". This kind of harmony is essential for sleuthing to be converted from a system into a living experience.

One of the purposes, or the main purpose of sleuthing is to draw the mind of the Man away from viruses of vice and direct it to better his living-life.

The soul-psychic sleuthing philosophy has to be peculiarly sensitive to periodic differences. For, whereas you can make replica of an ancient statue, there is no possible replica of an ancient state of mind. There can be no nearer approximation than that which a masquerade bears to real life. There may be understanding of the past, but there is difference between the modern and ancient reactions to the same stimuli.

According to Ludwig Wittgenstein, "Philosophy is not a theory but an activity," and according to Plutarch, "Philosophy is an art of living." If we combine the two thoughts, "Our philosophy of soul-psychic sleuthing is not a theory but an activity — the art of living; your present to result in the evolved future."

We have Walter Gropius saying: "Only work which is product of inner compulsion can have spiritual meaning," which makes us to believe that 'soul-psychic sleuthing' is a spiritual excursion. The compulsion of such excursions is evident from the present differential and varying living standards.

The objective of soul-psychic sleuthing is to rise above the subjective and objective living, and a couple of men of integrity can certainly lead us to accomplish the task. John Gardner believes: "Men of integrity, by their very existence, rekindle the belief that as a people we can live above the level of moral squalor."

Soul-psychic illumination is a powerful mechanism for guiding and directing the destiny of millions of men. Because, even pseudo-prophets are able to enlist huge crowds of followers and admirers, therefore, let us observe inwardly, analyze and act within the ambit of:

> To be spiritual is not to reject reason, but to go beyond it.
> — Sarvepalli Radhakrishnan

The soul-psychic sleuthig activity is basically the spiritual activity, however, initially it is introspection, retrospection, concentration, occult formulation and self-dominion.

1.1 Sleuthing Centre

Everything in Nature owes its existence to an expansion in all directions from an inner centre. Nothing develops inwardly from its periphery. Life itself grows like a pearl — the irritant of the grain of sand in an oyster may be likened to the initial movement of vibration from stillness of infinity, Astronomers theorize that the very universe began at a specific point with what they've named the "big bang": a mighty explosion that still continues to expand towards an unimaginable infinity.

Every point in this "centre-everywhere" universe is a central point of reference from which the universe can be understood.

A living man and/or God is a sleuthing centre, Man at the centre is surrounded by uncertainties which circle him into problems waiting to be identified and resolved with the grace of God.

> Man is the measure of all things.
> — Protagoras (the fifth century BCE)

God is a concept created by the human being and the human being wants someone to beg to for something. So the human being has created the concept of God, and then given him attributes, 'all-knowing, all-powerful, all-merciful'!

The highest ideal of every man is, thus, called God. Ignorant or wise, saint or sinner, man or woman, educated or uneducated, cultivated or uncultivated — to every human being the highest ideal is

God. The synthesis of all the highest ideals of beauty, of sublimity, and of power gives us the completest conception of the loving and lovable God.

However, the word God has become empty of meaning through thousands of years of misuse. By misuse, we mean that people who have never even glimpsed the realm of sacred, the infinite vastness behind that word, use it with great conviction, as if they knew what they are talking about. Or they argue against it, as if they knew what it is that they are denying. This misuse gives rise to absurd beliefs, assertions, and egoistic delusions, such as "My or our God is only true God, and your God is false," or Nietzsche's famous statement "God is dead."

God is one and many at the same time. He is big as well as small, near as well as far, within us and without.

Some people now use the term Goddess instead of God. They are redressing a balance between male and female that was lost a long time ago, and that is good. But it is still a representation and a concept, perhaps temporarily useful, just as a map or a signpost is temporarily useful, but more a hindrance than a help when you are ready to realize the reality beyond all concepts and images. What does remain true, however, is that the energy frequency of the mind appears to be essentially male. The mind resists, fights for control, manipulates, attacks, tries to grasp and possess, and so on. This is why the traditional God is a patriarchal, controlling authority figure, an often angry man who you should live in fear of, as the Old Testament suggests. This God is a projection of the human mind.

God's reality does not stand apart from our perceptions but is woven into them. A mother can see her newborn child as wonderful and worthy, and through her perception that baby grows up to become a wonderful, worthy person. This is one of the mysteries of love. A subtle give-and-take is going on at the deepest level between parent and child. In the same way God seems to grow directly out of our deepest inner values. There is similar give-and-take below the level of mere belief. Peel away all the layers of an onion, and at the centre you will find emptiness; peel away all the layers of a human being, and at the centre you will find the seed of God Particle!!

Power of God is beyond the comprehension of man. He directs the law of Nature. Of course, it is too difficult to attempt to solve the mysteries of nature.

God created this world by HIS will alone. HE thought, "I am one, let me become many," and the world came into being. This power also exists in man, although in a smaller proportion. Man's creation is dependent upon action, whereas God's creation does not require any action.

There has been, from the beginning of the world, a perfectly well-defined plan under which the human species is brought into existence. The plan of creation is exceedingly simple, easily understood, and can be verified in every person you meet. You do not have to take anything for granted, nor believe in anything you cannot see or touch or hold in your hand, consequently, in this very practical and realistic age, the most advanced materialist can embrace the soul-psychic sleuthing without offending in any way his sense of propriety.

Man is a composite of Body (Soma), Mind (Psyche), and Soul (Pneuma, or Essence, or Nous, some call it spirit, though others write it with capital "S"; at the same time they indentify "Spirit" with God, and God with "Self" of all beings.) An estoriast differs when he begins to penetrate into the human being as he is bound to reverse the order and attaches to the soul, a personality consisting of mind and body.

The soul has seat of position in the heart, and the mind has it in the head. And, function of the soul is to force into a body at the time of birth, disburse the movement and control while in the body, and then flee out of the body at the time of death. Functions of the mind are to find, fret, fume, frighten, and formulate strategies for survival.

The human body is one of the most accomplished chemical laboratories of the creation, and is equipped with all sorts of sensors, microprocessors, control valves and relays, disguised displays, etc. Besides: "The human body has one ability not possessed by any machine — the ability to repair itself," says George Crance. The hands of the Man are simply performing under communication, command, control and intelligence (C^3I) of mind.

The head of ours is like a cave filled with gold and jewels, against which boulders of false beliefs have been piled along with jagged rocks of misunderstanding and long-entrained hurts of past injustices. Then, there's the debris of doubt, despair, disgust, and disappointment piled high enough against the gold of conscience, the pearls of wisdom, the diamonds of intelligence. Also, there is your own heart full of the rubies of true love, and emeralds of humility, waiting for you to lift your hands to disburse the precious possessions. Your hands, though heavy and hard, are guided by the tender hand of the Unseen.

Thus, human being is a combination of the fabulous treasures of head, heart, and hands. You are incomplete if you neglect functioning of any one of these three — head, representing intellect; heart, representing love; and hands, representing performance.

The body of man is a chariot, his mind the driver, his senses the horses. The man of intelligence, who keeps watch over himself, travels on his way like an owner of a chariot, happy and contented, drawn by well-trained horses.

> You are what your deep, driving desire is.
> As your desire is, so is your will.
> As your will is, so is your deed.
> As your deed is, so is your destiny.
>
> — *Brihadaranyaka Upanishad*

According to Nisargadatta Maharaj, "The mind is the wife of the heart and the world their home — to be kept bright and happy." Use your hands in harmony.

> Man is citizen of two worlds, one of them the kingdom of God and the other the world of sensibility. As a member of the kingdom of

God man is exalted, as a member of the world of sensibility, he is humbled. — Kant, Immanuel

Great thoughts come from the heart. — Vauvenargues

Thus, working thoughts are fired by the heart; in other words, the thinking process is seeded by our souls. APJ Abdul Kalam[2] says, "The soul is at the root, pure potential; potential for consciousness, knowledge, experience, life, growth, learning, expansion, and so on. Rather, we are potential itself, pure potential." Henceforth, we consider soul-psychic combination as all-powerful.

It is a well-known fact that the matrices of life, mind and soul are inter-related, which lead us to a culture of face-to-face communitarian living close to nature. In this process of living, problems are bound to arise!

Shakespeare, that prince of philosophers, whose thoughts will adorn English literature for all time, laid down the well-known axiom: "There is tide in the affairs of men which, taken at flood, leads on to fortune." The question has been asked again and again: Is there some means of knowing when the moment has come to take the tide at the flood?

An answer to this question is, that the great Architect of the Universe in His infinite wisdom so created all things in such harmony of design that He endowed the human mind with some part of that omnipotent knowledge which is the attribute of the Divine Mind as the Creator of all.

It is this desire for knowledge implanted in the mind of humanity that places mankind above the animal creation, and makes men and women as 'gods' in their desire 'to know'.

However, man is a pseudo-self, and is a bargainer, giving only in the hope of getting. The real-Self gives for the joy of it, expecting nothing in return.

---

2. APJ Abdul Kalam, Arun K Tiwari, *Guiding Souls: Dialogues on the Purpose of Life*, Ocean Books Pvt Ltd, New Delhi, 2005, p. 19.

Man is the part of the universe and one with its Maker. As Gray says, in *The Advancing Front of Sciences*, "This curious, prying, stumbling, aspiring, persistently hopeful creature, Man: Half brute that clings to the cloud; half god who looks through distant light-years where the Sun is shining." It is this god-side of man that inspires us to believe that we have a right to use our creative energy in sleuthing.

According to Tauler: "Man is in truth a compound of eternity and time. The more he is attached to temporal things and rests in them, the farther he grows from things eternal; they seem to him petty, just as great objects appear small when we see them from a distance, and he can never attain to real peace."

We are the temple of the living God — Corinthians

Each man ought to say to himself, advise the Upanishads, "I was the creator, may I become again what I was."

Shri Ramana Maharsi says: "God is not separate from you or the cosmos." He adds: "Infinity and perfection do not admit of parts. If a finite being is apart form Infinity, the perfection of Infinity is marred."[3]

God created man, and vice versa. God is the outcome of human contemplation on the Nature. Also, God is the product of human dreams. God is creation of sanity in this world of insanity — the world of meetings, eatings, and cheatings. The sanity is to be re-established.

Nevertheless, men are travellers on a cosmic journey — they are stardust, swirling and dancing in the eddies of whirlpools of infinity. Life is eternal. But the expressions of life are ephemeral, momentary, and transient. God (≈Man) is the centre and cosmos is the sphere of activity.

1.2 Sleuthing

God is a good worker but He loves to be helped, according to Basque proverb: God has created 'Human' to help Him. Therefore, we have to be a good worker and God will help us as if sleuthing was his work.

---

3. Osborne, Arthur, *The Teachings of Bhagwan Sri Ramana Maharshi in His Own Words*, Ramanasramam, Madras, India 19, p. 48.

Sleuthing means watching, intelligence gathering, patrolling and maintaining law and order to obtain and be a part of a civilized society and system.

The Perfect Plan of God demands us to live a life conscientiously and consciously. The conscience is the function of the soul, and conscious of the mind (psyche). And therefore, soul-psychic sleuthing is a necessity of the civilized society and evolved individuals. For this, knowing, perceiving, understanding, learning and proper living are essential functions of the soul-psychic sleuthing.

What is civilized society? An unsung seer from Lebanon Yusif El Fakhri[4] has described the nineteenth century scenario in these words:

> This civilization is an old and corrupt tree, strong and terrible, whose roots are locked into the obscurity of the earth and whose branches are reaching beyond the clouds; but its bossoms are of greed and evil and crime, and its fruit is of woe and misery and fear. Crusaders have undertaken to blend good into it and change its nature, but they could not succeed. For multitude humility is a sort of weakness, and mercy a kind of cowardice, and snobbery a form of strength.
>
> Hypocrisy will always remain, even if her fingertips are coloured and polished; and Deceit will never change even if her touch becomes soft and delicate; and falsehood will never turn into Truth even if you dress her with silken robes and place her in a palace; and Greed will not become Contentment; nor will Crime become Virtue. And Eternal Slavery to teachings, to customs, and to history will remain Slavery even if she paints her face and disguises her voice. Slavery will remain Slavery in all her horrible form, even if she calls herself Liberty.
>
> The West is not higher than the East, nor is the West lower than the East, and the difference that stands between the two is not greater than the difference between the tiger and the lion.
>
> Civilization is vanity and all in it is vanity. . . . Inventions and discoveries are but amusement and comfort for the body when it is

4. Kahlil Gibran, *English Edition*, Publishers and Distributors (India) Pvt Ltd., Mumbai, pp. 23-25.

> tired and weary. The conquest of distance and victory over the seas are but false fruits which do not satisfy the soul, nor nourish the heart, neither lift the spirit, for they are afar from nature.

A hundred years later the situation is in no way different, no way better, rather worst. Everyone is trying to acquire position of power and pelf. Simply look at one of the sections of the media — newspapers.

Newspapers are becoming show windows which are decorated with attractively dressed mannequins. Even journalists have a price tag on their pens and conscience. One reason that is responsible for the behaviour of the media is the repressive state itself. If a television channel shows something that the dictator does not like, then the telephone lines and electricity are cut. It is guessed the print and visual media must have decided that they might as well quietly make their pot money if they can't make a difference anyway.

The progress of technology has brought us a mixed blessing. In some way it has helped us; we no longer need to work from dawn to dusk just to continue to exist; and this coupled with ever-advancing medical technology, has improved the quality of our lives and increased the amount of time we have to spend.

Other effects of our headlong plunge into the technological era have been less pleasant. Some of the outward signs are obvious, of course: industrial pollution, overcrowding, and the nuclear sword that hangs over all across the world over our heads.

The integration of weapons of mass destruction (WMD) to the world-connectivity further aggrevates the situation. Even the exploration of the space is hardly to bring any succor to the sufferings and ills of the society and the system.

Lutzenberger[5] said: "Modern industrial society is a fanatical religion. We are demolishing, poisoning, destroying all life-systems on the planet. We are signing IoUs (Instruments of Understanding) that our children will not be able to pay . . .. We are acting as if we were the last generation

5. Jose Antonio Lutzenberger, *Sunday Times*, London, March, 1991.

on the planet. Without a radical change in heart, in mind, in vision, the Earth will end up like Venus, charred and dead."

To sum up the present scenario, we have a quote

> The means by which we live have outdistanced the ends for which we live. Our scientific power has outrun our spiritual power. We have guided missiles and misguided men.
>
> —Martin Luther King (*Strength to Love*)

We were born wet, naked and hungry. Then it got worse — the miseries that we go through in the process of our understanding and the scientific advancements, are much more than those of primitive age.

Beings with a human form are bestowed with an opportunity to develop a sense of purpose and responsibility towards one's family, society, nation and the world. Sleuthing is an essential tool to make best use of this opportunity.

We need more reasonableness, tolerance, neighbourly love and, above all, a wiser intelligence to overcome the menace and make a happier world. But how can the first three virtues which entail a certain readiness for surrender and sacrifice, charity and catholicity develop in the masses when keen competition, not only among neighbours but also among states, for a larger slice is the order of the day. And how can "intelligence" grow "wiser" when, denied the faith in spiritual order and everlasting life, it must look only to the extremely short span of its early existence, with no hope in a Beyond, for the satisfaction of its inherent passions and lusts. Noble virtues and saving wisdom do not arise from inventions or from an over-abundance of the goods of Earth. They rest in the gift of the spirit alone. This is the truth which the agnostic intellect has still to learn. Not one but all the mighty empires of the past floundered on the granite rock of this Truth and sank never to rise again. To make himself virtuous and wiser is not in the power of man himself. For these he must look into the still unfathomed depths of his own consciousness.

On account of the lure of worldly goods and the errors of reason, empire after empire and culture after culture crumbled to the dust, because the knowledge of the secret gained was not applied to regulate the life of the intellect which prevents the erudite now from accepting the existence of superior intelligent forces in creation that rule the fate of humanity, and exact obedience to the Law of Evolution at any cost, was prevalent in the ancient times also. But, it was never so rampant as it is now, and never before was there such a threat to the survival of the race as it stares us in the face at this moment.

Darwin, the father of the doctrine of evolution, in one of his famous writings asserted: "Over the very long run, man's fate on the average is predestined by the Malthusian disequillibrium. Man procreates in a finite world. Man's continued scramble for finite resources condemns him to eternal social instability, to violence and to brutishness."

We are all aware of the historical background of the Malthusian Prophecy and its futility as one could see it today. Science and technology have provided many solutions to save the mankind from eternal social instability.

With the idea of internal sleuthing comes the question of language of sleuthing. The sparks ignited by objective living experience and subjective feedback from various sources have to be the abiding sparkle and, with time, have to blaze forth in splendour. The medium, i.e. the language of sleuthing must develop and expand and the world's treasures must be brought into its possession and through it within the reach of every man.

Sleuthing's main objective is to gain knowlege — here, in the present context, the knowledge of one's inner self. And, the knowledge is only indifferent perception of objects. Feeling is emotional reaction of man's heart to those objects. It is not a mere perception of objects, but the innermost realization of the soul. Pleasure and pain are its common evolutes; desire and aversion, love and hatred are its phenomenal consequences; and delight is its ideal.

Whether your need is the alertness to jump out of the way of a skidding automobile or the consumption of right food for your own body needs, the Divine Intelligence within you is ready to supply it. Things you need to know will be brought to your attention. This Powerful Intelligence is always ready. It asks of you just one thing, that you take time to become aware of its presence and application.

You are aware that the senses always show you a dual state, both good and bad, with their numerous variations. This is why all sense testmony must be set aside during soul-psychic sleuthing. Stop all the cringing, timidness and spacious imaginings. These feelings do you no good, whatsoever. Make up your mind that you do not have to feel uneassy, apprehensive and anxious.

You may look to God for all the good you desire such as love, appreciation, gratitude, sincerity, pleasantness and peace.

When the going seems to be rough and tough, place your attention upon the Universal love which is giving you what it is. This gives you the understanding of others, which has been, up to now, lacking in you. Your intellect has not always correctly interpreted what the eyes see, but your mind, your soul, which is the Wholeness — God takes over the intellectual powers, giving them strength and knowhow, and enables you to be understanding.

Social and moral "laws" were put forth by the sense beliefs of man, and the sleuthing provides you a journey that every man can follow, as it is an exploration of the personal world of your own mind and soul. It is all within you. The arrow of soul-psychic sleuthing pierces all the way.

> The gates of hell are open, night and day;
> Smooth is the descent, and easy is the way. — Aeneid Virgil

The sort of man you have made of yourself, how you will be regarded by the world, whether people will admire and respect or despise you, whether you will get the approval or the condemnation of your Creator, — all this is in your own hands. No matter where your lot may be cast, no power on the earth can keep you from making a man of yourself, a superb character — a masterpiece, a shining soul.

Many people seem to think that they are under obligaion to make life as complete, as successful as possible. But this is precisely what we are here for — to evolve as the real man or woman for the Creator is involved in each of us. We cannot be true to ourselves and shirk this obligation. Each was sent here with a divine message, to honour it loyally, not to distort or mutilate it. The message is the work of a lifetime — the evolution of a superb manhood or womanhood, the grandest achievement of which a human being is capable.

The object of our human life should not be merely living–getting. This was mere incidental in the Creator's Plan, only an inferior motive compared with the grander motive of making life. Self-expression, self-enlargement, self-growth, the calling out of the man or the woman, the exercising of one's powers of mind, body and soul — this should be the real meaning of life.

Making life a masterpiece does not necessarily mean that one must engage in some high profession, some great special work of learned calling. All honest labour is dignified and ennobling. Many men have made masterpieces of their lives as cobblers and have lifted this occupation into dignity and respect. Multitude of farmers are raising farming to the height of a grand profession by mixing brains and character with the soil, and are making masterpieces of their lives.

There is an oriental saying, "If you have two loaves of bread, sell one and buy hyacinths to feed your soul."

The objective of sleuthing is, thus, the conception of a heaven, a place of indescribable beauty where no sense of unrest, discord, disaster or unhappiness ever enters. It is a place or condition where no one is envious or jealous, where no one tries to take advantage of another and where all are interested in each other's welfare. In this dream heaven, each is joyously working at the thing s/he loves best to do. Harmony and love illuminate every face. Happiness so fills the atmosphere that there is no room for discord. Unrest, anxiety, worry, disappointment are unknown. The shadow of fear never enters her. Love reigns superme, and — that dream place is possible right here, on this planet of ours.

Heaven never lacks customers because of man's "burning

impatience with Infinity." The rich and poor, commoners and kings, jetsets and stay-at-home, capitalists and communists, civilized and primative, all are roped in by its glittering merchandises. The soul-psychic sleuthing may help you to get there! Then, you can smell the garden of the heaven, hear into the Universal Intelligence and share your developed soul-psychic attributes.

The objectives of sleuthing are incorporated in the enquiries: "As a matter of fact, is there any finer aim in this world than to make oneself a nobler citizen. Is there anything more inspiring than the ceaseless endeavour to be somebody worthwhile in the world, to stand for a little higher ideals in your community, to leave the world at least a little better for having been in it? Is there any finest goal there than to leave the world as an awakened and liberated soul? — All the great souls who have worked up from obscurity have held their spared moments sacred to culture, to mental expansion."

> The mysteries of life are revealed to one who keeps his mind vigilant all the time of life. — *Yajurveda*

And, this vigilance has to be always alert in the three areas of head, heart and hands, because: "Success goes to our head, failure to our heart and money to the hands."

> Sleuthing seeks schedule and serenity: Think in the morning, act in the noon, eat in the evening, sleep in the night.
> — William Stake

> Do well and right and let the world sink. — Herbert

> Every noble activity makes room for itself. — Emerson

> Our good and evil deeds follow us continually like shadows.
> — Lord Buddha

> Let not the fruits of action be the motives of your action, otherwise you might be disappointed and leave the path of right action. — *Rigveda*

Reasearch into the art of problem-solving has brought to light a number of interesting facts regarding this process. Of these, by far the most important point discovered is this : most people have difficulty in finding right information, which can be reached by sleuthing techniques to be discussed in the following section.

Most real problems deal with people rather than things, and as a result it is sometimes quite difficult to isolate what is real from what we may wish to be true.

We have to be very careful indeed to be sure that we apply thought — facts to problems, rather than feeling facts.

A thought fact — a real fact, in other words — is something that can be verified independently. It is not something that is open to question or dispute; either it is true, provably true, or it isn't. If it is not provably true it is not a fact.

A feeling fact — a statement or point of information that we may desire to be true (and which in fact may be true) — is more properly an opinion; there can be many differing views as to how true it is, and it is open to question.

It is a thought-fact that Dr Radhakrishnan was a President of India; it is a feeling-fact that he was the best (or worst) President we ever had.

Determining the difference between fact and opinion is absolutely crucial to solving problems of any kind; as we have stressed and will continue to stress, the quality of your solutions is directly dependent on the quality and truth of the information reaching.

Feelings are as valid and necessary as thoughts in helping the mind to work efficiently and truely; in problem-solving, though, we have to make decisions about their values if we are to consider them as units to build towards a solution.

There is a silent judge in each of us, weighing and measuring our acts, approving or disapproving. We cannot bribe this judge. If we do wrong we are punished. If we do right we are rewarded. Nothing less than our best, not spasmodically, but all the time, will satisfy this exacting inward judge. Only the best on every occasion can lift our lives and give us enduring satisfaction.

The only way to experience satisfaction and truth directly is to look within, to observe oneself. All our lives we have been accustomed to look outward. We have always been interested in what is happening outside, what others are doing. We have rarely, if ever, tried to examine ourselves, our own mental and physical structure, our own actions, our own reality. Therefore, we remain unknown to ourselves. We do not realize how harmful this ignorance is, how much we remain the slaves of forces within ourselves of which we are unaware.

This inner darkness must be dispelled to apprehend the truth. We must gain insight into our own nature in order to understand the nature of existence. Therefore the path that Lord Buddha and other enlightened souls showed is a path of introspection, of self-observation. Lord Buddha said, "Within this very fathom-long body containing the mind with its perceptions, I make known the universe, its origin, its cessation, and the way leading to its cessation." The entire universe and the laws of nature by which it works are to be experienced within ourselves. They can only be experienced within oneself.

Any attempt to observe the truth about oneself immediately reveals that what one calls "oneself" has two aspects, physical and psychic, body and mind. We must learn to observe both. But how can we actually experience the reality of body and mind? Accepting the explanations of others is not sufficient, nor is depending on merely intellectual knowledge. Both may guide us in the work of self-exploration, but each of us must explore and experience reality directly within ourselves.

Looking in will require of us great subtlety and great courage — nothig less than a complete shift in our attitude to life and to the mind. We are so addicted to looking outside ourselves that we have lost access to our inner being almost completely. We are terrified to look inward, because our culture has given us no idea of what we will find. We may even think that if we do we will be in danger of madness.This is one of the most resourceful plays of ego to prevent us from discovering our real nature.

So we make our lives so hectic that we eliminate the slightest risk of looking into ourselves. Even the idea of meditation can scare people. When they hear the words "egoless" or "emptiness", they think experiencing those states will be like being thrown out of the door of a spaceship to float forever in the dark, chilling cold. Nothing could be further from the truth. But in a world dedicated to distraction, silence and stillness terrifying us; we protect ourselves from them with noise and frantic busyness.

The sleuthing methodology recommended here is to put the mind (psyche) in a state of concentration and meditation. Even an aspirant who is not able to discriminate or reason about theological problems is to cultivate this habit. For, to fix the mind on one subject for a long time is difficult task and cannot be accomplished without years of hard practice.

The human mind chatters. There's always something going on in our minds. It's like a busy street corner in a metropolis; all kinds of emotionally toned thoughts, hopes, fears, and memories crisscross and jump into each other, tugging on our attention and distracting us from our focus. In order to stay in the present, we must do two things simultaneously: pay some attention to the chatter, and maintain some degree of detachment.

We have to pay some attention to the chatter because it contains signals from the soul. Each of the memories, fears, hopes, regrets or fantansies that scurries about has some degree of emotional charge. The emotional colouration and intensity tell us the significance of the specific content of consciousness, and the content often identifies or symbolizes the area of life concerned.

We also have to maintain a degree of distance, from an "observing ego", as it is called. "Feelingless objectivity" is not the appropriate degree of distance. Total disconnection from the emotion leaves only our rational minds on the job. Feeling is a function of the incarnated individual soul, and we must be aware of our feelings if we are to attend to our souls! Only when we are able to observe and feel, do we have the possiblity of understanding the messages of the soul. When we let the heavy traffic that sometimes fills our minds run us down and carry us away, we lose the necessary degree of detachment.

The second necessary element for attending to our individual souls is noticing the whispers to the soul. We must take time to reflect actively on what is going on in our lives — outer or inner. We must also make space in our busy lives for active reflection. It's as important as regularly brushing our teeth. Actively reflecting is a habit we need to form. It requires that we stop, look, and listen before alarm goes off, before a complex erupts, before a relationship goes sour, before we fall ill.

Our complexes, our relationship fascinations and antipathies, our dreams and fantacies, synchronistic events, and medical and psychiatric symptoms are all important messages from the soul that offer us information on the condition of the soul. It is important we actively reflect on these messages the soul sends us.

The third necessity for attending to our soul is time. We have to take time to notice what is going on. We have to take time to reflect on what we notice. When an emotionally coloured thought or image or experience of whatever degree of intensity completely fills our consciousness, we do not have the degree of detachment neccessary to reflect on it. Setting aside the time to reflect, safe from intrusion and distraction, creates the space in which we can ponder the whispers of the soul, and explore the meaning for our lives.

Maintaining these three prerequisties — being in the present, noticing the whispers of the soul, and making time to reflect — is an ongoing challenge, we don't get it perfect the first time. All three elements demand patience and discipline. With practice, we can steadily improve our skills and increase our harvest of insight.

There are also several other approaches that are of value in sleuthing. Silence, meditation, spontaneous writing, journaling, active imagination, and divination.

William James, the great American psychologist, spells out the significance of sleuthing skill: "The faculty of voluntarily bringing back a wandering attention over and over again is the very root of judgement, character and will. An education which should include this faculty would be the education par excellence." James was not guessing. He tried to teach himself this skill, at least as it applies to everyday affairs, and he succeeded well enough to lift himself out of a life-threatening depression. In this pivotal achievement he grasped the connection between training the mind and mastering life.

Sleuthing demands a great deal of perception, insight, into the fact of your life, how one lives one's life. After all, philosophy means the love of turth, love of wisdom, not the love of some abstraction. J. Krishnamurti (1895-1986), a world teacher, in the course of very serious and devoted contemplation and exploration undertaken with great passion, indicates that pinning our hopes on organized religion, science, political ideology or the market economy not only fails to address basic human problems but also actually creates them. The way out of our difficulties, Krishnamurti states, can only start in the mind of each one of us, in an awareness of the way we actually perceive life, ourselves and others.

But, man is an altogether different proposition. He is influenced by his emotions, ego, prejudices, and his faulty inadequate knowledge. His awareness not having reached the super state, it is layered in different planes such as his conscience and his mind. He thus requires, in his evolution, an elaborate system of receiving, decoding and interpreting data.

Under those conditions, the continuous stream of beeps or messages or knowledge of the Lord that passes through man is either ignored by the gross mind of man or is faultily interpreted. The Truth now becomes relative.

Due to his changing mind, and the threatening feel of fragmentation and competition, and the lack of the divine qualities of the Lord, man is subject to marred enjoyment, faulty interpretations and undesirable action. Man's deep involvement in life is exposed to misery and dissatisfaction, varying in degree according to his own understanding which in turn depends upon his sleuthing ability.

'Living' cannot be ignored. Living brings with it grief, disappointment, rage, etc. These do not disappear. These cannot be wiped out. But, grounded firmly in the sublime bliss reached through soul-psychic sleuthing, the disappointments of life acquire a fleeting, a less consequential, a less intense, a more tolerable, a surmountable gravity. One's composer is maintained even through difficult phases in life. Even calamities are rendered less grievous.

Introspection is way of knowing one's mind. In other words, it is a probe into one's inner feeling. There are two types of introspection. They are as follows : (i) one may resort to direct scrutiny of conscious states and processes at the time of their occurrence; (ii) one may resort to the recovery of the past states and processes by a retrospective act. The modern equivalent of the term "introspection" is reflection or "inner sense."

Introspection as a method is opposed to behaviourism. The latter relies on the overt or apparent behaviour of the individuals in analyzing the psychological states of an individual.

One cannot achieve real greatness in the mundane life without being able ot monitor and control his states of mind and sense organs, and without having a correct awareness of himself/herself and the world. In fact, to enjoy the world in a detached but lively way is the real art of living.

The movement of the mind from a state with resistance to a state without resistance is called the quantum jump of the mind from logical and scientific reason to unfaltered philosophical reason; or from relative state (conscious state) to an absolute state (superconscious state); or it is a leap from the lower plane of relational knowledge (intellectual knowledge) to a higher plane of ultrarelation knowledge (intuitional knowledge). As there is no matter which is self-effulgent, so we assume that the neurons of the mind receive illumination from the self-effulgent

Self, the *Atman*, the Universal Consciousness. The state of mind with resistance is capable of receiving partial illumination, a state of mind without resistance is capable of receiving full illumination from the self and as such is fully illumined with the pristine glory of the self, and as such is fully bathed with truth. The state of mind without resistance is capable of pure perception and as such the mind perceives the persent moment of the chronological space-time continuum, and there is a continuous flow of the present moment only, this is the vision of the Absolute where there is neither time, space, nor causation. This is the realization of the eternal values in the chronological space-time continuum, which means the attainment of the state of detachment, selfless service and eternal love for the entire humanity.

Therefore, in soul-psychic sleuthing practice all preconceived ideas and notions have to be investigated, removed and replaced, if necessary, by another set of ideas based on facts, related to body, mind and spirit.

Einstein went beyond the area of preconceived and accumulated knowledge. He picked up something from the intuitive dimension, brought it back and spent his life-time rationalizing it. It is very difficult to spend one's life rationalizing an intuitive insight, but that is what sleuthing is also aimed at — expansion of creativity.

Soul-psychic sleuthing implies 'evolution' that is accompanied by the acquisition of senses and powers beyond the five normal senses of seeing, smelling, hearing, tasting and touching. With the activation of the *chakras* by yogic exercises, the hitherto dormant regions of our brain start awakening gradually. With these awakenings, the individual can acquire psychic powers — ESP (extra-sensory-perception), telepathy, clairvoyance, clairaudience, prophecy, levitation, out-of-body experiences (OBEs), healing, etc., depending upon one's interests and practices.

Wealth or creative comforts, health or longevity, powers of intellect or other talents, enjoyment of the most intense pleasures and even the possession of psychic powers — each and all of them can never be the end in themselves; they cannot be the 'goal' one seeks in the sleuthing practice. Rightly and discriminately used, they may serve as temporary stepping-stones or passing 'milestones' on the path of soul-psychic march, at the best.

The soul-psychic sleuthing is to be ordained conscientiously and consciously. Conscience means true faith in "Atman-Parmatman", translated into English "soul-God." It incorporates spiritual norms, ideas, and ethics occulted by sages, saints, savants, and seers since the dawn of the Universal Intelligence into the minds of the mankind, which are in turn "plugged in" into the Universal Consciousness.

> Wise man is instructed by reason,
> Men of less understanding by experience,
> The most ignorant by necessity,
> And, beast by Nature. — Kalhana

Meditating monks manage the mind magnificently. Moran present the other end of the spectrum of sanity. Mystics cover the whole range of the formulating and functioning spectrum of the mind. It should be the aim of every human being to be mystical, but soul-psychic sleuthing will certainly lead man to achieve the status of the hierophant. Though the road is capricious, but it is worth taking pains and to practice soul-psychic sleuthing, which is the first stage of a journey towards self-realization; it is just to perform a capriole — most of us are catechumen.

The soul has three potential faculties, viz. memory understanding and will, whose supernatural objectives are the three theological virtues, hope, faith, and charity or love respectively. These three virtues are the means by which the soul unites with God, each one creating a vacuum and darkness in its respective faculty: hope in memory, faith in understanding or intellect, and charity or Love in the will. The understanding is to be perfected in the darkness of faith, memory in the vacuum of hope and the will buried in the lack of sensual love, to go towards God. When these faculties are perfected, the soul is enwrapped in love — soul can unite with God in this life neither through reasoning, nor by enjoyment, nor through imagination, nor through any other sense organ, but only through faith, hope and love.

Hope all humans — savants or simple — will be guided by their soul-psychic suggestions, if the universe of ours is to be made a paradise.

Man by nature is a disorderly creature. Left to himself there would be anarchy in society. In the modern world, law and order is maintained by strict policing aided by modern communication technology. In olden days, this was difficult, and in future, it is going to be more and more complex, and then soul-psychic sleuthing may become a necessity.

> know thyself and thou shalt know the universe and the gods.
>
> — *Inscription of the Temple of Delphi*

> There is nothing greater than the practice of the percept which says "know thyself".
>
> — *Antoine the Healer*

Even the psychically expansive sleuthing activity has no meaning if not animated from within by soul-inspiration. Unfortunately, the tendency of human nature is to view all things as "circumference everywhere, centre nowhere" when the mind's attention is focused too much outside itself, it becomes superficial.

Maybe the sleuthing goal will be achieved in exploring the unchartered frontiers of inner space of our minds, our hearts and our souls. This sleuthing ability is within you, you don't have to rush to the nearest bookshop for the new-age salve for the soul — just read on to build up sleuthing faculties, after an appropriate understanding.

Sleuthing is not some kind of a trick of manipulating the intellect, or a way in which something you cannot see is prevailed upon to "heave-ho" and jump gladly to do your bidding, but you can instruct those foolish thoughts to "be still or fade away." As you travel from senses to mind to soul, many more wonderful things will be revived in your mental awareness.

Thus, the principle of soul-psychic sleuthing is the link which enables man to contact reality. That principle may be overlaid with any colour of the rainbow because it can be laid hold of by any person of any denomination, any colour, creed or country. The principle is universal consciousness which eternally is peace, tranquillity, power, love, faith, harmony, health, wholeness and evolution.

Soul-psychic sleuthing was prevalent during the Vedic era. "Veda" literally means wisdom — the knowledge of truth — which is based upon direct perception. It is not theoretical knowledge but the truth that comes to the individual in the state of pure consciousness. It means universal knowledge, not the dogma or opinion of any group.

The sleuthing is not only the foremost of the outer sciences which deal with the nature of the physical universe, it is one of the most important of the inner or spiritual sciences which deal with the mind and soul. It shows the cosmic source and the background of the working of forces in any field of endeavour. It can be used to help understand all spheres of life.

The sleuthing technology has many branches and sub-systems and allows for a great diversity of approaches. This knowledge itself is based on the freedom and creative intelligence of the individual being. Hence, every true practitioner of it will have his or her own particular version of it. The Vedic tradition is the tradition of the creative adaptation of eternal wisdom. Those who put limits on it, reduce it to one appproach only, or claim authority over it, deny its very basis. Hence, the reader is asked to examine this knowledge critically to see if it works and to apply it creatively in his or her own self-unfoldment. It just requires a little patience and contemplation, a willingness to open up to a new way of looking at things — perhaps a doorway into the infinite. However, there is no final way of finding order and harmony in the cosmos.

The essential principle of the sleuthing science is self-knowledge. As great sages, both modern and ancient, have repeatedly stated: "self-knowledge is the basis of all knowledge." Yet self-knowledge is something more than psychological analysis. It is not the knowledge of our inner consciousness or unconditioned being. Analysis of memory confines us only to a superficial aspect of our being. Self-knowledge is also something more than knowledge of past lives; this is only a more extensive memory still caught in the veil of form and limitation of time.

Self-knowledge is the knowledge of who we really are, of our true being, which is the light of awareness and not an external identity. This is the self of which all incarnations are masks. It is found not only by knowing who we were or why we became this or that; it is found by negating all identity and reintegrating all life, all the world within our own hearts. This requires seeing all lives within us. Such seeing is more than memory; it is a recognition of the Divine presence in all times and in all places. In it our continuity from life to life is experienced as part of a network that links us to all life. In it we learn the true lesson of life's experience — the truth of unity.

Sleuthing can be used to examine all domains of life. From it we can learn about our health, wealth, career, relationships: our body and mind, our material, mental and spiritual manifestations. It shows the entire structure of energies through which we must act. As such, it is the most comprehensive science we have. Yet on its highest and proper level, it is part of the science of the spirit or the practice of concentration and meditation. Its purpose is to guide us beyond the net of these outer forces to their source. This source is not in the heavens — it is in our own clear, free and quiet mind.

Thus, the soul-psychic sleuthing is the methodology of travelling to an island of peace in the turbulent, chaotic ocean of life, as we know it today, where we may locate pearls of prosperity and wholeness.

1.3 Sleuthing Techniques

The human personality contains a deep dormant psychic potential within its framework. This potential is within the reach of everyone, provided they have knowledge of particular system by which it can be tapped.

It requires to go deep into our consciousness. As we go deeper into the consciousness, the energy which is dormant, or the potential or qualities of mind of which we are not aware at present, become active. Many things begin to happen spontaneously, for instance, healing or an idea which materializes itself without any effort — may be due to natural instinct, or intuitive feedback, or extra-sensory perception (ESP).

With such an active state of mind, when we look at people we can see their whole personality turned inside out, even their thoughts can be seen. We know without asking what the other person is thinking about. This is called telepathy. Or, we may be thinking about something happening back home. We may see certain events taking place in a dream or a vision, either while we are relaxing or sleeping. Later on, we realize that these events were really happening, we were actually there. This is called clairvoyance. We may be sitting in one room and someone may be talking in another room, when our mind suddenly goes there. We perpetually hear with our ears what this person is talking about. This is called clairaudience.

We may be fiddling with, say, something antique, in the silence of our study and suddenly our mind starts seeing scenes of some tregedy or comedy which we may come to know were really associated with the antique article. This is called psychometry.

The ESP, telepathy, clairvoyance, clairaudience, psychometry, are some of the techniques, to tap into the unknown reality.

The trinity of head, heart, and hands is well known, the culture of the head (mind), the culture of heart (soul) and the culture of hands, have been cribbed, cabined, and caged in the hoary scriptures of Hinduism. This trinity plays an improtant role in sleuthing the unknown terrain.

Sleuthing incorporates head — mental realm development for telepathy; attributes of heart — love, compassion and controlled breathing for clairvoyance; and psychometric sensitive hands obtained through rubbing fingers of the two hands.

Open your mind to telepathy, clairvoyance, psychometry, ESP, lucid dreams; open your sensitivities to new experiences and be prepared to see an entirely new world and undergo magnificent revelations of the world we live in.

It is by virtue of telepathic, clairvoyant, ESP, intuitive, and instinctive faculties that our souls hold communion with the Supreme, put self in resonance with the infinite — cosmic consciousness, so that the superconsciousness within us experiences truth and reality.

Besides the above-said techniques, there are a few additional ways of sleuthing. These are advanced practices that you should engage in only under the guidance of a competent practitioner.

I-CHING

It is one of the classic Confucian and Taoist wisdom texts, and is perhaps the world's oldest book. The *I-Ching* has been a cornerstone of the Chinese culture for several thousand years. The *I-Ching* (pronouced "Yee jing") consits of sixty-four six-line figures and a number of attached commentaries. The six-line figures, called hexagrams, represent the momentary interaction of the two primal forces in the universe (Yang and Yin) as those forces relate to the question you ask. For example, hexagram 62 addresses the significance of small things, which form the golden threads leading to the soul.

Since the commentaries on the hexagram itself and on the individual lines, are usually in the form of images rather than explicit statements (not "Do this" or "Do that"), it takes considerable skill and practice to accurately understand the *I-Ching's* response to your question. Therefore, it is wise to have an experienced guide.

TAROT

Another valuable tool through which the soul can speak is the tarot. Traditionally, the tarot consists of a deck of cards, the twenty-two cards of the major arcana, and the four fourteen-card suits of the minor arcana. The tarot cards, like the hexagrams of the *I-Ching*, represent archetypal situations and processes in pictures. The correspondence between the cards in a tarot spread and our question is not based on causality. Rather, like the hexagrams in the *I-Ching*, the connecting link is not "magic," but shared meaning: the cards we draw and our life-situation have the same structure and pattern of meaning.

SAND TRAYS

This method accesses the inner child. When you are invited to create a diorama in a sand box using the miniature toys provided by the therapist — or yourself — the soul speaks through the created image and informs your consciousness of its depths. Serial images created over the duration of therapy are like a serial X-ray of the soul and its state of spiritual development and incarnation in outer life.

ACTIVE IMAGINATION

This approach is different from the *I-Ching* and the tarot in that you actively engage in a dialogue with the figures and situations the soul presents in imagination, similar to the one presented in the clairvoyance and psychometry. Active imagination is a technique that C.G.Jung[6] developed. In active imgination, you choose an image or a figure from a dream (for example), and engage it in a dialogue, just as we would with a flesh-and-blood person. This interior dialogue can move very rapidly, so it is important to keep a written record as you proceed. Otherwise it is too easy to forget the exchange; and since the other in us often tells us things we would never listen to from another person. Our "ocular evidence" counteracts our tendency to deceive ourselves that nothing important took place. It is well worth the effort to come to terms with the other in us, because in this way we get to know the essential facets of our personality, we otherwise might never confront.

As with the *I-Ching* and the tarot, the value of a guide when doing active imagination lies in having someone who can help you meaningfully relate the vivid images to the realities of your current

6. C.G. Jung; *Mysterium Conjunctionis*, The Collected Works , vol. 14, Princeton University Press, Princeton, 1996. p. 706.

life. It is very easy to make too much or too little of a picture; either extreme overshoots the mark, and you can lose the message in the exaggeration.

However, the human mind is the world's largest filtering device. When used properly during the active imagination, it filters out what you perceive as unimportant and gives you only the information you are looking at the time — combining psychic function with the soul signals.

INTERNAL GUIDANCE

Each of us has an internal guidance system by which we can know all there is to know about life. All that's really improtant to know about life. And if we listen to that internal system, we'll find ourselves led to the right and perfect people, places, and circumstances that are prepared to give us an opportunity to express the grandest part of who we are.

Neale Donald Walsch[7] says: "I always advise people to just move into the process called 'decision-making,' and step toward something. As soon as you definitely decide to do or not to do a thing, to choose or not to choose a thing, as soon as you move in one particular direction or another, within moments your tummy will tell you whether or not that's the palce you should go. It's an internal guidance system. For me it's in my stomach; for others it's located may be as a thought in their head. But all of us have that internal guidance system."

> Only from his own soul can he demand the secret of eternal beauty.
>
> — Farrid-Uddin Attar

BRAINWASHING

While investigation is conducted into what your soul speaks, and before your soul speaks, it is made to twist and turn, as it is done in brainwashing.

---

7. Neale Donald Walsch, *Inspirational Living*, Jaico Publishing House, Mumbai, 2007, p. 56.

In many countries of the world investigation officers follow certain practices aimed at extracting confession from their captives and also changing their personalities, if needed. By a judicious choice of physical and moral deprivations and by persuasions, the old personality is broken down and new personality is established in its place. The man under investigation hears so many times repeatedly that he is an enemy of the state and a traitor to his country, that a day comes when something breaks down in him and he begins to feel with full conviction that he is a traitor, a rebel, altogether despicable and deserving the direst punishment. This process is known as brainwashing.

We know that the religious and yogic practices are very similar to "brainwashing". The same physical and mental deprivation, solitary confinement, a powerful sense of sin, despair and desire to escape through expiation and conversion, adoption of a new image of oneself and impersonating that image. The same mechanism operates — the mind is made to concentrate on some particular idea to the exclusion of all other ideas and concentration is powerfully reinforced by rigid discipline and painful austerities; while developing soul-psychic abilities.

There may be many more techniques and processes for sleuthing of which some are preferable over others. The necessary choice is to be made. According to Confucius: "By three roads we can reach wisdom: the road of experience, and this is the most difficult; the road of initiative and this is the easiest; and the road of reflection, and this is the noblest."

> The soul when it has arrived at unity, acquires a supernatural knowledge. — Lao Tse

> The virtue of a man who has attained to the height of perfection, extends even to foreknowledge of the future. — Confucious

Tsu Tse says, "A seer's faculities are so ample, so vast, so profound that it is as if immense source from which everything issues in its time. They are as vast and extended as the heavens; the hidden source from which they issue is deep as the abyss."

Hildegard (1098-1149), a female hermit of Benger, says Serivias,[8] "Use all your faculties to appreciate God's creation. Use the soul within you to understand the soul within all living beings. When you see God in the beauty of what he has made, you are not looking with mortal eyes, but with the eyes of the soul. When you hear his wisdom within this beauty you are not using mortal ears, but listening with the ears of your soul to the wisdom He has implanted within you. Use your body to sympathize with other people's bodily experience. Use your emotions of anger and revenge to understand war. Appreciate goodness through distinguishing it from evil. Appreciate beauty through distinguishing it from ugliness and deformity. Define poverty by contrasting it with wealth. Rejoice in good health by comparing it with sickness."

> You cannot see the whole sky through a bambo tube.
>
> — Japanese Proverb

> Venture all; see what the fate brings.
>
> — Vietnamese Proverb

Therefore, you may try more than one technique to accomplish the sense of fulfilment. When we are to observe the spiritual aspect of our being, the bambo tube which we use must be the best possible one. The idea of mortification, that is, giving discipline to the body and mind, is to prepare them for this end. We must bring them to a state of such perfect harmony with our spiritual aspiration that they will never rebel, but will work in accordance with our higher purpose in life.

> Deep within man dwell those slumbering powers; powers that would astonish him, that he never dreamed of possessing; forces that would revolutionize his life if aroused and put into action.
>
> — Orison Swelt Marden

Still, more information may be drawn from the 'collective unconsciousness'; this is likely to be of universal character. In all cases,

8. Robert Van De Weyer; *366 Readings from World Religions*, Jaico Publishing House, Mumbai, 2006, p. 346.

however, there can be strange confusion when human consciousness tries to reconcile the unknown with the known, the timeless with an earthly time-scale. Beware of it.

Out of many strategies, tactics and techniques of soul-psychic sleuthing, only three of them, viz. telepathy, clairvoyance and psychometry will be highlighted in the following chapters.

1.4 Sleuthing Sojourn

We postulate: "Soul gives to mind the data-bank of previous lives at the time of birth of the present incarnation, and takes back the updated data-bank at the time of death for the consumption of future lives. (The major part of this data-bank remains burried in our unconscious minds — making us uninformed of our past or future lives)." There is credit and debit phenomenon (Karmic Law), which can be viewed in the following terms: "You are cut off from Being/God, Self as long as your mind takes up all your attention. When this happens, and it happens continuously for most people — you are not in your body. The mind absorbs all your consciousness and transforms it into mind-stuff. You cannot stop thinking. Compulsive thinking has become a collective disease. Your whole sense of who you are, is then derived from mind activity. Your identity, as it is no longer rooted in the Being, becomes vulnerable and ever-needy mental construct, which creates fear as the predetermined underlying emotion. The one thing that truly matters, is then missing from your life: awareness of your deeper self — your invisible and indestructible reality — the Spirit/Soul."

To become conscious of Being (God), you need to reclaim consciousness from the mind. This is one of the most essential tasks on your spiritual journey. It will free vast amounts of consciousness that previously had been trapped in useless and compulsive thinking. A very effective way of doing this is simply to take the focus of your attention away from thinking and direct it into the body, where Being can be felt in the first instance as the invisible energy field that gives life to what you perceive as the physical body.

All the spiritual teachers of humanity have told us the same thing, that the purpose of life on earth is to achieve union with our fundamental enlightened nature. The 'task' for which God has sent us into this strange, dark world is to realize and embody our true being. There is only one way to do this, and that is to undertake the spiritual journey, with all the order and intelligence, courage and resolve for transformation that we can muster.

> The pilgrim should never be discouraged; though he should struggle for a hundred thousand years without success to behold the beauty of the Beloved, still he should not give way to despair.
>
> — Baha-ullah

However, there are hurdles; and distractions are the biggest hurdles in unfolding of your psychic potentials. Beware of them, and eliminate all distractions one-by-one. Consider the example of a Tibetan master who lived around the turn of the last century, a kind of Himalayan Leonardo da Vinci, called Mipham. He is said to have invented a clock, a canon, and an airplane. But once each of them was complete, he destroyed them, saying that they would only be the cause of further distraction.

> The more thou shalt advance, the more thy feet shall encounter bog and morass. The path which thou walkest, is lighted by only one fire, even the light of the audacity which burns in thy heart. The more thou shalt dare, the more thou shalt obtain.
>
> —*Book of Golden Precepts*

Distractions are to be completely dissolved, destroyed and eliminated before you reach a state of 'self-dominion'. The self-dominion means complete control over mind (a state of quiet mind), thought and action. And then, you can remain on sleuthing sojourn for the period you are to have hold on your mind.

The mindset of everybody is fixed to function on certain frequencies, beyond which it does not function fruitfully. In order to make it function on wide-band of sleuthing journey *vis-à-vis* telepathy, clairvoyance, psychometry, one has to tune it, finetune it, by practising self-control. To begin with, you must have desire, determination and dedication to achieve 'self-dominion.'

We can perceive thoughts only after they develop a great deal, or after they become actions . . . . If we can get hold of thought at the root, before it has become a thought, before it has become action, then it would be possible for us to control the whole. Now, if there is a method by which we can analyze, investigate, understand, and finally grapple with those finer powers, the finer causes, then alone is it possible to have control over ourselves, and the man who has control over his own mind assuredly will have control over every other mind. That is why purity and morality have been always the object of religion; a pure, moral man has control of himself — a complete self-dominion.

A race is as great as its individual members are self-determined. "He that reigns within himself," says Milton, "and rules his passions, his desires and fears, is more than a king." Self-mastery is the foundation for an evolving life.

Self-mastery does not consist merely in being able to control one's temper and emotions. It also means that you do not tremble in the face of danger, that you remain unmoved amid temptation, that you do not shrink when poverty shakes the skeleton wand at you, when trials and difficulties crowd upon you, when, in short, nothing can touch that serene self-poise which characterizes the God-men, in all storms of life!

The man who has once learned to control his thought forces, knows that true self-mastery becomes a matter of course. He knows how to protect himself from his mental enemies as well as his physical ones. He knows, for instance, that when the brain is in danger of a passion fire, it will not do to add more fuel to fan the flame by storming and raging, but will quietly put out the fire by applying an antidote — the serenity thought, the thought of peace and prosperity.

Take bad temper, for example. This is the result of false pride, selfishness, or cheap vanity, and no man or woman is worth the name who continues to be governed by it. There is nothing manly or womanly or noble in the quality that lets loose the "dogs of war," which in an instant may make enemies of friends, ruin a home, or bring shame and disgrace on oneself and one's family.

The man who has not learned to control his temper or to resist his appetite, who is the victim of the slightest temptation or impulse, who is led by feeling, emotion, and not by the steady light of principles, will never make a leader of men, for he cannot lead himself.

It is generally said by different moralistic traditions that one should not get angry, that it is bad to get angry. However, there are certain natural expressions in our life, and anger is one of them. Anger is a safety valve for the pent-up energy that has to be released at times in one way or the another. If we do not open that safety valve and energy remains bottled up inside, then the pressure will seek some other outlet. May be in the form of hypertension, heart ailment or anxiety.

What happens, however, is that with the expression of a negative emotion, the anger, a feeling of guilt is attached. That guilt should not be experienced in a harmonious life. If life is disharmonious, then guilt arises, then inferiority or superiority complexes arise, then the idea of high-class and low-class living and working arises, then the idea of being overburdened with worries and anxieties arises. It all comes from the single aspect of guilt.

This applies, not only to anger, but also to practically every ambition and desire that we experience. We have evolved strange concepts of right and wrong which often go against our nature, mind and body? Because we are unable to come to terms with realities of our personality. Self-acceptance has to be understood in a very positive, systematic and constructive way.

Man is not necessarily criminal. But when the emotions, the sentiments, the feelings, the desires, or whatever it may be, are aroused, that the subject will lose self-control and often commit crime in response to the appeal of his passions.

It is worthwhile to note that what the mind causes, the mind can cure. By directing your conscious mind to dictate to your sub-conscious mind, you can break undesirable habits, confess crime and eliminate the guilt feelings, develop personality, will-power, strength, health, physique, overcome fear, and accomplish almost anything. Result will fascinate you.

People who are miserable and inefficient are so, chiefly because they are not masters in their mental realm. They fling open the doors of their mind and admit all sorts of conflicting mental currents which bring discord, meanness, hatred, and jealousy. Pandemonium reigns throughout their mental kingdom, and then they wonder why they are unhappy and impotent. It never seems to occur to them that it is because they do not control their thoughts, because they allow the enemies of their peace and welfare to etch their hideous images upon the walls of their mind, to make a menagerie of their mental kingdom instead of keeping it as a temple, dedicated only to the use of the highest and the most sacred things in their nature.

We are victims of our thoughts because we are willing to be subjected to them, for no mental influence short of actual manomania is so strong that we cannot resist it, or eventually send it flying, by the exertion of the right sort of determination. It is only the man with feeble mental muscles who cannot command the forces of his mind.

Any normal person can obtain command over any aggregation of mental weaknesses if the desire for conquest that thrills the soul is real, and is backed by an earnest and persistent effort.

Only a few great souls here and there obtain a complete dominion over themselves, and stand out like beacon lights in the history of race. Some of us get possession of a little of ourselves. We conquer a small portion of territory here and there in our vast physical and mental domain, but the greater part of ourselves we never conquer. The power that should preside at the helm is not always and everywhere the master.

Pure gold does not suffer any deterioration or loss from the severest fire test, because there is no dross, nothing that the fire can finish. If you have kept growing, broadening your mental horizon: if through experience, you have accumulated wisdom which is more precious than rubies; if through the years, you have constantly followed your highest ideal, then there is nothing that can affect your great interior wealth, with which no material resources can compare. If you have mastered the self, you are really rich; you have serenity, a mental balance, a poise which no calamity or loss can touch or tarnish.

Self-dominion is possible only if you can control your thoughts: "It is thought, and thought alone, that divides right from wrong. It is thought, and thought only that elevates or degrades human deeds and desires," says George Moore.

In case you are not able to control your thoughts, allow them to flow freely so that they come to some end — "The free man is he who does not fear to go to the end of his thought," says Leon Blum. If they still persist then stop them by deep breathing exercise.

It is suggested that you keep a relaxed attitude of mind. What is important is not to work against time, not to be in a hurry, not to be too much time-bound, not to look at watch too often; in fact, go in for little more leisurely pace of work and activity with calm and composure, without losing your temper. In other words, not to be at loggerheads with yourself but to be your own friend. To this end, hobbies, exercise, travel, music, meditation and soul-psychic sleuthing will help.

> A man who is master of patience is master of everything else.
>
> — Lord Halfin

The mind is like a naughty child; it does the opposite of what you want to do. So, if you try to shut-out sense impressions, the mind automatically makes them more intense. If, on the other hand, you force the mind to think of external things while the eyes are closed, it will, after some time, tend to lose interest in the external sounds, etc. and will not associate with sense impressions. This state of mind is exactly we want for inward looking — sleuthing.

You have to discipline yourself. Many of you think that if you become disciplined you will lose your spontaneity, your creativity — as if to be instinctive is to be creative! Well, maybe so. But the things that are created out of an instinctive state of mind are most horrible. That is not true creativity: it is mediocrity, even less than that — it is insanity. Creativity is a big thing. There is only one creator and that is God, and unless you go very close to God, to say you are creative is nonsense. Discipline is necessary. Why? If you want to be truly telepathist, clairvoyant or psychometrist, you have to get rid of the bad habit of letting your energies run out.

Let us look at self-acceptance now. The natural expressions of the human personlity have to be accepted. If an elephant were to fantasize and try to live like a goldfish, or a peacock like cow, then it would be very disharmonious expression of their natural being. In fact, one would classify them as ridiculous. Do you see any such correlations in yourself ? We are often like an elephant trying to become a goldfish or a weak mouse trying to be a roaring lion.

Such fantasies pervade the thoughts and lives of all individuals. We all try to change our nature and the nature of others. We try to create a sugar-coated personality by ignoring our negative and limiting qualties, our detrimental expressions and actions.

We have to open ourselves so that we can experience the harmony of life, and in order to open ourselves totally there has to be a degree of self-acceptance. This self-acceptance is based on proper analysis and understanding of the qualities, weaknesses and strength that is within us.

If we make thorough analysis — SWOT (Strength, Weakness, Opportunity, Threats) analysis — and, include psychic talents and application of psychic talents, i.e. sleuthing techniques, we shall be better off. For that, i.e. for the development of psychic talents, we have to have self-control.

Scout your own life, while you are in reviewing reverie, do this in any case sooner or later to see if you are getting to "self-dominion" before starting the practice for developing psychic talents.

It is therefore, necessary to perfect one's body, mind, personality and awareness to such an extent that there is total control over the forces of nature and the fields of psychic domain.

The carousel of time seems to spin faster and faster; time is a "Great Charlatan," not a great healer — keep it in view; life is less than it could be — and all because we don't use our brain authoritatively. Nevertheless, the human being is a very tough character. He is so confoundedly tough that he has whipped the whole animal kingdom and he can shake the stars.

Man is intended to be self-determined organism. That is to say that as long as he can make evaluations of his data without artificial compulsions or repressions he can operate to the maximum efficiency. When man becomes exteriorly-determined, which is to say compelled to do or repressed from doing something without his own rational consent, he becomes a pushbutton animal.

The clearest thinkers have always been brought eventually face-to-face with self-evident truth that Man's inward states influence his outward conditions. It is a remarkable fact that each of them has finally arrived at the place where he has seen that Man either controls his mental states or they control him. Where they control him, he is the slave of circumstances and conditions; where Man controls them, he is the master.

To acquire mastery over all our forces, we may observe austerity and/or self-discipline. As we do this, however, worldly powers and occult faculties will develop. When a man has learned to control his speech, for instance, whatever he says is bound to come true. The power is gained through silence, by controlling the energy which is now being wasted by unnecessary speech. The truly wise ones do not speak, unless by their words they can accomplish something. If a person is indrawn and speaks seldom, everyone pays attention to him; but he who is constantly talking, no one heeds his words. What a blessing it is when we have the power to govern our speech; for so much harm is done by unnecessary words. How often the things are better left unsaid! Therefore, if we can practice silence even a little, we shall have greater power. When a man learns to regualte his speech and thus avoid waste of energy, his intuition and ESP grow keener, his voice becomes stronger, and his language gains a new beauty.

One may often have noticed the feeble, 'wishy-washy' way most people talk. One may have tried hard to follow some rambling statement, but have found at the end that one hardly knows 'what it was all about,' or that the person who has tried to interest you has made an impression on you, whatever. This has been due to the fact that the man or woman has no power of concentration and consequently no force behind his/her flow of words.

It is the same when such people write a letter — again there may be lot of words, even expressions and sentences well put together, but the letter has no effect on you, and very likely you toss it aside and think no more about it.

On the contrary, another person may say only a few words but those words take effect; or they may write, and their sentences strike home — the secret of this mystery is concentration of mind.

The simplest way of developing this power is by the use of soul-psychic search and to bring tranquillity of mind. Go straight for what you want without shilly-shallying or hesitation of any kind.

Having had our mind mingled with matter; energy entrapped into emotions; emotions sinewed with the soul; thoughts seeking salvation; and our consciousness conditioned and curated for comforts, but carped into caprice, and cramped into crime; we have to achieve self-dominion, and then step-by-step surmount the sleuthing techniques.

We must seal the process for self-dominion and give it a firm form and structure in our daily activity. We need the consistency, concentration and seriousness to bring things to conclusion. This requires dedication, calm, coolness, and willingness to persist in the face of adversity — to greet even suffering or opposition as friend. It requires detachment, the capacity to be alone, and the ability to abide in stillness. This is a moment by moment awareness that does not overlook anything, but which remains at the essence.

We must confront the hidden side of the life on the psyche. It is not enough to clear things up on an outer or superficial layer, or even on intermediate or deeper level. We must eradicate the seeds of falsehood from the deepest recesses of the mind. We must deal with the illusion power of the mind, the power of secret or hidden desires. We must face all ghosts and demons of our subconscious, including the most elemental fears and desires upon which this world of ignorance has been built. We must understand all the habits, addictions and dependencies upon which our attachment to the world of appearances is based.

> Nothing great will ever be achieved without great men, and men are great only if they are determined to be so.
>
> — Charles De Gaulle

The mind of man, specially subconscious mind, will not, and for many, cannot remain idle. If you don't plant desires in your subconscious, it will bee upon thoughts which reach it: idle mind is a devil's workshop. So dominate your mind like a tyrant to establish your greatness.

Until and unless greatness is attained, knowledge is gained, there is ever the ebb and flow, the constant see-saw between the animal and the man in every human being. The beast or brute is never completely absent or overcome except through a final Divinisation of the individual. As long as there is the human, side by side there will be animal also; now one having the upper hand, now the other. It is only when the man gets above and beyond both these and gets transformed and established in the third and the hitherto dormant aspect of nature, namely the Divine aspect, that he transcends both the sub-human and human limitations. Then outwards, there is no more of this tug-of-war between the animal and man natures to gain precedence and dominate over the field of human-consciousness.

There are many means to gain control over the senses and mind, but anyway discrimination is the best. You must constantly discriminate.

"The mind becomes engaged in the objects of its liking. It wants everything to be pleasant. Therefore, you should always keep discriminating between what is permanent, or eternal, as opposed to what is temporary, or ephemeral; what is beneficial to you and what is harmful. Self-mortification does not work on the mind; the mind can only be controlled by discrimination," says Swami Muktananda (1908-1982).

The mind is such that where nothing exists; it makes you see the whole universe, as one sees a snake in a rope or water in a mirage. It makes you see forms in the formless. It causes relativity to manifest in the Absolute.

The same mind makes a friend into a foe and a foe into a friend. It takes you from heaven to hell or from hell to heaven. To focus the mind outside is bondage and to focus it within is liberation. The pleasure and pain of the body do not affect the self. The self is free from what the body has to go through.

In order to experience one's true self, one should remain in solitude for some time each day. If possible, one should go into complete seclusion for about seven days every two or three months. During these periods of solitude, one should abandon all thoughts and practise watching what is happening within. In this way, one gets into the state of witness-consciousness, and self-dominion.

As we turn within more and more, the senses become correspondingly subtler and more powerful, and the mind becomes one-pointed. However, the subtlety of senses increases in direct proportion to your degree of control over them, whereas a more subtle sense is more pervasive. Therefore, through the control of the senses, sounds emanating from far-off places can be heard, remote objects can be seen, and distant odours can be smelled. It is also possible to know another person's thoughts. Similarly, the power and effectiveness of your words increases in direct proportion to the silence that you observe.

As is true for all attempts to mature and grow emotionally and spiritually, we must cultivate moral imperatives: non-injury, truthfulness, self-centric discipline to scrutinize ourselves, and the desire to reach the goal.

In addition to cultivate these moral imperatives, we must balance the subtle masculine and feminine energies that move through the body along specific pathways. "Subtle energy" is the energy of the non-physical body, also known as astral body or subtle body, that appears to clairvoyants as the aura surrounding a person's physical body. Whether or not we see the human aura, we experience the effects of another person's subtle body, or aura, when we feel, for example, that a person is "warm" or "cold", hostile or friendly. When our aura mingles with the aura of another person, we have a sense that we are connected with this other person. Our pets are usually more sensitive to the subtle energies that we radiate, than we are.

Dr. John Hagelin, a world-renowned quantum physicist, says: "I see a future of unbounded potential, unbounded possibilities. Remember we are using, at the most, just five per cent of the potential of human mind. One hundred per cent human potential is the result of proper education. so imagine a world where people are using their full mental and emotional potential. We could go anywhere we would do anything. Achieve anything,"[9] with self-dominion.

Whether it is the mind of man acting on matter (psychometric impressions), or matter acts on mind (psychometric readings), or matter acts on matter, or whether mind acts on mind, the methods of arriving at certainty could be the same in principle as in the scientific investigations. The laboratory experiment of the bell-jar, test-tube or crucible, the control methods of the biological laboratory and the normative methods of the statistical apprach to certainty have all behind them a critical attitude of mind which could be kept alive even in the world of the study of the self of Man. Mental experimentation and domination could follow the same disciplinary outlines as laboratory experimentation.

---

9. Rhonde Byrne; *The Secret*, Beyond Words Publishing, New York, 2006, p. 181.

We have great authority over our possessions and our faculties. If you tell your eyes to close, they close; if you tell your finger to bend, it bends; if you give your feet an order, they obey. And when you get that kind of authority over your brain, your tongue, your self-image, and your enthusiasm, you may be well on your way towards great accomplishment.

> You may control a mad elephant;
> You may shut the mouth of the tiger;
> Ride the lion and play with the cobra;
> By alchemy you may earn your livelihood;
> You may wander through the universe incognito;
> Make vassals of the gods; be ever youthful; You may walk on water and live in fire:
> But the control of mind is better and more difficult.
>
> — Thayamanavar

In order to maintain self-dominion and even ground it, we must keep in the company of evolved souls; for they carry helpful aura. Each person carries his own vibrations and they correspond to his type of life, his thoughts and feelings, his doings, his consciousness. They may be good and helpful or not good, and therefore unhelpful, if not positively harmful. Then there are those whose atmosphere vitiates spiritual aspiration. Verbally or otherwise, they create doubts, introduce stresses of disequillibrium and in many ways set in motion waves that are inimical to your progress. You need to be vigilant and avoid the company of such people. There are, further, some who are like vampires; they suck your vitality and leave you tired, dry. They may be interesting in their conversation, fascinating in other ways, but they leave you exhausted. You must make it a point to be away from such persons.

Further, there are books containing the writings or utterances of God-realized persons and they are full of their spiritual vibrations. Such books carry their charge, each word is instinct with their power of spiritual dynamics. Make it a point to devote some time daily to reverant study of such authentic literature. Disciplined study and practice is a long prescribed way to prepare oneself for 'self-dominion';

capable of developing occult faculties like telepathy, clairvoyance, psychometry, etc. and for integral perfection of life.

1.5 Sleuthing Scope

Soul-psychic sleuthing scope extends from zero to hero, like in the case of Lord Buddha; from ignorance to enlightenment; from minus infinity to plus infinity, i.e. eternal; from sinful life to free-soul life with all 'karmas' dissolved.

God created man. Man did not know who he was, what he was, and where from he came. In the quest of these answers man created God, and man did not know whether God is the first or he himself is the first? And still, men do not know themselves with certainty who is the first, except what scriptures and evolved souls have said from time to time, or what occultists and seers have told us. Were the persons world stage's Big-B's, we mean the scientists Big-Bang proposers!

Nevertheless, God created the man because He was feeling alone. HE is still feeling alone in spite of the fact that cosmos He created with infinite entities is not too big for Him to communicate with, command and control — world has become chaotic (The followers of certain religions are harvesting[10] souls from other religions, because they feel that their God, Lord, Father needs more worshippers to reach Him and fill the prayer halls). But God feels cosmos is too small, and so, He keeps it expanding — physicists suggest that cosmos is expanding since the Big-Bang. This inspires God to become more creative. Similarly, Man is also becoming or wants to become more creative and evolve further.

The creativity and evolution necessitate for man to gather more intelligence, which in turn puts premium on soul-psychic sleuthing.

That makes the sleuthing scope very wide and vivid — from solving basic problems of the simplest man's life through controlling nature and evolution of human life to enlightenment and *nirvana*. However,

---

10. Arun Shourie, *Harvesting Our Souls, Missionarie, Their Design, Their Claims*, Rupa & Co., New Delhi, 2006.

the present text is limited and circled by suggestions-cum-solutions offered by common sense, conscience, telepathy, clairvoyance, and psychometry, exclusively and combinedly (Hightened ESP).

If you ever turn your mind inwards for sleuthing, you perceive such wonderful things that you would not like to look outwards at all. It is said that if anyone has caught a glimpse of what is within, he will never again seek anything outside. That is a fact. Even if, because of your previous habits, you are inclined to look outwards, you find all the joy has gone from these outside things. You go through the habit of looking out and become restless, but there is no joy, no glamour left in the outside world, nothing is left. And very soon you come back to your inner quest, and you make further and further effort, to reach the most wonderful reality!

And one thing you must not forget: all that you see here is the effect; the cause is always more potent than the effect; the cause is hidden, subtle, it is not in the outside. We run after all these things; they exist for one moment — the next moment they are gone. We can never hold on to them. But the causal thing, that from which all these have come — that is permanent. If we can persuade ourselves that this hidden thing is the real thing, then sleuthing becomes easier for us.

There are many possible mechanisms at work in gaining knowledge of the unknown and of the future — but in cultivating your own aptitude for solving problems and prophecy, you can leave the "mechanics" of the process to the unconscious mind. However, you have to encourage the unconscious mind by giving it opportunity to develop its powers, as through the changes in lifestyle, and through the fun and enjoyment of the various ESP games; on the base of "self-dominion".

We have to make perpetual effort to spiritualize the cells of our body into such a refinement, sensitiveness and delicacy that we may become more and more perfect "wireless stations" to receive finer vibrations. That will give us such happiness as the gratification of the coarser senses can never secure. All our senses may be kenned to finer perceptions. The cultivation of our higher ideals will lift our lives.

It is a well-known fact that some of the disoriented products of excessively rigorous spritual disciplines, mystics, possess uncanny psychic gifts of telepathy, clairvoyance, prediction and the like. For this reason crowds of people visit them to seek some favour or a solution to their problems. Their performances, at times, are amazing and their clairvoyant gifts are so extraordinary that the visitors are dumbfounded. Some men of this type are even found in mental hospitals both in the East and the West.

Deterioration in the quality of consciousness does not only occur in mystics, but in the case of men of genius as well. William James, who designates the unhealthy condition as the sickness of the soul, cites the case of Goethe (*c.* 1824 CE), Martin Luther, Tolstoy and others, who had attacks of melancholia towards the end of their lives. The borderline geniuses include some very notable examples, as for instance, Nietzsche, Rimbaud, Van Gogh and others.

Kundalini mechanism is the force responsible for the soul-elevating ecstacies of the mystic and the dark fits of depression of the maniac. It is a well-observed fact that in most cases of madness, periods of gloom alternate with spells of lucidity or intervals of violent agitation with periods of relative calmness.

The information and intelligence gathered through our senses, i.e. without the help of soul-psychic investigation — without involvement of instinct, intuition, psychism, telepathy, clairvoyance, psychometry, etc. — is most of the times far from "Truth". Because, we have been barraged with the opinion of others, many of which we have adopted as our own. Haven't you heard political speeches which "set your teeth on edge?" Or, read something in the newspapers which has upset you so much that you were unable to sleep? Do you know that it is possible for a news reporter to leave out part of the facts, or worse, to combine two true facts in such a way as to arrive at a completely different meaning.

Soul-psychically enlightened person is dynamic. His ethical and moral standards are high, his ability to seek and experience pleasure is great. His personality is heightened and he is constructive. It is not yet known how much longevity is added to a life in the process of becoming knowledgable. He is entirely self-determined. And his creative imagination is high. He can do a swift study of anything within his intellectual capacity, which is inherent. His vigour, persistence and tenacity to life are very much higher than anyone has thought possible.

As soon as, through soul-psychic sleuthing, the Man is apprised of the facts of the natural order of the cosmos, s/he will stop misusing what was given to her/him for her/his benefit.

The main purpose of the sleuthing is to curb all tendencies to react negatively. What is negative or what is conscientious and ethical can be explored by tantalizing your mind to the level of superconsciousness.

The development of the soul-psychic techniques of telepathy, clairvoyance and psychometry, will certainly lead you to crossover the first threshold of spiritual ascendancy — from 'meditating monk' to 'mediumistic monk'; and finally to the 'mystic'.

When you have developed occult powers, and mastered the sleuthing techniques, never brag about them. Ostentatious display of unusual powers is decried by masters. A Persian mystic, Abu Saiid, once laughed at certain *fakirs* (Muslim ascetics) who were proud of their miraculous powers over water, air, and space.

"A frog is also at home in the water!" Abu Saiid pointed out in gentle scorn. "The crow and the vulture easily fly in the air; the Devil is simultaneously present in the East and in the West! A true man is he who dwells in righteousness among his fellow-men, who may buy and sell, yet is never for a single instant forgetful of God!" On another occasion the great Persian teacher gave his view on the religious life thus: "To lay aside what you have in your head (selfish desires and ambitions); to bestow freely what you have in your hand; and never to flinch from the blows of adversity!"

The nature has strange ways of keeping account of one's good and evil deeds and potentials. In spite of it, we have learned to understand our own behavioured responses to weather extremes; the irritability that comes with hot, humid days; the paranoia that builds up with long hot, dry spells, etc. For example, we hunger for more foods rich in fat and protein in the winter because the body needs more of these substances for warmth and sustenance in the absence of the Sun.

Similarly, we must understand and learn all the soul-psychic sleuthing techniques ourselves, and practice regularly to solve the problems related to health, harmony, humanity, quiet-mind, truth and the universe.

In the contemporary world, there has been a qualitative change in the dimensions of problems facing mankind, while social organization is becoming more and more complex. Increase in the population, high level of demand and rising aspirations of some sections of society which for centuries remained depressed and underdeveloped, have been partly the result of growth of knowledge and technology. On the other hand, the growing problems have further strengthened the urge to develop soul-psychic sleuthing techniques.

Man's life is like a loom where sorrow and happiness are interwoven like the warp and weft. There are ups and downs in the life of a man as the Wheel of Time turns. When he is in difficulties he is dejected and when in joy he is elated. Sorrows are caused by many factors such as physical ailments, family problems, desires and high ambitions. To cure his ailments or solve his problems, or when his wishes are not fulfilled, man turns to God for His help. As Saint Kabir has said people remember God only when they are in distress and drowned in worries but during their hay days they fail to remember Him. But the Divine God or Goddess never lets down anybody who earnestly prays to them and asks to remove his sorrows and fulfil his desire.

We can solve almost every one of our problems by learning to love — to love our jobs, to love the company we work for, to love the people we work with, to love life, to love excellence, to love God. Anyone who works with other people will encounter problems and differences of opinion. But all of the problems can be solved — through understanding acquired by sleuthing, and of course, love.

The roll of destiny unfolds itself and actualizes the inevitable. You cannot change the course of events, but you can change your attitude and not the bare event. The world is the abode of desires and fears. You cannot find peace in it. For peace you must go beyond the world. The real course of the world is self-love. Becuase of it we seek pleasure and avoid pain. Soul-psychic sleuthing will make you replace self-love by love of the Self and the picture changes. *Brahman* the Creator is the sum-total of all desires. The world is instrument for their fulfilment. Souls take whatever pleasure they desire and pay for them in tears. Time squares all accounts. The law of balance reigns supreme.

From our point of view the world is a vale of tears, a place to escape from, as soon as possible, and by every possible means. But to enlightened beings the world is good and it serves a good purpose. They do not deny that the world is a mental structure and that ultimately all is one, but they see and say that the structure has meaning that serves a supremely desirable purpose. What we call the Will of God is not a capricious whim of a playful deity, but the expression of an absolute necessity to grow in love and wisdom and power, to actualize the infinite potentials of life and consciousness.

Life and death do not create problems; pains and pleasures come and go, are experienced and forgotten. It is memory and anticipation that create problems of attainment or avoidance, coloured by likes and dislikes. Truth and love and man's real nature, and mind and heart are the means of its expression.

It takes a fairly strenuous course of training to obtain a mental state of peace. It is disciplined life, like the life of a soldier. The perfect state is reached only when the mind, body and speech are in proper coordination. Every problem would lend itself to a solution if we are determined to make the law of truth and peace the law of life.

Every person must be himself a sleuth and be his own spiritual leader, must make his own journey of discovery, and find his own peace.

2

Our Sleuths

MAN is a highly sentient being among the vivid species of organisms; to our knowledge having the most complex mental structure, so far evolved on Earth. We enjoy our life through head, heart and hands.

Our two main senses are 'seeing' and 'touching', i.e. eyes and hands. However, Prof. Calligaris, a famous Italian specialist of experimental psychology believes that there are three 'communicating discs' in human body and they are: cortex of the brain, the heart and the index finger of right hand. These represent the head, the heart and the hand.

Watching function is executed by the eyes. It is not proper to depend on external watching for proper functioning necessary for perfect living of the life and its evolution. External watching brings transformation in living standards; still, it simply remains a substitute for internal watching; the watching that is provided by the mind and soul. Internal watching is the premier quality watching.

If somebody watches us, our entire body language changes — we become self-conscious and shy. Albert Einstein said that the movements inside an atom were totally different when he was watching them from when he was not. The point is that even matter, which is lifeless, undergoes some change when it is being watched.

In the temple before the deity we feel that God is watching us. This soon brings substantial transformation even if only for a short while. We get access to the witness who is beyond ego. For a short while the ego loses its limitations.

We have to acknowledge that the change which occured in our consciousness on the altered state of consciousness that we experienced before the deity was an excuse. The change that occured in consciousness was no different from the state of consciousness we feel watching a beautiful sunset or a majestic mountain. It is a type of self-hypnotization. This transformation can be described as a kind of spirituality.

Vedantic philosophy describes at length, the distinction between the seer and seen, the subject and the object. The 'seer' is the perceiver, identified with the subject and is of the nature of consciousness. The 'seen' is the thing perceived, identical with the object.

There are five senses for a 'seer': gustation or taste, olfaction or smell, vision or sight, auditory or hearing, and kinesthesis or feeling. We make most of the decisions that affect our behaviour primarily using only three of these senses: the visual, auditory, and kinesthetic systems.

There are still another four senses — four "inner organs" like the mind, intellect, memory and the ego. Thus, in all there are nine sense organs of the human body; the first five are external, and the other four internal.

Of the four inner organs, mind is the most important and powerful. As said, it receives the rays of consciousness of the soul and then activates and controls the actions of all the external organs.

The seeing, listening and learning are related to each other. What is seeing, perceiving? Do we see actually, or do we see through a darkened screen? A screen of prejudice, a screen of our idiosyncrasies, experiences, wishes, pleasures, fears, and obviously our images about that which we see about ourselves. So, we have screen after screen between us and the object of perception. Then do we ever see the thing at all? Or, is it that the seeing is coloured or prevented by our knowledge, experience, by our images or the beliefs that condition the mind, the memories which the mind has cultivated so that seeing may not take place at all? And is it possible for the mind not to have these images, conclusions, beliefs, memories, prejudices, fears, and without having those screens just to look? This becomes very important because when there is seeing — real seeing — you can't help but act.

Thus, our perception is relative reality. We know that the Sun is far bigger than the Earth and yet appears only as a small disc. Sometimes, sense perception may reveal a limitation, while the fact is entirely different. Sometimes our feelings are not correct in an interpersonal encounter. Images seen in a dream appear valid in that dimension, yet may not be in the working state.

There are different coloured glasses through which we perceive the world. Sometimes the world looks very beautiful and pink, sometimes it looks very drab and dull. Sometimes we get carried away by the force and sway of thought or we begin to wonder about the rationality of a thought we have had — distorting the images for our consumption.

Our exciting, nervous, strenuous, existence tends to make us overlook the common beauties and interests of life. Even the trivial things in our everyday path are full of inexpressible beauty and meaning only if our perceptions were fine and keen enough to sense them.

There is a plant called the 'touch-me-not'. When you go near to it, even if you have not touched it, it closes its leaves. Plants can feel, they know. In the same way, animals have their own degree of knowingness. Dogs can sense things coming. Birds can sense something that is going to happen. If there is an impending earthquake, you can hear the birds making huge noises just a few hours before the event.

Most of our lives we accept what we see without a question. No one tells us that what we see isn't true. Until we see a theatre magician do his act, we have become quite accustomed to thinking that everything we see is the way it looks.

Moreover, although sight, as a means to knowledge and control of ourselves and others — a noble sleuth — is regarded as the most important of the first five senses, however, the other senses are equally important.

> Reason and intellectuality cannot make you see the Divine, it is the soul that sees. — Sri Aurobindo

Eyes have been described as the gateway to the soul, which is the mystry related to reality and cosmic-consciousness.

> Truth is generally seen, rarely heard. — Baltasar Gracian, (1601-58)

The senses never impart to you the true vision, it comes from the soul and the inner layers of the mind. Vision is an activity of the eyes. It is also an activity of the receptive power of the mind and it is also awareness. Becoming more and more aware is developing a broader vision in abstract terms. Vision may also mean distraction and dissipation of the senses and the mind.

A vision is meaningless unless it inspires us to shape a bright future. All we have to ensure is that the vision does not become an idler's wishful thinking. We have to wake up from the long slumber of centuries.

> He whose heart is not attached to the objects of sense finds pleasure within himself. — Lord Krishna

Seeing something for the first time is cognition. Bringing something to perception when that thing isn't in front of one to perceive is memory. Recognition is the combination of both earlier perception (or cognition) and memory, which is a clue to the continuity of 'soul'.

Our language, also, plays a role of a sleuth. The linguistic relativity hypothesis[1] of Benjamin L. Worf states: "The way people use lanuage determines how they see the world."

Thus, our sleuths are: head enclosing mind; heart — the seat of soul; hands with sensitive forefinger. Besides, there are our five senses, speech and hired sleuths (consultants).

---

1. Whorf, Bejomin Lee, *Language, Thought and Reality*; p. 320.

2.1 Carnal Eyes

In order to know a subject or a problem or an event we have to go on finding more and more truth about it. For example, an elephant presented to a number of blind persons will be described differently by them. Some of them may say that it is like a pillar, because they saw or felt by their hands its legs only. The others who may have touched its trunk may describe it as something else. They may go even to the length of saying that there is something like a stem of tree coming out of its mouth. Thus, there shall be a number of descriptions, but none of them shall be complete or wrong. If we, however, place them together intelligently we get a perfect picture of an elephant. We may not be blind or eyeless, yet our vision is too limited to have a perfect view of reality behind the great universe.

Our senses openly mislead us. There are cases of illusion (rope appearing as snake). Perception of movement outside the running train is another example of perceptual illusion. Hallucination (perception of apparitions and other non-beings), non-perception of stimuli due to darkness are the common experiences of our life. Further, our senses convey false knowledge in respect of stimuli of enormously large size. Due to largeness of the Earth, it appears as flat, though it is global in physical constitution. The list of visual limitations and false perceptions in fact, is quite long and serpentine.

Our sense organs are limited in their ambit. To clarify, our eyes have their field of vision, limited to certain wavelengths/frequencies. Beyond such wavelengths, they are helpless. A dog's vision cannot be same as that of human's. An owl can see great in the dark, where human vision is limited.

In viewing the universe with your carnal eyes, much may seem to be missing. Just as your vision is limited when you stand in a valley, and much more can be seen by your eyes when you stand upon a hilltop or a mountaintop.

If the eye wants to see all that can be seen, the paradox of the eye seeing itself has to be resolved. To this, Dr. Alexis Carrel described the marvellous mechanism of the visual organ[2] like this: "A strange phenomenon occurs in the embryo. The brain causes a part of itself, the optic nerve and the retina, to shoot out towards the surface of the body. The part of the skin overlying the young retina, undergoes an astonishing modification. It becomes transparent, forms the cornea and the crystalline lens and unites with other tissues to build up the prodigious optical system which we call the eye. The aspect of universe depends on the constitution of the sense organs and on their degree of sensitiveness. For instance, should the retina record infra-red rays of great wavelength, nature would take on a different visage. The colour of rocks, water and trees would vary with the seasons because of the changes in the temperature . . . . Heat rays being visible would conceal all objects. In winter, the atmosphere would become clear and contours of things precise. The aspect of men, however, would remain very different, their outline vague, their face hidden by red mist issuing from their mouth and nostrils. After violent exercise the body would seem to increase in size, on account of heat released by the skin and surrounding the figure with a large aura. In the like manner, the cosmic world would assume another appearance if the retina becomes sensitive to ultra-violet rays and the skin to the light rays."

Most men can't see beyound the violet. Under ultraviolet light, the human eyeball glows slightly, so that one sees a mist of light isn't there, but since we can't see ultraviolet light itself, an observer will not see the source of ultraviolet that is there.

Electromagnetic waves cover a scale of fifty-five octaves and a good mortal vision covers only one octave, to be precise — violet wavelength of 4200 AU to red wavelength of 6300 AU (AU=10^{-8}cm). Horses see clearly what we call ghosts, dogs smell a thief.

The acuteness of all our sense organs, also, matters. Why do we always use rectangular TV-screen, a black-board in classrooms and cinema-screen in theaters, because of acuteness of our eyes in that

---

2. Dr. Alexis Carrel, *Man, the Unknown*, Penguin Books, New York, 1935.

ratio vertical: horizontal:: 3:4. Similarly, the depth of image is dependable on the range of visibility.

Eyes have the ability to see. They can observe and witness, but they alone cannot decide, judge, act or move the mountains. Their main function is just to see. This observation is understood to increase the awareness of the luminosity of the self. For example, the more twigs that are thrown onto a fire, the higher and brighter the flames become. In the same way the nature of the faculty of sight is to increase the knowledge and awareness of the luminosity of the self.

According to the special luminosity practice of Dzogchen,[3] all the light of our wisdom-energy resides in the heart *Chakra* (centre), which is connected through "Wisdom channels" to the eyes. The eyes are the "doors" of the luminosity, so you keep them open during meditative practices, in order not to block these wisdom channels.

It has long been said that the eyes are the windows to the soul. Only recently, however, we have learned how true that is. There is no parapsychological mystry about it. Simply by being observant, by watching a person's eyes (even of animal's eyes), you can immediately see which representational system he is using at a specific time: visual, auditory, or kinesthetic.[4]

A similar, but vivid description of God's eyes as given by Deepa Kodikal, an ascendant towards divinity, is: "I saw the world with the Lord's eyes. These eyes saw things different from those seen by ordinary mortals. These eyes were liquid rubies and they emanated rays of a peculiar radiance. These were only half-open, they could not be opened fully. Behind them was the knowledge of being the Creator. The Great Lord God, the Almighty Creator of this astounding, marvellous universe. He in whom exist all the gods and deities; He of whom are born Lakshmi, Bhavani, and Saraswati! From whom cascade

---

3. Geshe Thupten Jinpa and Richard Barron, *Dzogchen: The Heart Essence of the Great Perfection*, Ithac Snow Lion, New York, 2000.
4. Robins Anthony; *Unlimited Power*, Free Press, New York, 1986, pp. 127-33.

forth knowledge and divine bliss, to permeate the known and the unknown universes. The Creator who is the eternity and the infinity; the cause and the effect; the supreme manipulator of destinies!"[5]

All our senses can be fooled. Even when they are very sharp and accurate, it is the mind at the back of them which understands and comprehends. Man has constructed a telescope which increases his visual range so greatly that it has brought within his vision worlds that are millions of miles distant, yet the greatest thing about that giant telescope and the worlds it sees is the mind behind the eye that looks through it at them, which is fooled.

Under certain circumstances eyes convey false knowledge of the stimuli to the mind. For example:

(1) A dust particle falls in the eyeball. The particle is so close to the eye, yet the eye fails to perceive it. Further, eyes fail to perceive their own eyebrow because of the same reason. In fact, the visual focus has a starting as well as termination-point. Stimuli at the pre-starting point fall without the range of visual perception. The termination-point of focus is extended in the case of radiant objects, such as the Sun, the Moon and the stars. In the case of non-radiant objects, the termination-point occurs much earlier. It is because of this tendency of visual termination that the sky falsly appears as canopy. The canopy-view of sky is nothing but an illusion that arises due to the termiantion-tendency of visual perception. Let it be mentioned here that sensory perception is confined only to such stimuli which physically exist. Sky lacks this qualification; it is devoid of all physical attributes. In Sanskrit language, the equivalent of sky is *sunya*. Void or *sunya* lies beyond the periphery of visual perception. Our knowledge of sky, therefore, is not perceptual; it is inferential. Like sky (space), the entity of time also lies beyond the periphery of visual perception. Yet it is

5. Deepa Kodikal, *A Journey within the Self — A Diary of Yogic Experiences*, Viva Books Pvt Limited, New Delhi, 2006, p. 45.

believed to be a piece of empirical reality. In fact, the origin point of the time-concept is traceable to the sequence of actual events such as sunrise, a sunset, hide-and-seek play of day and night, cycle of seasons and so on.

(2) In the state of attention, divided attention, sleep and other such mental conditions, eyes along with other senses cease to perceive any stimuli. In the state of inattention, linkage of mind with the senses is suspended.

(3) Our eyes fail to distinguish identical units from one another. We fail to distinguish one ant from the other, one fly from another, one bee from another, one wasp from another and so on.

There is an ancient adage, "what thou see-est, that thou be-est."

The blind person never fears ghosts — Burmese Proverb
The eye never forgets what the heart has seen — Scottish Proverb

We have all heard the expression "looking through rose-coloured glasses," applied to people for whom whole world seems wonderful and sweet. But we all wear glasses of one kind or the another, fitted with the lenses of our personalities. This is why two people can read the same book, see same film, hear the same politician, and each comes away from the event with a diametrically opposite view of what was presented — necessitating soul-psychic investigation.

In the animal kingdom some nervous systems are much faster than ours and others much slower. A snail's neurons pick up signal from the outside world so slowly, for example, that events any faster than three seconds would not be perceived. In other words, if a snail was looking at an apple, and you quickly reached in and snatched it away, the snail would not be able to detect your hand. It would "see" the apple disappear before its very eyes — a phenomenon good enough to explain 'teleportation' discussed in the following chapter. In the same way, quantum flashes are millions of times too rapid for us to register, so our brains play a trick on us by "seeing" solid objects that are continuous in time and space, the same way that a movie seems continuous. A movie consists of twenty-four still pictures flashing by per second, with twenty-four gaps of blackness as each frame is taken away and a new one put in its place. But since our brains cannot perceive forty-eight stop-motion events in one second, the illusion of movie is created.

Always check the observations; the observer may be wrong. But the actual observations made by physical means through mind's eye and the eye of soul, are never wrong.

> It is only with the heart that one can see rightly; what is essential is invisible to the eye. —Antoine De Saint-Exupery

2.2 Mind's Eye

Human life is considered to be evolved since it possesses the capacity to embody a separate sense called 'mind' along with other senses (touch, taste, smell, sound and sight), through this composite medium of cognition one can perceive the images of nature.

Human mind by definition, is 'the intellectual power in man' and 'Man' means visible body. The mind works day-n-night from sensitive sanity to virile vanity, irksome irrationality, and/or essential eccentricity.

Mind is understood in two different senses.

(1) The individual mind is the self or subject which perceives, remembers, thinks, wills, feels, reasons, etc. and which is functionally related to an individual bodily organism.

(2) Mind is considered to be a spiritual or metaphysical substance that pervades all individual minds and is often contrasted with material substance.

According to Descartes, Rene (CE 1569-1650), a French philosopher, mathematician, and physicist, the mind can exist independent of the body, and the body can exist independent of mind. Although mind and body are functionally independent of each other, held Descartes, they interact with each other in the pineal gland of the human body.

This gives rise to the concept of 'Disembodied Mind.' The disembodied mind is the mind that continues ro possess mental qualities such as feeling, thinking, perceiving and willing without being in a body. Something similar is the 'mobile centre of consciousness,' a phrase coined by Andrija Puharich, a leading American neurologist.

The nature of individual mind is such that potentially every nook and corner of the world can be reflected in it, and there are ways and means to experience this.[6] "Let me give you an example" says Andrija Puharich,[7] "you might say that you have never studied the circulation of red blood cells, under a microscope in a laboratory. Yet you have to look at the blue sky, relax your mind, and you will directly observe the flow of myriads of blood cells in the fine vessels of your eye. Or, you could be down at absolute rest in a quiet room in your basement where there is no light or other disturbance, and within an hour or so you would begin to see, feel, and hear things whose existence up till now had never been suspected."

Eternal knowledge lies not in the other world, but in the centre of consciousness. The human mind is the finest instrument which can be trained to realize the centre from which consciousness flows in various degrees and grades. It is the mind which shares joys and sorrows of others and contemplates weal and woe.

We see mind breaking through the barrier of space to reach another mind with an exchange of intelligence. We see mind going through a network of other minds and reaching its goal with a high degree of selectivity. We see mind extending outward with invisible threads to blanket hundreds of minds at one time to bring about a common or mass hullucination in the group. We have seen how mind

---

6. Raynor C. Johanson, *The Imprisoned Splendor*, Harp and Brothers, New York, 1953.
7. Andrija Puharich, *Beyond Telepathy*, Picador Pan Books Ltd, London, 1975, p. xiii.

can be relayed, stored, and even projected into the future, through the mediation of inanimate objects such as pieces of paper, pottery and photographs.

It is difficult to escape the conclusion that the mind at certain levels of operation is ubiquitous and can pass through the barriers of the physical world around us. In fact, there are times when it literally transcends time as it leaps ahead to cognize physical events not yet born, or leaps backward in time to reconstruct scenes long since perished from the physical realm.

New and nearly unchartered realms, Terra Incognita, the Human Mind, is a land which lies an inch behind your forehead.

According to a noted physician from India, Dr Yatish Aggarwal[8], "The human mind is simply awesome. With the cranium for its abode, a 1350 grams mushroom of gray and white tissue of geletine like consistency, and 100 billion nerve cells slaving for it 24X7, it simply has no boundaries. No other creation of this universe can match its majestic tread, the activity it enjoys. Even the fastest bullet trains, aircraft, rockets and space shuttles cannot outstrip it. Why, even H.G. Wells' Time Machine would be a poor second in its back and forth speed."

The physics of mind can be perceived through Neuro-Linguistic Programming (NLP). Physics deals with the structure of reality, the nature of world. NLP does the same thing for your mind. It was initiated by John Grinder, a linguist, and Richard Bandler, a mathematician, Gestalt therapist, and computer expert. NLP allows you to break things down into the component parts that make them work. People have spent a lifetime trying to find a way to feel totally loved. They have spent fortunes trying to get to "know themselves" with analysts and read dozens of books on how to succeed. NLP gives us the technology to accomplish these and many other goals elegantly, efficiently, and effectively — now!

The mind is like a naughty child; it does the opposite of what you

8. Dr. Yatish Aggarwal, *The World within, Symptoms and Remedies of Mind*, Raj Kamal Books, New Delhi, 2004.

want to do; this does not imply that if you ask the mind to do wrong, it will do right.

How hard it is to control the mind? Mind has been compared to a maddened monkey, drunken and bitten by a scorpion. The human mind is like that monkey, incessantly active by its own nature, then it becomes drunk with the wine of desire increasing its turbulance. After desire takes possession, the scorpion sting of jealous at the success of others comes. The demon of pride enters making the mind to think itself all important.

Mind is really two persons in one. One of these persons is a little person. One-ninth the size of the other, the big person. The active little person, the conscious mind likes to interfere, likes to be bossy, likes to control, as it has reason and logic but no memory. The big person, the subconscious has no reason and no logic, but it has the seat of memory. Everything that has ever happened to a human, even things that happened before birth, are retained within the subconscious, and under suitable types of relaxations (like sleep, hypnosis, astral travelling, etc.) that memory can be revived for consideration — through dreams, regression, and distant projection, etc.

The conscious mind governs and directs our daily normal life, and in the meantime recording every event, emotions, feelings, thoughts that encounter its action since childhood upto present moment. Its duty and functioning is limited and restricted to the things it already knows and its knowledge never exceeds the past (of the present life) and the present. For this reason no conscious mind, however intelligent or super-human it may be, can tell what will happen the next moment or what is going on next door. This restricted action of the conscious mind is only manifested when this mind is awake. Once it becomes lulled or dormant, as during sleep or in case of intoxication by drugs, it loses all control over the voluntary movements of body; that is why when one goes to bed with a book or cigarette and falls asleep, the book or cigarette drops without one knowing it. The brain being conquered by sleep loses its power over the grasping tendons of the hand and thus it drops objects.

When conscious mind is dormant, the subconscious mind starts to work. Unlike the conscious, the subconscious field of working is not limited, and that is the reason and main cause of dreams and other manifestation experiences during the absence of the conscious mind.

The lives of addicts, especially those who take big doses of narcotic drugs, cocaine, opium, etc. give a magnificent illustration of the absence of the conscious mind. In such cases the addict is found in a very peculiar state saying and doing fantastic things. He often sees houris or fairies or whatever his heart desires and acts in accordance with these halucinations and illusions.

Some magnificent writers, poets, composers and authors, and even artists, researchers are accustomed to taking drugs in order to awaken their subconscious minds which supply them with best ideas never attained in the case of consciousness. Some meditating monks, mediumistic monks and mystics are supposed to have followed this path.

The subconscious mind knows no barriers of space or place. Its action and duty are unrestricted. The most fascinating desires and ardent sensations only are brought to the surface and disclosed through subconscious activities.

The subconscious is highly sensitive to the dominant thought in the conscious mind, and performs its highest functions most brilliantly when the conscious mind is relaxed and quiet.

A tranquil and purified mind can transcend the barrier of sense world and reach the outermost frontiers of the world of time and space. It can glimpse what lies beyond the domain of senses. It gains extraordinary capabilities. It becomes all-knowing; it can know all the events of the past, the present and the future.

Broadly, the human body has three invisible parts — the inner-mind (subconscious mind), the outer-mind (conscious mind) and the intellect (some call it unconscious mind). You need a perfect coordination among them. The outer-mind does not accept any suggestion easily. Characteristically it argues. However, the inner-mind accepts any suggestion very easily and retains it for ever.

The unconscious mind is the base of man's normal and abnormal behaviour, it is a whirlpool of fantasies, confusions, and oscillations of creativity and doom. Human body takes nourishment and living energy from the soul. Mind takes unconscious from the soul at the time of birth and gives back the unconscious after charging it (with karmic records of the present living) at the time of death. Mind also takes experiencing and experimenting powers from the soul — soul, however, retains command and remains supreme.

Freud described the mind as having three parts. The ego includes that part of mind of which a person is generally conscious — the part that perceives, remembers and feels; the part that is used to figure out what to do today, tomorrow, and next week. The other two parts of mind — the super-ego and the id, Freud maintained, are largely unconscious (the unconscious should have been addressed as infra-conscious, because infra, meaning below, refers to consciousness at a different level, not its abcence). The super-ego includes parental, social, and moral injunctions, and tells people when they are good and when they are bad. When it is in conflict with something the individual has done or something he wants, the person might feel discomfort, shame, or anxiety. The id contains many desires, cravings and wishes, and can be in direct conflict with the super-ego. The ego acts as a referee between the desires of the id and the prohibitions of super-ego. What the individual says and doesn't say, does and doesn't do, are considered to be the product of this constant and unconscious process. These three parts do form an integrated whole, function as a whole, but the entire structure is like an iceberg — the tip above the water represents consciousness, and the vast region below symbolizes the unconscious mind. (Figure 2.1)

No one has seen the subconscious or unconscious mind, but most psychiatrists and psychologists conceive it with layers arranged like an onion. Ingenious labellers have named its divisions as perconscious, subconscious, underconscious, and supraconscious, whereas, some others have identified these layers as conscious, subconscious, surfy-unconscious, unconscious and super-conscious. This classification is given in the Table 1.

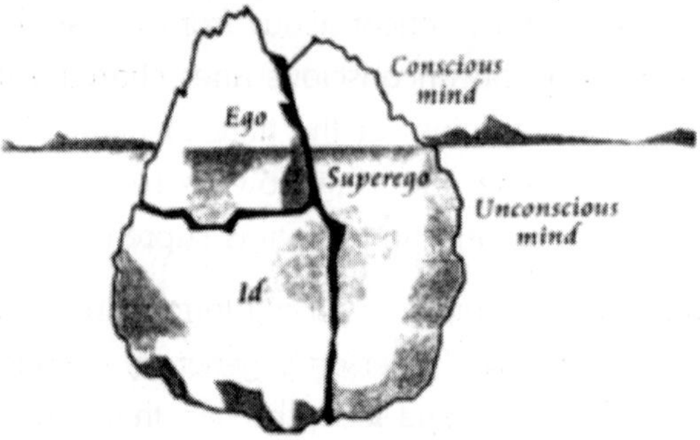

Fig. 2.1 Freud's model of mind

Table 1. Layers of Mind

S. No.	*Mind[1] Layer*	*Main Attributes*	*MEET-C*	*Awareness*	*Brain-wave*
1.	Conscious	Logic	Matter	Awake	β
2.	Sub-conscious	Memory	Energy	Relaxed, Meditation, Hypnogogic	α
3.	Surfy-[2] unconcious	Intelligence	Emotions	Dreaming,Creative, Intuitive, ESP	θ
4.	Unconscious	Mast-Malang[4]	Thought	Deep-sleep	δ
5.	Super-[3] conscious	Spiritualism[5]	Consciousness	Ecstasy	∝

Notes: (1) There are wide variety of nomenclatures for mind's layers besides given in this column — like analytical mind, reactive mind, somatic mind,[9] overmind,[10] etc.

---

9. L. Ron Hubbard, *Dianetics — The Modern Science of Mental Health*, Warner Paperback Library, New York, 1973, p. 58.
10. Waters, T.A., *Pschologistics*, Cornerstone Library, New York, 1977, p. 33.

Futher classification of the mind is by its two aspects: one is, working mind and the other is, thinking mind. The working mind functions only in the present moment. But the thinking mind, is always in the past or future, never in the present moment. Therefore, what happens in the case of an ordinary person is, while the working mind is trying to do a job to the best of its ability, the thinking mind keeps interrupting the working mind. Warning him, "What would happen if you fail?" And yet, there is another aspect: sensing mind or perceiving mind or experiencing mind. The perceptions and experiences relate to the past, the present and the future.

(2) May mean the unconscious which is ready to move to the conscious, as it happens in dreams and in acts of creativity. You may call it by any of the names: surging-unconscious, active-unconscious, evolving unconscious, stimulated unconsicous, upper-unconscious, outer-unconscious, under-conscious, saturated-unconscious, ripe-unconscious, and similar other names, etc.

(3) Super-conscious mind is the state of mind where individual mind is in fusion with the cosmic mind.

This yogic state, achieved by a few, is beyond attributes. It is a state of mind which is devoid of thoughts and images, and when one has overcome anger or is struck with wonder. Suddenly, for a fraction of a second, the waves of the mind are still. The mind perceives others but in this state it can also perceive itself — the mind being the consciousness in movement.

(4) Mast-malang is a slang in the Hindu-heartland; representing a state of mind reached before attaining '*Samadhi, Nirvana, Moksha*'; when emotions, feelings and existence lose their significance, and the Universal Intelligence is the subject of thought. There, the happiness and misery of this world do not have any effect on the mind. In this state the burden of destiny becomes light.

(5) Spiritualism refers to the fifth state of mind — 'transcendental' state — here mind ceases to be mind. In waking and dream states, one sees unreality instead of reality while in deep sleep one sees neither. In deep sleep, the individual soul is not conscious of "I" or "You"; it is unconscious even of non-duality. In the transcendental state, however, the entire visible world disappears, and one sees everything as Supreme-Self. There one sees reality, and there is an awareness of non-duality. One who has knowledge of the Self no longer sees the world as world. The various dualties such as right or wrong, the

> master and disciple, and bondage and liberation all become one. Such a realized person does not consider the triad of doer, deed and fruit of the deed as different from the Self. He sees everything as the Self. Such a person has no mandatory duties. Since he does not experience duality, he is always non-attached. This is the fifth state in Vedanta, called *jivanmukti* — Liberation. In superconscious state of mind, mataphysical and transcendental knowledge comes to the man. This state of going beyond reason, transcending ordinary human nature, may sometimes come by chance to a man who does not understand its science; he, as it were, stumbles upon it.
>
> In superconscious state there is no longer any perception of the subject or of the object.

And yet, there is another view of mind construct: the irradiated portion of our unconscious is subconscious. The irradiation has been done by our conscious knowingly as well as unknowingly, during this lifetime since birth; and during our past lives, which comes with our soul as 'memory of past'. The irradiation has also been done by 'universal consciousness', corresponding to our future and future lives. It is like a video CD which gets recorded in view of our conscious as well as in our state of unawareness.

Just as a CD recorder registers whatever has been lasered onto it, in the same manner every experience we undergo, consciously or even unconsciously, is registered by the unconscious mind. The deepest layer in which the information is engraved, we call it 'under-conscious' mind. The second layer of recording is not so deep. This is the subconscious level, where the data are in process of transition and manifestation. The third layer or the outer-most layer of storage on unconscious mind is in the process of fructification at the conscious mind level, is called the preconscious. Thus, our mind is: from the outermost circle — conscious/preconscious/subconscious/underconscious/unconscious/superconscious, the innermost (the seed or soul or *roüh* or blue diamond, etc.) It is simply play of words for nomenclature.

Unconscious intelligence which gets pushed up to surfy-unconscious, subconscious and preconscious can be accessed through clairvoyance and dreams. However, highly evolved souls are able to tap into entire unconscious with ease.

The superconscious (the centre of the CD) state of mind includes simultaneous awareness of the waking, dreaming and deep sleep states. There, simultaneous operation of the conscious, subconscious and unconscious sections of the mind results in a single, enlightened state of consciousness integrated and relaxed personality. Those who have realized this state do not dream at all. They have one state of being which does not alter: waking and dreaming are alike for them, because they are continuously, sometimes quantumly, experiencing the spiritual state of superconscious — collective unconsciousness; illumination of total mind or a state of self-realization — liberation of soul.

Superconscious mind is the state of mind where fusion of individual mind with the cosmic mind has taken place.

> It is the mind that maketh good or ill, that maketh wretch or happy, rich or poor. — Edmund Spencex

There are enabling states (neurophysiological) — confindence, love, inner strength, joy, ecstasy, belief — that tap great wellsprings of personal power. There are unresourceful/paralyzing states of mind — confusion, depression, fear, anxiety, illness, frustration — that leave us powerless. We all go in and out of good and bad states.

For centuries, mankind has been fascinated by ways to alter his state and thus his experience of life. He has tried fasting, drugs, rituals, music, sex, food, hypnosis, chanting. What if you could snap your fingers and go into the most dynamic, resourceful state at will — a state in which you are excited, you are sure of success, your body is crackling with energy, your mind is alive? Well you can have — constructive thoughts, positive emotions and fortitude.

Thoughts proceed from the visible mind and ESP from the invisible mind. The average waking mind receives and retains only a few of the lessons of life. It is largly filled with idle and incoherent thoughts that are soon forgotten. The same may be truly said of the dream mind. Many of our day thoughts are daydreams, just as many of night dreams are night thoughts. Our day deeds of evil or good pierce or see the conscious, just as our night symbols of sorrow and joy sadden or please the objective senses. Our day thoughts are filled with the warnings and presence of the inner mind and our night thoughts are tinctured and often controlled by our external mind.

The objective mind is constantly striving to penetrate the spiritual realm, while the spiritual mind is striving to enter matter, hence our actions have their subjective counterparts and their subterranean counterparts. The universal mind in harmony with the evolutionary plans and laws of the macrocosm, materializes through the fun time of the microcosm, imparting to each, with its routine of failure and success, its daily objectivity. The inner or passive dream-mind may perceive the subjective types or antitypes many days before they objectify through the microcosm.

> The powers of the mind are like the rays of the sun dissipated. When they are concentrated, they illumine. — Swami Vivekananda

> Little minds are tamed and subdued by misfortune; but great minds rise above it. — Washington Irving

> Language is the light of the mind. — John Stuart Mill

> Great minds discuss ideas, average minds discuss events, small minds discuss people. — Anoymous

> The mind grows narrow in proportion as the soul grows corrupt. — Rousseau

> It is mind that makes the body rich. — Shakespeare

The mind is like a radio that is being tuned. In the process of being tuned it suddenly picks up a station that is broadcasting in a funny language (as in lucid dreams, crystal gazing, ESP-onslaughts), and we start thinking about it. What was that I heard? Usually, we are not able to pick up the same station again because the radiowaves become too weak or the transmission stops or the mind-tuning drifts fast and we do not know when the next trasmission is going to be; anything can happen. It is that tuning into subtle frequencies which is the important aspect of the soul-psychic sleuthing.

All that we need is suspended, invisible to the naked eye in this electromagnetic library of vibrations. Hooking into this source of knowledge, by becoming receptacles to harness creative energy from the myriad shafts of light that ceaselessly move around us, will always be vast realm that awards our tapping. Each time you view television, that clarity of the picture or an image corresponds to the transmission of the beam as also the degree of how finely your set is tuned. The mind is similar in many ways, yet infinitely more fascinating in its working, as each of our individual experiences with it will clearly show.

To awaken the creative realms, we need to tap the awe-inspiring working of the inner-mind — subconscious, unconscious and superconscious. The inner-mind is located just behind the solar-plexus, somewhere near 3rd and 4th *chakras*, and is sometimes also referred to as abdominal brain! It is the irrational level of the mind. This phase of mind gorverns independently, twenty-four hours a day, all our vital inner processes like beating of our hearts, breathing, digestion and assimilation. Its working is not limited by the time or space dimensions. The inner-mind takes cognizance of its environment by means independent of the physical senses. It perceives by intention, imagination and its higher faculties of telepathy, clairvoyance, etc. It talks to us through hunches, inspirational flashes or insight to follow a certain course of action.

Your subconscious, unconscious and superconscious minds will never give you false information. Sometimes they will not wish to answer a particular question. Do not use pressure, as it is sometimes used on Ouija board or in the the pendulum healing oracle. Another thing to avoid is to ask the minds to make predictions.

The thoughts and feelings you currently manifest will shape your future, your health by directing the energy balance in your health by directing the energy balance in your awareness. If you want to change your universe, alter the way your mind views the world around you.

> The stronger the blow on the mind, the more vehement is its reaction.
>
> — Premchand, *Godaan*

Spiritual traditions accept different levels of mind as conscious, subconscious, unconscious, and beyond. We try to understand these levels because the idea of having very many subtle components within our mind is fascinating.

Psychology and psychotherapy have made small inroads into the subconscious and the unconscious mind, mainly for therapeutic purposes, whereas the spiritual traditions have gone far beyond the statge of psychotherapy or psychoanalysis. In actually discovering the experience and functioning of the different levels of consciousness, they lead to the highest level or the experience of the total mind. This is unknown as far as medical science is concerned, but is termed enlightenment, *mukti*, *nirvana*, etc. according to the different spiritual traditions.

Before his death in 1980, Joseph Banks Rhine, a First World War Veteran and botany student who became professor of psychology at Duke University, North Carolina, U.S.A., summed up like this: "It is shocking but true that we know the atom today better than we know the mind that knows atom."

Many more mysteries of mind are yet to be explored and experienced, and they are to be searched through unconscious and superconscious states. The experiences of super-mind, of mind in the state of the superconsciousness are thought to be related to soul — when the mind does not see, think or feel, the mind is bypassed.

Without thinking of it, a "split personality" problem, you could imagine the super-mind as another you — a you who knows everything you do, and who sits up there in your mind watching everything that happens to you, logs on the information and does its own problem-solving — most of the time without giving you the slightest indication that this silent spy exists.

Nevertheless, the inner-mind processes data and produces new information at a rate much higher than that of the conscious mind. It isn't too difficult to picture this flood of information from the inner-mind pouring in and overwhelming ordinary consciousness with ESP.

Our minds are full of concepts, beliefs and ideologies, that one has made all kinds of assumptions from an early age. But as we understand today, there is great difference between the idols of the human mind and the ideas of the divine. That is to say, between certain empty dogmas, and the true signatures and marks set upon the works of creation as they are found in nature.

The entire work of the understanding be commenced afresh, and mind itself be from outset not left to take its own course, but guided at every step; and the business be done as if by machinery. "The mind, free from the impediments of prejudices and generalizations, can by knowledge attain sovereignty over nature," said Francis Bacon (1561-1626), a lawyer and member of the British Parliament. This holds good even today, after 400 years.

The mind should be sentenced to solitary confinement to increase its power. If the mind constantly runs after sense objects, it becomes unstable, but if it remains quiet and concentrated, it becomes more powerful. The mind can also be quietened by controlling *prana*, and then thereby one's own sleuthing power unfolds.

When the mind is focused externally on some object, it is called gaze; when it is focused internally, it is called concentration. The power of a focused mind is immense.

We know, mind exercises its suzerainty through *samskaras* — conscious actions, whether cognitive, affective, or connative — assuming the potential and hidden forms below the threshold of consciousness.

2.3 Eye of Soul

Soul is beyond matter, space, time and causation. It is beyond the reach of material science, and is beyond the realm of physical science.

Man is a soul wearing a physical body. Soul is extremely subtle. It is subtler than ether, mind and energy. Soul is the immortal part in man. According to Gustar Stromberg, "The soul is superconscious energy, and is always in search of peace and happiness."[11]

> Within each of us burns a spark of the Divine; our individual Soul.
>
> — Lynn Catlin, *Honoring the Sacred*

Every human has an individual soul, distinct and seperate from the body, yet related to it in a mysterious way, possessed of super-natural power. Soul is like a fluid, which takes the form of anything it is poured into. It "makes things" out of what it is. "Soul never leaves you, but you can leave it only in thought" says Radhakrishnan.[12]

Soul is beyond birth and death, time and space. Soul is like a tree of life, the source of pure intelligence, completeness, and pure and perfect ideas. It is pure awareness, a witness, whose mere presence enables the body to carry out its obligations. All sense perceptions take place because of the spirit, but the spirit is not affected or tainted by their activity. All the instruments of knowledging action, bodily maintenance, mind, and intellect are innert matter only. "It is an eye of the eye, an ear of the ear, tongue of the tongue, a mind of the mind, and also life of the life."

Soul knows exactly how to lay down cell after cell in a million cells of a fingernail and make each one perfect, as it is doing at this moment. No one knows how to put the fragrance in a single flower, yet this soul is touching a million flowers daily with its magic wand, and distilling their subtle essences into perfume from the soil, water, air and sunlight. Man boasts of every tiny discovery he makes — this soul knows them all before he gropes along his faltering way toward them.

Soul does not have limbs or parts as the body has, and therefore, no contact with it is possible, as in the case of sky which has no contact

---

11. Gustar Stromberg; *The Soul of the Universe*, McKay, Philadelphia, 1948.
12. S. Radhakrishnan; *Eastern Religion and Western Thought*, Oxford University Press, New York, 1969.

with the pot in its pot space. As such, any attack by weapons cannot harm the sky/space which has no limb or part. As the space itself cannot be destroyed by anything, similarly, the soul, within which the space is there, cannot also be destroyed by the elements such as water, fire, air, and earth.

For the support of the body, food, air and water are incorporated into it. When the structural support of the body is removed, the body perishes. But the soul which has no such support, supports everything else. Even when the body is destroyed, the soul survives, being an unattached and unsupported existence. As all the types of destruction do not cause destruction to the soul, it is free from destruction, and so is eternal.

> Distinct from the gross, subtle, and causal bodies, being beyond the fire sheaths, abides as a witness to the three states of experience of the form of existence, consciousness, bliss is 'I', soul, the Self.
>
> — *Tattvabodha*

If the human soul is a self-existing, immortal entity, then how does it exhibit radical difference in the quality of its awareness during different stages of life, say the embryonic, the adolescent, the mature and the obsolescent stage at the end? What happens to this virile, eternal substance in the grip of age so that it often regresses to the mental condition of an infant, blubbers and salivates at the mouth? And even if it is held that the soul is the product of a still inexplicable activity of the biological organism, operating through the brain, then there must be some element or elements in the body or the brain, which have capacity to exhibit consciousness in varying degrees. In other words, there must be certain highly complex and sensitive substances which in an organic structure combine to give rise to awareness in the form in which we see it exhibited in animals and man.[13]

Soul is an infinite source of knowledge, wisdom and strength. . . . Those philosophers themselves who made the essence of the soul to

---

13. Rollo May, *Man's Search for Himself*, W.W. Norton and Co., New York, 1967.

consist in cogitation, and again, the essence of the cogitation in clear and express consciousness, cannot render it in anyway probable, that the souls of men in all profound sleeps, lethargies, and apoplexies . . . are never so much as one moment without expressly conscious cogitation; which, if they were, according to the principles of their philosophy, they must, *ipso facto*, cease to have any being. . . . It is certain, that our human souls themselves are not always conscious of whatever they have in them.

Kahlil Gibran says: "Your soul is oftentimes a battlefield, upon which your reason and your judgement wage a war against your passion and your appetite. Your reason and your passion are the rudder and the sails of your sea-faring soul. If either your sails or your rudder be broken, you can but toss and drift, or else be held at a standstill in mid-sea. Therefore, let your soul exalt your reason to the height of passion, that it may sing; and let it direct your passion with reason, that your passion may live through its own daily resurrection, and like the phoenix rise above its own ashes."

Your body is the harp of your soul, and it is for you to bring forth sweet music or confused sounds — *samskaras* (karmic imprints). Our soul always sways between the wonders and strangeness of existence and concealed mysteries of life. However, spirituality is ever springing in the soul, even while the hands hew a stone or tend a loom.

According to Hindu philosophy, the soul (Atman) enters the human heart at the time of birth, transfers the 'akashic records' — the records of past, present and future to the mind, and remains there as a life-activating energy till death, when it leaves the body with the akashic records, incorporating the revised listing of experiences, plans for actions and executions. The soul is consciousness, life-energy and akashic records. According to some schools of thought, the soul belongs to God, and needs to be safeguarded from psychic attacks by demonic entities, ghosts, apparitions, discarnates, polterghosts (noisy ghosts), who spite God.

> For what shall it profit a man if he gains the whole world, and loses his own soul.
>
> — Mark, 8.36

> Money is lost, nothing is lost;
> Courage is lost, much is lost;
> Honour is lost, most is lost;
> Soul is lost, all is lost. — Mohammed Ali Jinah

All of the shamanic traditions are based upon the philosophy of "search for the lost soul." George Iranovich Gurdjief (1877-1949), an obscure but influential teacher of mystic philosophy, wrote a treatise *Man the Machine* in which he encourages the search for an immortal soul.

The soul is not only the creation of man, but it is the real man. It is the inner imperishable double of imprint of what has outwardly and inwardly transpired. All thoughts, desires and actions enter the soul through the objective mind. The automation of the body responds as quickly to the batting of eyelids as it does to the movement of the whole body. By it the footsteps of man and the very hours of his head are numbered. Thus, it becomes his inner-part. It is therefore the book of life or death, and by it he judges himself or is already judged.

> Look upon all the animate beings as your bosom friends, for in all of them there resides one soul. — *Rigveda*

> Self is the only person that can ever bind the soul.
> — Henry Van Dyke

> What is regarded as a soul is another manifestation of the functions of the body as a living thing. — Nirad C. Chaudhury

> Soul pervades the body and God pervades the soul.
> — Swami Dayananda

> This is the technique of the soul. The individual must die so that nations must live. — Subhas Chandra Bose

> The *Atman*, subtler than the subtle, greater than the great, is seated in the heart of each living being. He who is free from desire, with his mind and the senses composed, beholds the majesty of the self and becomes free from sorrow. — *Kathopanishad*

The following lines of Evelyn Underhill can serve as sample:[14]

> Since the soul, according to mystical principles, can only perceive a Reality in proportion as she is real, knows God by becoming God-like, it is clear that this birth is an initial necessity. The true and definitely directed mystical life does and must open with that most actual, though indescribable phenomenon, the coming forth into consciousness of man's deeper, spiritual self, which ascetical and mystical writers of all ages have agreed to call regeneration or rebirth. Nothing that is within him is able of its own power to achieve this. It must be evoked by an energy, a quickening spirit, which comes from beyond the soul and secretly initiates what HE openly crowns.

In India the concept of rebirth has been current from the Vedic times, some 3000 years before the birth of Christ and is the basic tenet of the Hindu and Buddhist faiths. But what is this energy, this quickening spirit which "secretly initiates what God openly crowns" continues to be a secret even today.

If mystical ecstasy represents the superme effort of the soul to merge into the ocean of All Being and the effort has no intimate relationship with the body, then age or disease should have no adverse influence on the achievement of this union. However, it is the exhaustion or the impure condition of the aura which leads to the dark night of the soul among the mystics and blank periods in the case of geniuses.

The whole life experience is also considered to be false and unreal, because the spiritual traditions believe the soul to be beyond the experiences of pain and pleasure. They have described the soul as the real nature, the real identity of the individual, which is not subject to birth or death, decay or disease.

Eye of the soul, the centre of consciousness in man is at a point between and behind the two eyes. This centre is known as the 'third-eye', and in Hindu mythology, the third-eye of Lord Shiva is the most powerful sight.

---

14. Evelyn Underhill, *Mysticism*, Methuen and Co. Ltd, London, 1911.

Hidden deep inside the centre of brain, it is no bigger than the size of a pea, yet it sees all and knows all. For Hindu and Buddhist mystics[15] it is the third-eye, while for ancient philosophers, the site of the pineal gland was nothing less than the soul, the spiritual heart of the body.

Some religious sects still believe that this tiny ball of living tissues is the departure point for the soul after death. But despite the reverences that have surrounded the pineal gland over years, doctors and scientists are only just unravelling some of its deep mysteries.

However, according to some para-psychologists, the third-eye is the state of mind, which is heightened, rarefied, penetrating, and integrative intelligence that sometimes leaps into human mind from where — God knows.

According to Max Heindel,[16] the occult scientist, the power which moves the heart, does not come from outside, but is inside the heart. There is a chamber in the left ventrical, near the apex, where a little atom swims in a sea of the highest ether. The atom is called the "seed atom" or soul. The force within it moves the heart and keeps the organism alive. All the other atoms in the whole body must vibrate in tune with this atom. Without the force of the seed atom, the minerals could not form matter into crystals; the plant, animal, and human kingdoms would not be able to form their bodies.

The inner sounds, flashes of lights, astral voyages and visions are merely the preliminary indications of a new area of highly extended awareness obtained during soul-psychic sleuthing practices (like, silence, concentration, attention, meditation, etc.). In rare cases one may attain the perennial state of superconsciousness, living constantly in an effulgent world of infinite being and bliss, both in working state and dream. In order to achieve this sublime end, the sustained activity of a powerful current of the *kundalini* force is necessary for varying periods

---

15. Tuesday Lobsang Rampa, *The Third Eye*, Corgi Books, London, 1967.
16. Max Heindel, *Occult Principles of Health and Healing*, Indigo Books, Cosmo Publications, New Delhi, 2002, p. 253.

which may extend to years — the rise of *kundalini* to the Crown *chakra* is desired for the opening of the 'third-eye.'

> The soul contains in itself the event that shall persently befall it. The event is only the actualizing of its thought. — Emerson

The soul arranges synchronistic events to draw our attention to a constellation of energies, events, people, and circumstances in such a way that some aspects of our soul potential can be embodied in our life at that moment. It is a mysterious and sacred moment when cosmic force of our soul energy, and events and people in outer life are in optimal alignment for some invisible aspect of our soul to become visible. We only need to acknowledge it, attend to it, and act upon it in a conscious manner.

2.4 Hands

Psychometry is based on sensitivity of hands, as our hands can easily sense energy changes and differences. We all have experienced some aspects of this. When we touch someone or shake his hand, we get definite impressions about him. Our sense of touch helps us to attune ourselves to that individual's energy.

Aristotle said that the hand is "the organ of the organs, the instrument of the instruments." And, Casimir Stanislash of Arpentingy,[17] a distinguished French cavalry officer and a scholar (born March 13, 1798 in Normandy), the man who weaved the science of Chirognomy, wrote:

> There are hands which naturally attract us, and there are hands which excite in us repulsion. I have seen hands which seemed covered with eyes, so sagacious and so penetrating was their appearance. Some, like those of Sphinx, suggest an idea of mystery; some betray recklessness and strength, combined with activity of body; others again indicate laziness, joined to feebleness and cunning.

William G. Benham,[18] a noted scientific hand reader, writes:

17. Comte O. De Saint-German, *The Study of Palmistry*, Ajay book Service, New Delhi, 2003, p. 17.
18. Benham, W.G., *Laws of Scientific Hand Reading*, Taraporevala, Bombay, 1962, p. 21.

> You will find that every pair of hands has eyes; that they seem to look at you, asking pity, maybe, for their owners, or that they have mouths, and beseech you to hear their story.

He further adds,

> There are located at the ends of the fingers a great number of nerve cells which make possible the sense of touch possessed by this part of the hand, and it is evident that one use for the nails is to protect and shield from harm this concentration of delicate nerve filaments. In order that the sense of touch may be extremely acute, the nerves must be as near the surface of the skin as possible. If there was no protection afforded by the nails, this could not be, and with the nerves of touch deeply imbedded under the skin, the sense of touch would be blunted one. The Creator intended us to read from them for the benefit of the human race.

Quintilian, speaking of the language of hands, says:

> For the other parts of the body assist the speaker, but hands, I may say, speak for themselves; they ask, they promise, they invoke, they dismiss, they threaten, they entreat, they deprecate, they express fear, joy, grief, our doubts, our assents, our penitence, they show moderation, profusion, they mark number and time.

We will now give our attention to the skin, the nerves, and the sense of touch. Speaking of the skin, Sir Charles Bell once said: "The cuticle is so far a part of the organ of touch that it is the medium through which the external impression is conveyed to the nerve." The extremities of the fingers best exhibit the provisions for the exercise of the sense of touch.

It is impossible to deny that the sense of touch, concentrated in the hands and especially in the finger tips and the centre of the palm, constitutes the most of the five senses and can almost take the place of other four. The blind, the deaf, the dumb, the unfortunate one deprived of the senses of smell are still kept in communication with the world and their fellow creatures if their sense of touch is unimpaired, if their hands are still in possession of their full capabilities. This undoubted supremacy of the hands prepares us for any revelation that will demonstrate its paramount influence in the psychometric readings. In fact, it is the hand whose extreme nervous sensitiveness carries to the brain the double principle that gives birth to thought; it is the hand again which executes what the other senses have merely advised or prepared.

2.5 Consultants

Nowadays, we have an unfortunate tendency in our culture to bring every problem to an expert, and pass on to him or her (or the agency, the company, the government) the responsiblity for its solution. A great many of undesirable characteristics of time might well be traced to this tendency. How drug-dependent we have become; how easily led into war we are; how quickly persuaded we are to spend our present income and mortgage our future earning power as well; how addicting we find the popular spactator sports and other mass entertainment programmes.

We should go to professional consultants — clairvoyants psychometerists, astrologers, palmists, numerologists, card readers, tarot card readers, etc. only when our own sleuthing process fails to respond. Having consulted all of them, or only some of them; we should, if possible, indulge into TAROT (Trend Analysis by Relative Opinion Testing) exercise. Opinions of all the consulted experts need to be analysed in the light of parameters (all the circumstanes) best known to ourselves and reach to the solution.

A querist is subject to his past *karmas*, or deeds in his previous lives and their fructification or otherwise. It is for the fulfilment of those deeds that native is compelled to think on a particular line that he does and goes to a particular occultist. In other words, the question, the querist and meeting of the particular occultist are all subject to the Divine designs and in keeping with the grand comprehensive scheme of things. There is nothing like a chance in such things. While it may not be possible to say anything about the Divine scheme of things, but in practical life, human actions or thinking have invariably been found to be in consonance with the Divine will. Sometimes even the Divine grace physically compels the person — God does everything for our good.

For example, in the period of Rahu a querist does not go to the astrologers practising *mantras*. He goes, during that period to tantrics, because Rahu signifies *tantra* and not *mantra*. It is only during the Jupiter's period that he goes for *mantrika* remedies. The native does not go to a *mantrika* during Rahu period but unconsciously waits for Jupiter's period to commence. It may sound quite strange to many persons but it is true, as statistics suggests.

There are many more such instances, but one of the similar instances is worth narration. D.P. Saxena,[19] an astrologer, was going for some important work and just stopped by the roadside hawker to purchase some fruits — bananas. They were meant for his own consumption. Suddenly, a monkey came from somewhere and sat on the bananas of the hawker. The hawker and many others who were purchasing the bananas offered the monkey one or two, but he did not accept them. Just to try his luck Saxena also offered one to him. The monkey took that one and ate itself and quietly went away. Saxena that day got his work done so easily and quickly that he himself was surprised. Thus, to say it in few words, God supervises all our actions at all times and asks us to follow a particular path. Saxena is a devotee of Lord Hanuman, the monkey-god.

The one thing that can be observed is that no event is an isolated event independent of other events. A chain of events takes place at a particular time with extreme precision as regards time and space.

There is a cosmic consciousness all around us. The whole providential design is in its womb and it is unfurled and manifested as and when 'time' for it comes. The 'time' when personified is nothing but the cosmic consciousness, all-pervading and omnipotent like God Himself.

---

19. Saxena, D.P., *Principles and Practices of Hoary Astrology*, Ranjan Publications, New Delhi, 1996, p. 18.

The 'time' (in Indian terminology is understood as 'Honi' for bad events and 'Muhurta' for good events), maybe all-powerful, but it has one limitation. The limitation is that it is also governed by our own deeds and misdeeds. When our good deeds fructify, time gives us the boon, and when it is the other way round, the same time awards us the punishment. We would have been independent of time had we known the period of fructification of all our deeds and misdeeds. The all-pervading consciousness knows it or, we may also say, grants it at opportune time. This discretion does not mean any discrimination on its part. It simply means to coordinate the activities of the universe in accordance with the Providential Design. There is nothing like the accident or chance in any of the events taking place in the world. We call such events as accidents whose causes are not in our sight and the deeds whose fructification was deferred for some reasons for too long a time to be remembered by us at that moment.

It is on account of the uncertain period of the fructification of deeds that we should always be vigilant of time and, if possible, catch it by the horns to serve us faithfully.

The question arises whether the specific question which comes to our mind or the question asked by any querist and the solution sought also owe their birth to the time and movements of planets just as the birth of an event and of a human is subjected to. The great Badarayana holds that what a particular person thinks has a direct relation with the planets and the time.

An occultist may be called upon to judge the course of events that began at a particular time; or he may be called upon to choose an auspicious time for beginning a particular enterprise — a job generally handled by astrologers — however, a person with a clear vision may be better. He aids in attunement to cosmic law and thus helps human affairs to flourish in harmony with it.

The investigations made by various occultists and occult agencies may invariably be different in perception, quality and contents. Besides, a profound yogi, Swami Shivananda, (1887-1967), used to say:

"When there is one doctor there is one prescription, when two there is consultation, and when three it is cremation." Therefore, it is advisable not to resort to problem-solving with the help of many occultists, as far as possible, thereby eliminating the use of TAROT analysis altogether.

> We should seek the company of the sage who shows our faults, as if he were showing us a hidden treasure. — *The Dhammapada*

Consultants are advised to give an honest, open and unbiased picture of the impressions gathered through the sleuthing techniques. But when, during psychic readings and investigations, where you are going to avoid "giving a stone when you are asked for bread," adapt a semi-humorous, semi-serious method of judgeing people's dispositions from a cursory examination of their hands, faces and body language without letting them suspect that they are under examination.

Speak honestly, truthfully, yet carefully to your sitter. You can tell the plainest truths, but you need not shock or hurt your sitter by doing so. Be as careful with that complicated piece of humanity before you as you would be handling a fine and delicate piece of machinery. Above all things, you must be sympathetic; take the deepest possible interest in every person — your sitters; enter into their lives, their feelings and their natures. Let your entire ambition be to do good, to be of some benefit to the person who consults you. If this be the foundation of your work, it will never tire or distress you; on the contrary it will sustain you. If you meet enemies, be not argumentative for the sake of argument. Think of your work first, of self last. An occult consultant should feel his responsibility towards humanity, nation, society and his clients.

We know, some persons are born 'sleuth-hound' and one should not hesitate to seek their help in solving intricate problems. But, before these hounds give opinions/readings, they should make themselves aware of the psychology of the sitter, only then, they can bring certitude in the minds of their clients.

Also, a consultant must know himself; as according to what Confucius says, "Whoever knows essentially his own nature, can know also that of other men and can penetrate into the nature of things. He can collaborate into the transformations and in the progess of heaven and of earth."

Sitter must accept, as the *Mahabharata* suggests, "Accept what is good even from the babbling of an idiot or the prattle of a child as they extract gold from a stone."

> Do what thy Master tells thee; it is good.
>
> — Ptah-hotep (Egyptian Thinker)

3

Telepathy

TELEPATHY is transportation of non-verbal thought from one mind to another mind. It is neither simultaneous ideation of thoughts between two minds, nor coincidental convergence of thoughts between the telepathically connected minds. Telepathy is defined as action of one mind on another mind that does not involve the five physical senses. Simply, it is thought transference.

Telepathy[1] in essence is psychic stimulus, which is sharp or scanty but sweet or stingy. The more psychically sensitive an individual is, the greater the likelihood s/he will be influenced by the emotions and thoughts of others. This is particularly true with significant others. It was scientifically established in 2009.

Therefore, many people claim to have experienced it, producing much testimony in favour of telepathy, notably between the loved ones at the time of crisis. During such times, the strong, especially troubling thoughts and emotions of your family, friends and even of foes travel telepathically to inform you, affect you or stimulate you to act fast.

Since thoughts expand, spread and travel much faster than electromagnetic waves, in moments of crisis, telepathy is only communication system, which may bring some succor in time.

"Time is money" is one of the great maxims of commercial success. "Take care of the seconds and the hours will take care of themselves,"

---

1. Soal, S.G. and F. Bateman, *Modern Experiments in Telepathy*, Yale University Press, New Haven, 1954.

is just as true as take care of pennies and pounds will take care of themselves. Therefore, it is claimed: "A timely telepathic command is worth fortunes."

Telepathy, thus, is the psychic ability to communicate with another person without the use of the physical senses. Ideas, thoughts, feelings and images get transferred mentally without the use of any physical resources like telephone, mobile or picture phone services and systems. Telepathy is a communication between two (or even more) human minds — two sets of trans-receivers — however, communication is sent one-way at a time, very rarely they change roles during the event, for the event is short-lived. Sometimes transmitter is powerful and at other times receiver is sensitive, and verily both transmitter and receiver modules, two functions of the mind, are hi-fi — a sensitive and pure and trained or gifted mind constitutes such a set.

Telepathy is the most secure and reliable communication system, when established. For, without words, in telepathy, all thoughts, all desires, all expectations are born and shared, with joy that is unclaimed. In 1894, a Scottish theologian, Henry Drummond claimed that telepathy was "theoretically the next stage in the evolution of language." "It affords a rational basis for prayer and inspiration and gives us a distant glimpse of the possibility of communion without language, not only between men of various races and tongues, but also between every sentient creature, which if not attainable here may await us all in that future state when we shall 'know even as we are known'."

Telepathy is the only mode of communication on the astral plane where one's soul is moving to, soon after his/her death and remains there until the next birth of the subsequent life. On the astral plane you may meet your dead relatives and friends and get to know their true feelings and making them known of your true feelings, as there is no hypocrisy on the astral plane.

Telepathy has its origin in the Greek words: tele — distant, and pathe — occurence. This word was originally coined in 1882 by a leading Cambridge scholar and investigator, F.W.H. Myers; and the first major study of experiences — the *Census of Hallucination*, published in 1890 — examined replies to about 20,000 questionnaires. But science needed to examine telepathy under more controlled conditions.

Sir William Barrett, the pioneer of scientific research into telepathy and professor of physics at the Royal College of Science, Dublin, conducted a large number of experiments in this area, and finally became satisfied that telepathy was real.

But despite many discoveries and the outstanding individual results that some experiments have produced, not all the researchers are so successful when they attempt to duplicate telepathy tests.

In 1924, the German psychiatrist Hans Berger embarked on a telepathy experiment that led to his developing electroencephalograph (EEG), an instrument that measures and records the brainwave pattern.

Use of the EEG led to the discovery of a process known as brainwave entrainment. Simply stated, the human brain has a tendency to take on any dominant rhythm in an individual's immediate environment. The rhythm may be visual, audible, or even tactile and is what causes strobe-light epilepsy — in susceptible subjects. The reality of entrainment has been established experimentally by monitoring the brainwaves of subjects exposed to rhythmic stimuli, but the phenomenon of telepathy has been known experientially since the dawn of history.

A highly telepathic race is said to have existed in Lemuria. The Lemuria was a continent stretching between Asia and Africa, it went to the bottom of the ocean due to violent volcanic activity, some 1,00,000 years back, according to the occult study researchers.

Our physical research people give us conclusive proof of mental telepathy or telegraphy between finite minds. The communications or impressions are conveyed many miles across from one mind to another. This communication is easier when one or both of the subjects are in a state of somnambulence or asleep.

Telepathy is often involved in some types of foresight, forethought, simultaneous event occurence with concurrent reporting, and in prediction. The creative scientific discoveries have been said to have occurred simultaneously in different parts of this world.

Telepathy is particularly the case when someone seeks a forecast on the outcome of what should really be personal decision. The unconscious mind of the questioner frequently knows the answer to a problem of this sort, but is not allowed to transmit its knowledge into consciousness because of an emotional reaction, perhaps of guilt or fear, blocks the way. Then answer is picked up telepathically by bringing the unconcious decision into consciousness.

Sometimes it is possible to "read" through the unconscious mind of one person, things concerning another person — with whom the first person has a psychic link.

While the words are working on a person's conscious mind, the physiology is working on the unconscious. That where the brain is thinking. . . . Hey! this person is like me. He must be okay. And once that happens, there is a tremendous attraction, a tremendous bond. And because it is unconscious, it is even more effective. You are not aware of anything but the bond that has been formed. You have received some sort of telepathic message "I like you, as you like me." You become friends, or you initiate a partnership deal or you have picked up your life-partner, or a mirror to your unconscious decision.

Making an observation on telepathy, Swami Vivekananda remarks:

> Have you ever noticed the phenomenon that is called thought-transference? A man here is thinking something, and that thought is manifested in somebody else, in some other place. With preparation — not by chance — a man wants to send a thought to another mind at a distance, and this other mind knows that a thought is coming, and he receives it exactly as it is sent out. Distance makes no difference. The thought goes and reaches the other man, and he understands it. If your mind was an isolated something here, and my mind was an isolated something there, and there

> were no connection between the two, how would it be possible for my thought to reach you? This shows that there is a continuity of mind, as the Yogis call it. The mind is universal. Your mind, my mind, all these little minds are fragments of that universal mind, little waves in the ocean.

Thus, when one feels his unity with mankind, all these minds become trans-receivers through which he can work at will. That is how all evolved-men are adept at telepathy and clairvoyance. A spiritual master (one who has union with God) knows almost everything and can penetrate every heart. That is how he can send telepathic messages faraway. His awareness merges with the universal awareness and becomes one gigantic whole.

However, it is not yet possible for one human being (ordinary man, not a yogi) to receive the thought waves of another man just by concentrating or tuning to those waves. On materialistic level, no receiving set for brainwaves have yet been invented. It is hoped, none ever will be. It would make life an unbearable torture, if everyone could know what we were thinking just by turning on a machine.

Yogis do not poach on your thoughts. And some yogis as well as savants observe that telepathy is basically internal communication with oneself. While,

> It is far more useful to commune with oneself than with others.
>
> — Demophilus

Others consider, commune with oneself is the telepathy with God.

> I want to know God's thoughts . . . the rest are details.
>
> — Albert Einstein

The telepathic communication can rise from mineral plant, animal, and human kingdoms of this world; from other worlds and astral planes; and even from God. However, to summon the power of psyche to receive telepathic communications or to transmit the communications when need arises, is by no means a parlor's game learn-it-in-one-evening course. Yet, it is not something that requires a lengthy apprenticeship. If we could only lower the barriers created by our constricting sense of individuality, or 'I'-based thinking, perhaps telepathy would occur more frequently.

3.1 Intuition

Occasionally, we infer a telepathic reception as an intuitive signal. Therefore, it is in order to understand briefly the phenomenon of 'intuition'.

Whatever intuition is, it operates to give a mental impression from one person to another. However, the knowledge received is impeccable.

Intuitive people are endowed with the faculty of receiving ambient impressions directly. These persons will tell you that they "feel it in their bones." They are "psychic." They will have visions, dreams, strong impressions of impending danger, and will see signs and believe in omens. They can obtain the greatest proficiency in occult studies and practices.

The intuitive information and knowledge from ambient consciousness comes down in a flash in the form of intuition and ESP, which may be telepathic or clairvoyant in nature. It is not always there with us the ordinary humans and if it comes to someone regularly and at all the times, he is spiritually an evolved soul, a sage and a saint. Intuition is often very true.

'Intuition' is an inner experience of soul; while the intellectual knowledge is experience of outer senses. Intuition has been said to be "being taught from within," and it really is immediate perception, an instinctive knowledge that comes without reasoning. But, what so frequently passes for intuitive knowledge is hypnotic suggestion, sometimes coming from an individual, sometimes from race consciousness.

Intuition comes from contemplation of the word "Truth." You can learn to become intuitively aware, at all times, of whatever you need to know.

Spontaneous and intuitive awareness of the self, manifests in only about two per cent of our consciousness. Even here, we often doubt whether the intuition we have received is true or false. So we wonder whether the instruction we have received is from God or devil (a figure of our fantasy or false imagination), and what we should do about it. Should we do as our mind tells us, or should we think twice about it and see what happens? Should we go ahead or should we hold back? True flash of intuition is very rare. One experiences it in states of deep meditation, when the rational boundary and the intellectual concepts of mind are transcended, and when there is intense self-awareness generated inside. That intuition has to be awakened because it represents the other half of our personality, the unmanifest side of consciousness, wisdom, understanding and knowledge.

Intuition is our inner voice to lead us to our unique path. We must develop and learn how to trust and follow our intuition from the earlier stages of our lives.

It must be emphasized that the word 'intuitive' is used to denote a type of knowing which is instantaneous or rather timeless (a temporal), and not as is 'women's intuition' wherein it is used to denote a sort of 'sixth sense', a vague feeling, hunch or foreboding. It is same type of knowing which Ken Wilber has called the 'second mode of knowing' and which has been also variously called 'insight'.

It is well known that females are more intuitive than men. According to Pamela J. Ball: "The sea is representation of cosmic consciousness, a wild sea, the chaos of creation, but also the breadth and depth of feminine intuition, which many have cause to fear."[2]

Intuition is really a sudden immersion of the soul into the universal current of life, where the histories of all people are connected, and we are able to know everything, because it's all written there.

The intellect is subordinate to intuition, dogma to experience, and outer expression to inward realization. Because, intellect examines,

---

2. Pamela J. Ball, *10,000 Ways to Change Your Life*, Arcture.

calculates, decides, accepts, and rejects all that is happening within the spheres of mind; and intuition is an uninterrupted flow which dawns spontaneously from its source down deep within. It dawns only when the mind attains a state of tranquility, equilibrium, and equanimity. That pure intuition expands the human consciousness in a way that one starts seeing things clearly. Life as a whole is comprehended, and ignorance is dispelled. After a series of experiences, direct experience becomes a guide and one starts receiving intuition spontaneously.

About intuition, Albert Einstein wrote, "There comes a time when the mind takes a higher plane of knowledge but can never prove how it got there. All great discoveries have involved such a leap."

Intuition is the best form of knowledge. The deepest mysteries of life are known through intuitive apprehensions. Intuition means immediate knowledge and direct insight; and it is the full expression and extension of regions beyond all senses. However, deep intuition is utterly silent.

According to S. Radhakrishnan, intuition is a creative energy and all men with intuitive knowledge are creative. It covers the whole spectrum of life. Here is consciousness at its full and simulataneous realization. The upward urges are the creation of higher creative intuition which unveil the layers of unlimited possibilities inherited in man.

3.2 ESP

Telepathy and clairvoyance are the two major offshoots of ESP — extra-sensory perception — the elusive and tantalizing 'sixth sense' arising in the human mind; the mind being sensitive to sensations perceptions, and thought transference.

ESP is a general term for all cases where knowledge of events or things is acquired by a person without the use of ordinary channels of awareness like the five senses, logic and memory. Intuition can be callled ESP as it is not a mental process that involves any sense organ. Intuition is a direct experience of something. Thus, ESP formulates to a complex capability of the mind.

ESP is believed to be a universal faculty but is not equally developed in all living beings. However, some are gifted with well-developed ESP. Evidence suggests that the gift of ESP is inherited rather than acquired, as it has been seen in numerous cases of savants and saints. Yet, studies have established that almost everyone has it to some extent and it is more prominent upto an age of six to seven years; it slowly fades away with calcification of pituitary gland. This view is supported by the fact that cases of 'past life memories' are generally seen in early childhood, and are forgotten by the time the child reaches adolescence. According to a survey, most people have at least one ESP experience in their lifetime.

In the study of humans exhibiting ESP-cognition it has been found that better orientation can be achieved if the sensitive (psychic) comes into tactile contact with some object belonging to or related to the target area or subject (sitter) in the question.

We have all, at some time or another, visited a place for the first time and had the spooky feeling we know what we will see around the next corner or who we are going to meet next — strange manifestations of the subconscious — ESPs.

Daily exposure between two persons often results in considerable ESP between them. They can predict what the other person will do or say. Though, some may write this off as simply knowledge of the other person's habits and behaviour.

As would be expected, it follows that there is no way of monitoring ESP, even among those who seem to be quite strongly gifted with ESP. The ability appears to come and go for no particular reason, and we just don't know enough about it yet, to make ESP workable on a regular basis.

Millions of people, an estimated seventy per cent around the world, will confess to experiencing some form of ESP. Einstein's ESPs are well documented. He had vision of relativity while visualizing himself walking along a sunbeam; putting in other words, he accelerated his awareness to the speed of light: to observe a rod moving with speed of light as to whether it is looking as long as it was and saw it not shrinking; whereas an observer in normal and stationary state of awareness, would see the rod shrink to the negligible length.

> If the doors of perception were cleansed, everything would appear . . . as it is, infinite. — Blake, *Marriage of Heaven & Hell*

Perceptions become usually brilliant and intense when LSD (Lysergic acid diethylamide) is consumed. Colours and textures seem richer, contours sharpened, music more emotionally profound, and smells and tastes heightened. Colours may be heard or sounds seen. Alterations in time and space perceptions, and visual hallucinations are common. Emotions become intense, suggestibility is heightened, and exaggerated empathy with or detachment from other people may arise due to ESP.

With your eyes you see, but with your mind's eye you have ESP. According to Congolese people, "A priest sees people at their best, a lawyer at their worst, but a doctor sees them as they really are." Everyone sees persons or events from a different point of view. But an individual endowed with ESP can see in totality. This inherent sensitivity or perceptive ability may vary widely and wildly from person to person.

We can see an object, smell a flower, hear a sound, or experience a taste or touch. These are called sensorial experiences. For this, we must have an object to cognize or perceive. If there is no flower, our eyes cannot see it. However, there can be experience without objects which we have called inherent sensitivity, extensively known as extra-sensorial perception (ESP). Even a blind man can see, and deaf man can hear — by developing corresponding ESP centres in the brain.

ESP acquisition is neither an art nor a science, but a practice and priestcraft. Authentic and impartial researches show that priestcraft owes its origin to tantarism and witchcraft which were an inseparable part of the old rites, rituals and ceremonies together with their paraphernalia of *soma-rasa* (or other psychodelic substances), sex and vice; various strange ways in which men have tried to discover what lies beyond the range of normal perception.

ESP can be developed with desire, determination, dexterity and discipline. Many have succeeded with regular practice with ESP-cards, and have demonstrated it on demand. Tarot cards, also, are claimed to have endowed ESP to their readers.

Most of the mystics are adept in ESP by birth, behaving as a mad man or a meditating monk at times, but are perfect clairvoyants and are continually in contact with men and matter — telepathically. "ESP is the Spiritual Awareness, and has tremendous healing power for mental health specifically and somatic health in general", says Jay R. Brikman in his book *Reflections in a Pumpkin Field and Reflections in a Lily Pond*.

Reports on animals' "Sixth Sense" in detecting impending hurricanes, earthquakes, tsunamis and volcanic eruptions long before earth starts shaking, go back to centuries — rats racing from buildings, sparrows taking flight in flocks, dogs howling incessantly, etc. It is an impressive track record though anecdotal. An eyewitness to the phenomemon, a Danish man stated "dogs were running away up to the hilltops long before we even realized about December 26, 2004, tsunami" when he was staying in Ao Sane Beach, north of Phuket (Thailand). Science is iffy on a subject like that, for obvious reasons, as it is difficult to replicate it in a laboratory. And there are always explanations and theories that mitigate the mystery of the anecdotes.

Some scientists are looking for explanation of why some species behave strangely before catastrophies, by correlating the animals' sensory abilities with microscopic and invisible sensory stimuli.

However, Ben Hart, professor of Animal Physiology, told that animals' pre-quake behaviour is inconsistent. It is a fact that animals can sense anything, including very minor changes that happen before earthquakes, but there is so much background noise during an earthquake, that it is unclear what stimuli the animals are reacting to.

Thus, it may be concluded that such responses of animals may be helpful in controlling huge losses due to natural disasters in the near future. We are also hopeful that detection of bladder and prostrate cancer might be possible through trained dogs which is under investigation.[3]

Although there is a great deal of evidence for the existence of ESP, there are virtually no explanations of how it works — or, indeed, why?

Louisa E. Rhine researched 10,000 cases and concluded that ESP occurs in five ways: intuitive, realistic dreams, unrealistic dreams, hallucinations, and in a state of shock/trauma when subliminal barriers are easily broken.

Ken Wilber, an authority on transpersonal psychology, writes: "ESP and other such occurrences occupy those bands of the spectrum of consciousness where the boundary between self and the other has not been completely crystallized."[4]

J.B. Rhine, psychology professor at Duke University, North Carolina, U.S.A, was among the first to admit that ESP can be inaccurate. According to him: "It is notoriously vague, so that when intuitive people receive warnings about major disasters, there is insufficient information to prevent loss of life."

The phenomenon of ESP, according to the Eastern concept, belongs to another reality. And, Quantum physics has admitted the existence of the reality other than the 'material universe', and calls it 'non-material universe'. This makes us remember Plato, who said: "Science is nothing but perception."

In a 'true' ESP, knowledge is replaced in a strange way by something that has nothing to do with thought and less and less to do with vision, something superior which is a type of new perception. It's far above

---

3. Don Oldenburg, *Scientists Investigate Wildlife's Possible Warning Systems*; Dawn-International, 10th January, 2005.
4. Wilber, Ken, *The Specturm of Consciousness*, The Theosophical Publishing House, Wheaton Illiniois, U.S.A, 1985, p. 120.

the thought, above vision, it's a kind of perception: there is no more differentiation of the organs. And it's a perception, which is total: it is vision, hearing and knowledge at the same time. Something that is a new type of perception. So then, your know. It replaces learning. A perception that is so much truer, but so new.

About this perception, Mother[5] says:

> When I look at people, I don't see them as they see themselves: I see them with the vibration of all the forces within them or going through them. That's what is making my physical sight not disappear, but change in character, because, for me, the physical precision of normal physical sight is false. But that does not stop me from seeing physically. If, for instance, I try to thread a needle while looking at it, it's literally impossible, but if it is necessary for me to thread a needle, it threads itself, on its own! I have nothing to do with it: I hold the needle, hold the thread, and that's all. I think that if this state gets perfected, one should be able to do everything by the OTHER MEANS, the means that doesn't depend on external senses, and then, obviously, it will be the beginning of a superamental expression. Because it's a kind of innate knowledge that DOES things.

Like this, Mother had perceived most of the modern scientific discoveries, in advance.

However, this type of the perception is very very hard to get — may be developed through the superconscious mind-tapping.

3.3 Thought Waves

In the language of occult practice, brainwaves sensitized by our soul and modulated by our mind, are termed 'thought-waves' or 'psychic-pulses'. The brainwaves travel at the velocity of light ($3x10^3$ meter/ second) but the thought-waves (or thoughts) travel many more times

---

5. Mirra Alfassa Born in Paris in 1878, Known as Mother in Aurobindo *Ashram* in Pondicherry, India, from 1950 till her death in 1973.

faster than that — a velocity and corresponding frequency band are yet to be ascertained.

Thoughts are the product of our mind and brain, which are the two different entities having different role as well as function. In the long run, the mind is much more primary than the brain in creating all perceptions. But for now, the brain is our only concrete way of entering the mind. In cartoons a light bulb shows up over somebody's head when he has a bright idea; this isn't so in real life. The mind without the brain is as invisible and unprovable as God.

The working of different organs of the brain, was originally explained, very well, in the *Rigveda*, supposed to have been composed about 5000 years ago.

Our popular belief is that the brain functions like a Macintosh built from organic matter (one researcher has called it "a computer made of meat" (a disturbing but unforgettable phrase).

Your brain eagerly awaits your every command, ready to carry out anything you ask of it. All it requires is a small amount of fuel: the oxygen in your blood and little glucose. In terms of its intricacy and power, the brain defies even our greatest modern computer technology. It is capable of processing upto 30 billion bits of information per second and boasts the equivalent of 600 miles of wiring and cabling. Typically the human nervous system contains about 28 billion neurons (nerve cells designed to conduct impulses). Without neurons, our nervous system would be unable to interpret the information we receive through our sense organs, unable to convey it to the brain and unable to carry out instructions from the brain as to what to do. Each of these neurons is a tiny, self-contained computer capable of processing about one million bits of information.

Brain cells are not constant. We are born with about half the complement of neurons found in adult brain; the rest develop between six months and two years of age. Each neuron is connected to every other through billions of threads that branch out into thousands of tendrils per cell, forming a vast network. These tendrils, known as dendrites, sprout at the end of the cell like a tree trunk sprouting branches (the word dendrite comes from the Greek word for tree).

Although it sounds fixed and stable, this network is constantly shifting. And even if a neuron could remain the same, growing no new branches, the signals streaming down the dendrites are never same from moment to moment. Electrical impulses surge everywhere, shifting as we think new thoughts; our brains are like a telephone system with a thousand calls taking place every second. The main difference is that the cable lines of our neurons system are unstable, constantly changing their molecules with every moment of experience — both inner and outer. The wires are notoriously non-stationary, since they are not made of copper (or fibre glass) but of fluid fats, water, electrolytes, and the electrical charges running through them. Having a single thought is more complex than sorting out one message from all the telephone calls in the world. While we are managing that feat electrically, the brain also surges with chemical messages. One dendrite isn't strung into another; there is always a tiny gap between them. Across this gap, known as a synapse, each message must find a way to cross; otherwise the neurons would be isolated and unable to communicate. Electricity doesn't jump across the gap — the voltages are much too tiny to accomplish this. Instead, certain chemicals are emitted on one side of the synapse and received on the other. These chemicals, called neuro-transmitters, include dopamine and serotonin.

Among these chaotic swirls of chemicals and electrons no one has ever found a memory. Memories are fixed.

Even though we can identify the memory centres of the brain, no one has ever proved that memory is stored there. We assume it is, but how? To store a memory in a neuron is like storing a memory in water. (In fact, the brain is so fluid that if homogenized it would have same water content as a bowl of oatmeal. Our blood is actually filled more with solid content than the cerebrum). The notion that we store memory the way a computer stores it, by imprinting microchips with bits of information, is not supported by the evidence; when neurologists try to prove it, they soon hit a wall.

It is the same wall that Einstein and the other founders of Quantum physics broke through. A neuron is a poor receptacle for memory because, at the bottom, its molecules are not solid; they are patterns of invisible energy grouped into the appearance of particles. These energy packets themselves survive only on the quantum level; go deeper still, into virtual level, and the patterns dissolve; the energy vanishes into ghostly vibrations and then into nothing. Can memory be stored in nothing? The answer is yes.

When you remember anything, you move from world to world, maintaing the illusion that you are here among familiar sights and sounds. Sometimes the connections are faulty — one might have come up with the wrong name or telephone number. Without understanding this journey, however, there is not much hope of understanding telepathic dialling.

The advent of CT scans and MRIs has afforded us a glimpse into the brain as a place where energy is constantly being generated. But the brain and mind are different. Sometimes brain surgery has to be perfromed with the patients awake, conscious, and able to answer questions. If you are talking to such a patient and ask him to lift his arm, he obeys like anyone else, even though a section of his skull has been removed, exposing the cerebral cortex to open air. Now take an electrode and stimulate part of the motor cortex so that the same arm suddenly moves. The action is exactly the same as when you asked the patient to perform this action. However, there is one huge difference. In the first instance, if you ask what has happened, the patient will respond, "I moved my arm." In the second instance if you ask what happened, the patient will respond, "My arm moved."

Despite the external similarity (the arm moved), the first act involved will and desire; a mysterious entity called "I" did the work, not simply the brain. Such an experiment[6] was actually performed by the pioneering Canadian brain surgeon Wilder Penfield, which led him to conclude that our minds and our brains are not at all the same.

---

6. Penfield, Wilder, *The Mystery of the Mind*, Princeton University Press, Princeton, N.J., 1975.

None the less, Penfield asked an obvious question. Where in the brain can you find any mechanism that possesses intuition, creativity, insight, imagination, understanding, intent, knowing, will, decision, or spirit. Indeed all the higher functions of the brain still cannot create the qualities that make us most human. Are we supposed to dismiss them as illusion or postpone discussion until someone discovers genes for the soul?

However, Penfield came to the conclusion that "it is the mind which experiences and it is the brain which records the experience."

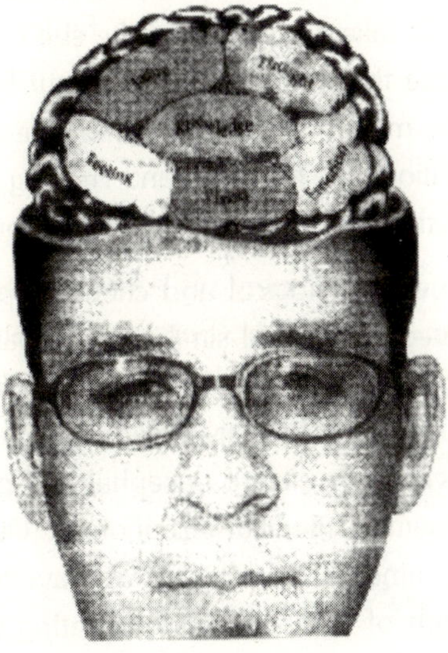

Times of India
15-10-2001

He concluded that the mind must be a kind of an invisible energy field that included brain, that perhaps even controls it.

The power of your brain to process information is staggering, especially when you consider that a computer — even the fastest computer — can make connections only one at a time. By contrast, a reaction in one neuron can spread to hundreds of thousands of others in a span of less than 20 milliseconds. To give you some perspective, that's about ten times less than it takes for your eye to blink.

A neuron takes a million times longer to send a signal than a computer switch, yet the brain can recognize a familiar face in less than a second — a feat beyond the ability of the most powerful computers. The brain achieves this speed because, unlike the step-by-step computer, its billions of neurons can all attack a problem simultaneously.

The human brain has capacity to produce answers faster than the "smartest" computer on the earth, even considering today's nanotechnology with computers that calculate in nanoseconds (billionths of a second). It would take two buildings, the size of U.N. Headquarters in New York to house the storage capacity of our brain! Yet this three-pound lump of gray matter can give you more firepower instantly for coming up with solutions to challenges and creating powerful emotional sensations than anything in man's arsenal of techonology.

In our skull, due to biological and chemical processes, electrical currents are generated, somewhat similar to the battery in our mobile phone set, to put it in simple layman's language. With thinking process imposed over it, these currents are variable in magnitude and are recorded as brainwaves or electro-encephalo-graphic waves (EEGs) — as these are known in medical terminology. Our brain is buzzing with activity, all the time. Regular pulses or wave-trains sweep across the brain every tenth of a second — amounting to 36,000 thought pulses per hour.

New thoughts come to us from the mind, not the brain. The most original new thoughts are called inspired; on the personal level seeing something new about yourself is called insight. When you feel inspired, more than ordinary thinking is involved. There is the sense of being uplifted, of suddenly breaking through. Old boundaries fall away, and one feels, if only for a moment, a rush of liberation. If the inspiration is powerful enough, one's whole life can be changed. There are insights so potent that years of patterned behaviour can change in an instant — you may develop powers of ESP, telepathy, etc.

> Only by falling back on our better thought, by yielding to the spirit of prophecy which is innate in every man, can we know what that wisdom sayth. — Emerson

> Love is an invisible, a sacred and ineffable spirit which traverses the whole world with its rapid thoughts. — Empedocles

> The universe is just a big Xerox machine. It simply produces multiple copies of your thoughts.
> — Neale Donald Walsch, *Conversation with God*

On an average day, the average person runs about sixty thousand thoughts through his mind, and in the most of the cases ninty-five per cent of those thoughts are the same. This is the tyranny of impoverished thinking. Those people who think the same thoughts everyday, most of these negative, have fallen into the bad mental habits. Rather than focusing on all the good in their lives and thinking of ways to make things even better; they are captive of their pasts. Some of them worry about their failed relationships or financial problems. Others fret over their less-than-perfect childhoods. Still others brood over more trifling matters: the way a store clerk might have treated them or the comment of a co-worker that smacked of ill-will. Those, who run their minds in this fashion are allowing worry to rob them of their life-force. They are blocking the enormous potential of their minds to work magic and deliver into their lives all that they want, emotionally, physically and, yes, even the power of telepathy, ESP, etc. These people never realize that the mind management is the essence of telepathic, clairvoyant, and extrasensory perceptions.

It is important to realize that man can create nothing unless and until it is first conceived in thought. Through vision, thought-waves can be gathered, assembled, separated and motivated into a plan of action and purpose that leads to success.

Few understand the power of thought, the basis of telepathy. If a man goes into a cave, shuts himself in, and thinks one really great thought and dies, that thought will penetrate the walls of that cave,

Table. 2: Brainwave Categories

S.No.	Wave Pattern	Frequency Band in Hertz	Electric Potential in Microvolts	Magnetic Field Tesla	Associated Mind	State of Mind	Stimulative Essence
1.	Beta-β	40-14	5-10	$\approx 2.5 \times 10^{-13}$	Conscious	Stimulated Steady Telepathy	Jasmine Rosemary Cardamom
2.	Alfa-α	14-8	50	$\approx 2.0 \times 10^{-12}$	Sub-conscious	Relaxed concentration ESP-cognition Clairvoyance	Lavender Melissa Chamomile
3.	Theta-θ	8-4	10	$\approx 5.0 \times 10^{-5}$ *	Tumescent -unconscious	Restful Expansive -vision Dreams	Neroli
4.	Delta-δ	4-0	20-200	—	Unconscious	Totally -unaware Sound-sleep	Rose Lilac Violet

* The theta wave magnetic field corresponds to the Earth's magnetic field pulsation of 0.5 gauss ($\equiv 5 \times 10^{-5}$ Tesla) at 7.5 Hz; the magnetic field drops as the frequency rises.

vibrate through the space, and at least permeate the whole human race. Such is the power of thought.

Scientists have also upheld the truth of Tantra claim that each thought-wave influences the mind; each mental vibration affects the life, and each emotion affects the soul.

Researchers have found that a distinct relationship exists between the frequency, voltage amplitude of the brainwaves and the state of mind of the individual. For convenience, the brainwaves have been grouped into four types: beta (β), alfa(α), theta (θ), and delta (δ). The reader must remember that these brainwaves are not the states of mind; they are merely a manifestation which allows one to know one's state of mind. Though much is still to be discovered regarding the relationship between these waves and the state of mind, the following is a brief summary of present day knowledge regarding these waves — given in Table 2.

These brainwave divisions are only broad subdivisions as the various states of consciousness display their own typical brainwave patterns. The states of consciousness of mind are the different manifestations of *prana*. And the brainwaves are the physio-electrical aspect of the *prana*.

In scientific terms, there are many more waves besides beta, alpha, theta and delta, such as mu, gama, vertex, spice, kapa, etc. corresponding to syncronized, desynchronized-high, low, orthodox, paradoxical phases of mind, and are of lesser significance.

The brain is similar to a tape on an adding machine, simply recording what has been visually observed, heard, smelled, tasted and touched. The life force enables you to do this.

As long as you identify yourself with the carnal mind of the senses, believing in both good and evil, your concept of self is as one person among billions: you are not thinking in your heart, but in your head — your brainwaves have not yet been modulated by the mind's eye, nor they have been sensitized by the soul.

Speaking physiologically, thinking is confined to the roof of the brain. We know, this life is the unseen "Intelligence", which is the 'real thinker', although our brain is coupled with the mind and its components: conscious, sub-conscious, unconscious and super-conscious.

Thinking is continuous oscillation between conscious and unconscious processes — conscious and unconscious being like warp and weft. True picture thinking is confined to manifestation of the unconscious — as in the dreams, the hypnogogic half-dreams, the psychotic's hallucinations, the artist's visions.

Thinking in the past is remembering; thinking in present is mainly problem-solving (as required in case of telepathy); and thinking in the future is anticipating (as desired in clairvoyance investigations) — the combined three processes work in dreams. A.B. Alcott said, "Thought means life, since those who do not think do not live in any high or real sense. Thinking makes the man."

> Thinking is the hardest work there is, which is the probable reason why so few engage in it. — Henry Ford

> There is no expedient to which a man will not go to avoid the real labour of thinking. — Thomas Edison

> There are two ways to easily slide through life; to believe every thing or to doubt everything; both ways save us from thinking.
> — Alfred Korzybski

Man has merely to recognize his thinking process, and know within himself that it is his for the enlarging of his life, health, happiness and prosperity.

A human being is born to accomplish a goal. As s/he grows, s/he gains coordination between his brain and sensory organs. Then coordination between the brain and mind arises. S/he begins thinking systematically, and his psycho-physical activities become goal-oriented.

The thinking process generates electric potential — EEG measurements are common feature in the hospitals, using metallic electrodes fastened to the skull. But magnetic field — MEG (magneto-encephalo-graphic) measurements are still rare. The MEG signals can be measered by the device having sensitivity in 10^{-13} Tesla range, where the telepathic singnals assume importance. To measure signals at those levels, an ultra-sensitive and sophisticated sensor to monitor the brain activity without touching the subject, called SQUID (Semiconducting Quantum Interference Device) is used. The sensor was developed by Wright Patterson of U.S.A. It consist of two coils supercooled by liquid helium to 4.2 K. At that temperature, the coils have almost zero electrical resistance. The charging currents are induced by MEG signals. [It is a strange coincidence that the nature also has a 'squid', a fascinating marine animal, which is again used to measure the electrical activity of our brain.]

The thought piloted aircraft have flown test flights. In the aircraft, the pilot exerts his control through 'thoughts'. If the background magnetic noise level in the cockpit is below that of the squids sensitivity, the plane will obey the thought command.

When the thought-waves can move the man-made machines, so they can move thinking-minds; the foundation of telepathy and telepathic process.

Two researchers have found that words have a charateristic electrical pattern in the brain. Neuro-physiologist, Donald York, of the University of Missouri Medical Centre, and Chicago Speech Pathologist Tom Jenson found that same patterns hold true from person to person. In one experiment, they were even able to find the same brainwave pattern in people who spoke different languages. They have already taught computers to recognize those brainwave pattern so they can interpret the words in person's mind even before they're spoken! These computers can literally read minds, much the way we can when we precisely mirror physiology. Thus, by mimicking another's physiology, one can experience new choices of thought, emotion and action.

The human brain is a computer, our "hardware". It is more efficient, gram for gram, than any inorganic device yet designed.

Yet, like all computers; it is at the mercy of the "software", the programming — that set of directions which tells it how to operate. Without proper input of information no computer can operate accurately, regardless of whether it is a window-2020 machine or the thought-producing brain of a man.

It is an established fact that the thought-waves travel through any medium and can cross even an iron-curtain, whereas electromagnetic waves do not travel through certain mediums, either they are partially or completly absorbed, or reflected back; depending upon the frequency band employed. This goes to say that telepathic communications go unhindered throughout universe(s).

The "thoughts" pop up in our mind — enter our mind, God knows from where. The thoughts probably have their origin in the 'Universal Intellignece', and therefore, it can safely be conceived that the thoughts themselves are 'telepathic communications' from the yet unveiled mysterious source.

Professor Calligaris, a famous Italian specialist of experimental psychology, says that "thought-waves" will be the means of enabling persons thousands of miles apart, to communicate with one another, as human beings march on the path of evolution. He believes in the three "communicating disks" in the human body — head, heart and hands.

In place of thought-waves/trains, M.K. Kaw has postulated the concept of "thoughton."[7] He defines thoughton as a thought which is encased in an emotion-field. Further, in the case of telepathy, thoughtons leave the sender, travel and stimulate the mind of another person, modify his/her energy-fields, and come back as modified thoughtons; leaving the messages or bringing back information package for sender so as to enable him/her to read the thoughts of the other person — thought poaching. And, in case of material objects, the

7. M.K. Kaw, *The Science of Spirituality*, Full Circle Publishing, Delhi, 2000, pp. 23 and 92.

thoughtons of sender leave an impression on the object; the impressions may be psychometrized by psychometry talented persons.

It is quite possible that just as lightwaves may travel for millions of years before they reach any object, so thought-waves may also travel hundreds of years before they meet an object with which they will vibrate, in unison. It is quite possible, therefore, that this atmosphere of ours is full of such thought[8] pulsations, both good and evil. Every thought projected from every brain goes on pulsating, as it were, until it meets a fit object that will receive it.

Our thoughts flit across like fireflies. Thoughts would spring up, flit across, and die down like the sparks from a roaring fire disappearing in mid-air. The thoughts flitting across can be scanned, entertained or rejected by a trained mind.

The microcosm reflects the macrocosm. Both are built on the same plan, both have the same origin. Thought created all. Control thought and you control everything. There is nothing mysterious or occult about that — soul-psychic sleuthing is the way and means.

3.4 Telepathic Nervous System

In the scheme of nature, men are the privileged species. Men have nervous system that is capable of becoming aware of the energy and informational content of a localized field. We experience this field subjectively as our thoughts, feelings, emotions, desires, memories, drives, beliefs, judgements, imaginations, instincts, intuitions, ESPs, and more. This same field is experienced objectively as the physical body — and through the physical body, we experience this field as the world. But it's all the same stuff. That is why the ancient seers exclaimed, "I am that, you are that, all this is that, and that's all there is." Some mystics went to the extent of saying. *sivo 'ham* — "I am Shiva," an ecstatic sufi poet-saint Mansur Mastana (CE 852-922) pronounced *anal-haq*, "I am God."

---

8. Robert Hughes, *The Cosmos is a Giant Thought*; Horizon, winter 1974, vol. xvi, No. 1.

For such seers and enlightened persons, telepathy, clairvoyance and ESP channels are always operative. They are above the levels of soul-psychic sleuthing and ever remain tuned to cosmic consciousness.

Your body is not separate from the body of the universe, because at quantum mechanical levels there are no well-defined edges. You are like a wiggle, a wave, a fluctuation, a convolution, a whirlpool, a localized disturbance in the larger quantum field. The larger quantum field — the universe — is your extended body.

Not only is the human nervous system capable of becoming aware of information and energy of its own quantum field, but because human consciousness is infinitely flexible through this wonderful nervous system, you are able to consciously change the informational content that gives rise to your physical body. You can consciously change the energy and informational content of your own quantum mechanical body, and therefore influence the energy and informational content of your extended body — your environment, your world — and cause things to manifest in it.

This conscious change is brought about by the two qualities inherent in consciousness: attention and intention. Attention energizes, and intention transforms. Whatever, you put your attention on will grow stronger in your life. Whatever, you take your attention away from will wither, disintegrate, and disappear. Intention, on the other hand, triggers transformation of energy and information. Intention organizes its own fulfilment.

The quality of intention on the object of attention will orchestrate an infinity of space-time events to bring about the outcome intended, provided one follows the other spiritual laws of success.[9] This is because intention in the fertile ground of attention has infinite power for organizing subjects and objects and events. We see the expression of this infinite organizing power in every blade of grass in every apple blossom, in every cell of our body. We see it in everything that is alive.

---

9. Deepak Chopra, *The Seven Spiritual Laws of Success*, Excel Books, New Delhi, rept., 2000, pp. 68-71.

What is remarkable about the nervous system of human species is that it can command this infinite organizing power through conscious intent. Intent in the human species is not fixed or locked into a rigid network of energy and information. It has infinite flexibility. In other words, as long as you do not violate the other laws of nature, through your intent, you can literally communicate unlimitedly.

Thus, human nervous system plays an important role during psychic phenomenon. A physiologist, the late Walter B. Cannon,[10] has made us aware that emotional condition of extreme danger, or a tendency to fight or flight, is associated with a massive action of the

Table. 3 Nervous system of Telepathy

S. No.	*Characteristic*	*Transmitter*	*Receiver*
1.	Role	Broadcasting	Radio-set
2.	System	Sympathetic	Parasympathetic
3.	Action	Prepares the body for exertion and drive	Prepares the body for relaxation
4.	State of mind	Fright; Fight-Flight	Relaxed, Day-dream
5.	Nervous state	Advenergia	Cholinergia
6.	Activated by	Norepinephrine	Acetylcholine
7.	Heartbeat	Accelerates	Slows down
8.	Blood vessels	Constrict	Dilate
9.	Coronary vessels	Dilate	Constrict
10.	Muscles of the pupil of eye	Dialate/ Constrict	Constrict/ Dialate
11.	Secretion	Sweat, dry mouth, urine, bile	Tears, Saliva, no urine or bile, no milk
12.	Blood Volume	Increases	No change of volume
13.	Efforts made	Determined	Causative
14.	Brainwave	Sharp beta-wave	Clean alpha-wave

10. Cannon, W. B., *The Wisdom of the Body*, Norton, New york, 1932.

sympathetic nervous system — suitable for telepathic transmission. The sympathetic system in general acts as an antagonist in the body to parasympathetic nervous system — suitable for ESP admission. Physiologically what one does, the other counteracts. However, here, the comparison between the two nervous systems — parasympathetic and sympathetic — is given in Table 3, from the perspective of telepathy.

Ashok Bedi,[11] a clinical professer in Psychiatry in USA, says: "Most sympathetic nerve endings secrete a harmone called norepinephrine that excites most of visceral structures and inhibits a few. The parasympathetic nervous system secrets acetylcholine, which, like norepinephrine, stimulates some organs and inhibits others. The norepinepherine forms a neurotransmitter line.

In the *kundalini* system, the sympathetic nervous system corresponds to an aspect of the *pingala-nadi*. This system is the "hot" system in that it prepares the body and the individual for the fight-or-flight response. In general, it excites the heart and blood vessels, increasing blood pressure, slowing the gastrointestinal system, and increasing the metabolism of essentially all the cells of the body. *Pingala* is the carrier of solar currents and intellectual-mental energy. It makes the physical body more dynamic and efficient, and provides increased vitality and "male" power. *Pingala* has a purifying effect, but its cleansing is like fire.

The *ida-nadi* corresponds to the parasympathetic system. The parasympathetic is the "cool" system that is responsible for calming, smoothing and renewing. It calms the heart, may lower blood pressure, enhances the gastrointestinal system, and is responsible for sexual stimulation and function. The *ida nadi* carries lunar currents, and is the channel of physical emotional energy. It is "feminine" in nature, and the storehouse of life-producing, maternal energy. *Ida* nourishes and purifies, but its purification is gentle.

---

11. Ashok Bedi, *Path of the Soul, the Union of Eastern and Western Wisdom to Heal Your Body, Mind and Soul*, New Age Books, New Delhi, 2005, p. 84.

The parasympathetic activation is associated with increased degree of sensitivity for telepathic reception. When this system is activated there is an increased amount of acetylcholine released into *ida-nadi* system, due to which blood pressure drops by twenty to twenty-five points, pulse slows down, skin is flushed, eye-pupils pin-point narrow and eyes shine brightly.

Scientists are now researching into the way our nervous systems function by means of PET (Positron Emission Tomography) scans and various other scientific methods including 'split-brain' experiments and other studies. These studies show that the left cerebral hemisphere, the 'talking' half of the brain (the hemisphere which controls speech) takes unrelated events and attempts to relate them by concocting a 'story'. It thus tries to make sense out of the multiplicity of sensory signals and perceptual images that the brain is normally bombarded with. The left hemisphere's job is to create a model and maintain it at all costs. The right hemisphere, on the other hand, tries to detect anomalies. When anomalous information reaches a certain threshold, it forces the left hemisphere to revise the entire model and start from scratch. This is called a paradigm shift. The left brain tries to cling to the existing model, the right tries to force the paradigm shift.

Thus, selective editing takes place and a threshold level is achieved. This level is different in different people. Depending upon the level of this threshold (what is, in simple words, the strength with which a person clings to his current thought), even obvious inconsistencies pointed out by the right-side brain may be ignored. But when this threshold level is surpassed — something dramatic happens — telepathic link is established, maybe with other human mind or even the Universal Mind.

Therefore, we know, in our brain the two (right and left) cerebral nervous hemispheres perform slightly different functions. In a right-handed person the left hemisphere is the 'dominant' one, now called the 'categorical'; and the right hemisphere is called 'representational'. When the energy flow occurs in the left hemisphere, things like logical thinking, calculations, functions related with vocabulary, grammar and technical ideas come out easily. Learning of such things also becomes easy. On the other hand, when the energy flow is relatively more in the non-dominant (right) hemisphere, things related with emotions, faiths and beliefs get the upper hand. Also, arts such as acting, music and poetry/gazals come easily. The non-dominant hemisphere has often been termed the "Heart" by the poets and literary persons. It is obvious that the right hemisphere perceives, believes and feels several such things that are uncomprehensible by the left hemisphere which thinks logically. These things are variously called supernatural phenomena or just blind faiths.

It is worth noting that the ancient savants have mentioned that when the air flows prferentially in the right nostril the understanding of difficult subject becomes easy. And, if you wish to indulge in telepathy, clairvoyance, etc., you better breathe through the left nostril.

However, the nervous systems — sympathetic, *pingala-nadi*, or the right hemisphere — parasympathetic, *ida nadi* or the left hemisphere — reach their working point through a process of slow growth and development, similar to the evolution of life itself. It therefore, follows that at the age of, say, twenty there may be the commencement of a development which may alter the entire life at thirty; but there is no age-limit at which to initiate soul-psychic sleuthing.

Telepathy, particularly, is a communication between the two trans-receivers — two human minds, and sometimes one mind to many receiving minds, as in the case of mass hypnotism. Sometimes sympathetic nervous system is powerful and at other times parasympathetic is active, and verily both the adrenergia and the cholenergia may exist simultaneously. Only in case of ingestion of hallucinating mushroom, the transmitter and receiver sets (nervous systems) become alternataly active for the person.

3.5 Development of Telepathic Faculty

Telepathic encounter is a recurring phenomenon in human life. The best example is the meeting of hearts. We know, speech is not the only means of understanding between souls. It is not the syllables that come from the lips and tongues that bring hearts together. There is something greater and purer than what the mouth utters. Silence illuminates our souls, whispers to our hearts, and brings them together. As tranquility descends it becomes a supreme thought, an overpowering emotion living in minds — a telepathic transaction has occurred.

Each of our thoughts, emotions, feelings and actions can be seen as an energy packet with distinct characteristics. These energies radiate out from the body into space in wave-like patterns of motion that slowly attenuate and dissipate. These patterns we may unconsciously or deliberately direct at another person — constitutes telepathic transmission.

The mind is never vacuous. Every moment a multitude of thoughts keep crowding it. As a result the thought or thought package on which we wish to lay emphasis does not get emphasized and, accordingly, it does not create the requisite impact on others.

Certain thoughts arise in our mind, and they concern the person sitting near. In that case the pressure it generates must make an impact on his inner mind, so much so that he feels compelled to follow these unspoken thoughts. But the postulate for this sort of transmission requires us to have only stable and mature thoughts. It needs clear and workable ideas, too. It is only then they will make a powerful impact on the inner mind of the person sitting nearby. S/he will accordingly begin to act on at our unspoken behest.

The thought packages which are to be transmitted must remain very firm and stable. It is possible only when we have, in our mind, only one prepondering thought, we shall be able to radiate it with full force and effectively.

On the contrary if your mind is cluttered up with a mass of all kinds of thoughts, including the one you intend to transmit to a certain person, it is very often seen that all the thoughts are reduced to common level including the one you wanted to transmit. Your force of action will get dissipated among the host of the thoughts running through your mind. The casualty is the thought which needed to be dispatched. It does not get the force and energy which is needed.

It is, therefore, essential that you practise the technique of dissociating your mind from thoughts and ideas. It, however, needs a regular practice. Mornings and evenings are the best time for this practice.

While practising transmission of thoughts one should advance one's practice gradually and steadily. It is no use why you should feel disappointed and put off if you are not successful in your attempts. You are certain to be crowned with success if you continue to practice for sometime with dexterity, determination and devotion.

As an example, when you receive a guest at your place, you start your practice right from there. In any case make sure that not a word and not a sound escapes your tongue. After a few moments the guest desires to have some hot drink, a suggestion planted by your thought-wave. He is actually getting slightly fidgety for some drink. If he does so, it should be taken as a pointer to the right transmission of your thoughts.

Say, as another example, you are in your office. Now you work up a suggestion that your boss comes to your cabin with a certain file and demands you to attend to the file. The boss is sitting in a cabin next to yours. You do not see him, for he is not seated opposite. Nevertheless, you try to plant on to his mind the idea which you propose to perform. Repeat the suggestion five to seven times.

Take note of the fact that the speed of the transmitted thought depends entirely on your will-power. If you have strong will-power, the transmission gains in velocity. Also, there must be full concentration on the thought. A crowd of thoughts will dissipate your energy and take away your capacity to concentrate on the desired thought. It simply does not get itself projected with any speed.

If you repeat the transmission of the thought ten to fifteen times, you will see your boss himself will arrive in your cabin armed with that file. While handing over the file he woud assign you the task as a priority item. He was going out so he thought he should get you to do this work. If you achieve this you could take it as a pointer to your success in the transmission of the telepathic signals.

At the same time make sure that you should not entertain in your mind mutually contradicting thoughts at a certain given time. For instance, you are seeking to transmit the idea that the boss will come to your cabin with the file. At the same time if you start entertaining the idea that boss being senior person will in no case come to your table, this negating instance, too, will make its own impact on the said officer (boss). This negative stance will certainly weaken your earlier positive transmission. As a result there may not be effective force in the thought transmission.

It is therefore, highly essential that you concentrate on a single thought and in no case entertain mutually contradictory thoughts.

> Learn to become focused, and to take your attention away from what you don't want, and all the emotional charge around it, and place the attention on what you wish to experience . . .. Thought flows where attention is targeted. — N. Vanvari

We know, a new Howitzer throws a shell more than twenty-five miles away. But, in order to do this there must be a tremendous propulsive explosive back up of the shell. It must be positioned and liberated in a certain manner. If the gunner should put in only half the required amount of powder the shell would never reach its mark. It would fall short just in proportion to the lack of energy behind it. Further, it is not only necessary to have ample powder in the back of the shell, but it must also be the best kind of powder, containing the maximum of energy. Similar are the requirements for the telepathic thought-targeting.

However, a positive and pleasing telepathic communication would need little fire. We know, a person bringing good news, behaves authoritatively.

He who brings good news, knocks boldly at the door.

— French Proverb

Another requirement is, when we seek to transmit our thoughts to a certain person, he may be near to you or far away from you; we should have his image alive in our view, simultaneously. Make sure that you also develop so much of strength that no other image emerges before you to distract your attention from the designated image.

When the image or picture is invoked and it comes before your eyes, suggest and transmit the thought into the image. You will find that you have succeeded. In the example given earlier, the image of the boss must have come off alive in your eyes. It is only then the transmission of thoughts is found to be feasible.

Suppose you have never seen the person to whom you are to transmit your thoughts. In this case, obtain his photograph or picture. If it is not available, try to construct a semblance of the person from whatever you have been told about him. Give it a concrete form and then try to transmit your thoughts to the form or the picture as the case may be. Fortitude will lead you to success.

If you have very strong will-power and a developed capacity to transmit your thoughts, it is certain that the thrust of thoughts will be felt by the intended person whether s/he is close to you or faraway, thousands of miles from you. You can transmit your thoughts to friends and relatives living abroad and make them do anything you might desire, but take care, it should be ethical, rational, lawful and for noble ends — you may even attain efficiency of 'SMS' on your mobile phone! It may need spiritual excellence!! But is worth practising!!!

At the initial stage you take to practice at 10 or 11 in the night. For at this time the outer-mind (conscious mind) of the target person remains asleep (or relaxed) and his/her inner-mind (subconscious and unconscious mind) goes active to the maxim. As a result whatever thoughts you would like to transmit will make a swift and powerful impact on his mind. And, you will have quicker success.

Further, the thoughts seeking some objectives or plans should be realistic. As an example, the thought of or resolution that we shall bring New York to the neighbourhood of New Delhi, is bound to end up as an exercise in futility, for it violates the determinants of time and space. It may also fail in asking your deity some favour?

The basic act of sending in telepathic message appears to be psychologically a centripetal one — concentration. In fact, the word "sender" in telepathy is a misnomer in that the sender does not send anything out, but rather serves a centre of attraction drawing to him the attention of the receiver. It is as though the sender creates a mental vacuum toward which the receiver's mind is drawn. The sender by his need and desire prepares a mental stage; the receiver in turn populates the stage with his own symbols and images.

Here is the "wow" factor. When you think about what you want, and you emit that thought-wave, you cause the energy of what you want to vibrate at that frequency and you bring it to you! As you focus on what you want, you are changing the vibration of the atoms of that thing, and you are causing it to vibrate to you. The reason you are the most powerful transmission tower in the universe is because you have been given the power to focus your energy through your thoughts and alter the vibrations of what you are focused on, which then magnetically draws it to you.

Thus, you develop the trasmitting ability. Sometimes, your receptive ability improves, without even attempting for it. But that is not enough to qualify you as a good telepathist. For that, you have to have reception ability somewhat similar to a wide space scanning radar. This requires you to increase the sensitivity towards incoming telepathic signals. This can be achieved by enhancing your postitive thinking, removing from your mind hard feelings and hurts, dispersing love for all, and regularly devoting at least ten to fifteen minutes for contemplative meditation — purification of conscious, subconscious and unconscious mind.

The human mind, freed from the disturbances or "static" of

restlessness, is empowered to perform all functions of complicated radio mechanisms — sending as well as receiving thoughts and tuning out undesirable ones. As the power of radio-broadcasting station is regulated by the amount of electrical current it can utilize, so does the effectiveness of human transmitter depend on the degree of will-power possessed by each person (The will, projected from the point between the eyebrows is the broadcasting apparatus of thought, also known as the mobile centre of consciousness.).

The receiver's mind should be as devoid as possible of verbal, symbolic or image material; either conscious or unconscious preocupation is not favourable. The presence of conscious cortical functions does not appear to favour telepathic interaction. Any self-consciousness tends to suppress telepathic reception. Alcohol, with its suppression of the cortical inhibitory function, has a most salubrious effect on the telepathic receiver. Conversely, fear, anxiety, or tension generated by the pressure of spectators is an unfavourable condition for full telepathic interaction.

A strong sense of concern for the known and unknown persons (not amounting to attachment) and general social welfare sense has to be awakend. Vegetarianism, orchestrated breathing, prayers, flower essences and rituals, etc. provide extra mileage. Perseverance is the key for progress.

For becoming an effective telepathic receiver, one may induce '*Yoga Nidra*',[12] a state of profound psycho-physiological relaxation and metabolic rest in which a fundamental release and readjustment in controlling mechanisms of the autonomic nervous system appear to occur.

Another technique for developing telepathic ability is to frequent with ESP cards. Here, a partner is required at later stages, who either acts as a sender or a receiver. In initial practices you simply try to read the cards — test subjects are asked to guess the motif on each card before it is turned up. In 1935, J.G. Pratt and Hubert Pearce, took

12. Swami Satyananda Saraswati, *Yoga Nidra*, Yoga Publication Trust, Munger, Bihar, India, 2003, p. 191.

part in experiments[13] which tested the strength of telepathic communication by extending the distance between them.

Telepathy is tested with ESP cards either in a group or individually. Solitaire telepathy with ESP cards is an advanced transdimensional stuff! Shuffle your deck of ESP cards and, holding them face downwards, scatter them over a table; then take any card at random, guess what it is, and write down your guess before looking. It is best to make guesses for a number of cards before looking; put carefully in order the cards you have used, and list your guesses sequentially. After a few sessions, when you look from time to time over your results, you will be able to discover some interesting facts about your powers and progress.

Telepathic talent demonstration is also done by an elevator experiment. We place the sender and the receiver, in two separate elevators in a tall building. The receiver, in the elevator which is going down, would be in the free-fall state, and, with respect to the elevator, floating. The sender on the other hand would be going up in a rapidly accelerating elevator and the gravitational force would increase on his body. If the accelerations of the two elevators are high enough, and the differential velocity is large enough, we would expect to find a marked increase in telepathic test scores under these conditions. Conversely, if we reverse the positions of the sender and the receiver with regard to the direction of their velocity, we would expect to get a decrease in telepathy scores.

When performing telepathic practices, try to reduce intellectualization as much as possible. Merely let the mind follow the mental actions necessary for execution of the practice. While contemplation is in progress the thought dives deeper into the mind, and takes the mind beyond the realms of rational thought. When this occurs, telepathic communication with the contemplated soul will get established, be it a living soul, departed soul, imaginary soul, your deity, and even God.

---

13. J.B. Rhine, *Extra Sensory Perception*, U.S.A, 1935.

3.6 Telepathists

All the Lemurians were telepathists — it was 1,00,000 years old epoch. Presently, almost all the infants are telepathists — you will invariably observe them smiling in their sleep — they are in touch with God. Also, highly evolved souls are in touch with God all the time. Thus, in case of infants and spiritualists, one of the telepathic terminal is God.

God is at the head of telepathic conference during the "Near-Death-Experiences (NDEs)" and naturally occuring "Out-of-Body Experiences (OOBEs/OBEs)", while you are in the human body and still living in the world of universal construct.

A closer look at these paranormal phenomena will reveal that we all can be telepathists par excellence if we awaken our inner-self. If you delve deep, it is a telepathic link between your conscious and subconscious/unconscious mind on one side and superconscious mind on the other side. Deep meditation and *yoga-nidra* (dynamic sleep) help you to enliven this telepathic link.

> There is always one man who more than others represents the divine thought of the epoch. — Emerson

It is to be noted that a telepathist is different than a psychopath. A psychopath is a neurotic person, who randomly communicates rightly; he can be treated as a lower-grade telepathist as compared to a telepathist having God-given gift of communicating with other lives (even animals, amphibians and birds and beasts).

3.7 Trance-mediumship

A trance-medium is simply the one who has learned how to disengage his attention from the relative world, and by causing to cease for a time any voluntary movement, allows utterances of ideas and beliefs.

The trance-mediumship is not a weird act, as uninfromed persons are inclined to think. It is a telepathic action, mind to mind, and the medium tunes in to a specific vibration. S/he is always faced with the possibility of reading only the thought-realm of the questioner, or "sitter" as they are called. A trance-medium is frequently both clairaudient and clairvoyant, and exercises these abilities in perfectly normal state, that is, awake and moving.

Mediumship is a psychic phenomenon, in which the medium comes in contact with the allaged non-physical entities, or God Himself. One channelizes the universal life force through himself or herself, which can be used for a variety of purposes, such as problem-solving, healing, talking to dead relatives, etc.

> A link was wanting between two craving parts of Nature and he was hurled into being as the bridge over that yawning need.
>
> — Emerson

A distinguished British physicist Sir William Crookes spent much of his time studying the powers of individuals with mediumistic gifts, and obtained satisfactory results. One of his long studies carried out in 1870s was on the medium Florence Cook. While in deep trance, she (Florence Cook) was able to produce the visible apparition of a girl who called herself Katie King. Crookes was not satisfied with his visual observations of this apparition, and demanded of Katie King that he be allowed to photograph her presence. This was arranged in due time, and Crookes worked out the technique that would be least harmful to the medium.[14] Altogether Crookes could have 44 negatives, some inferior, some indifferent, and some excellent.

For mediums, a soul is like a fluid, which takes the form of anything it is poured into. Soul "makes things" out of what it is. It is the source of pure intelligence, completeness, and pure and perfect ideas. A medium takes over one of such souls, for example, s/he takes soul of Mahatma Gandhi, Martin Luther King, Picaso, Vincet Van Gogh (1853-1890), J.F. Kennedy. A trance-medium, through his disciplined thinking, calls forth a "helper-soul" of a real being. This is not done willy-nilly, therefore the helper-soul helps the medium to investigate and solve the problem of the sitter.

Energy from the beyond works through the medium: the medium

14. Miller, Paul, *Science in the Seance Room*, Psychic Press Ltd., London, 1945, p. 121.

has no power of his/her own. There are two main categories: physical and mental mediums. In the physical category, there is movement of objects in different forms, and the medium demonstrates phenomena of telekinesis, levitation, etc. when the medium of communication is mental, the communication takes place through inner vision and hearing, automatic writing or speech.

Where mediums are physical, their seances will be peppered by inexplicable noises, levitation of objects or the movements of items arround the room. Daniel Dunglas Home, (1833-1886), was one of the most famous physical mediums to ever live. He performed feats that made scientists bite their nails. Once Home stretched his body to reach a height of 6' 6", some 11 inches more than his normal height (5' 7"). He also shrank to a height of 5 feet. He could separate his head from his body and so on. . . . But despite his reputation he depended on patronage and remained poor.

The elements of mental mediumship include clairvoyance, clairaudience, automatic writings, speech, etc. Mental mediums may sink into trance and assume the voice, facial expressions, gestures, and working specialities of their spirit guides. Some reach an altered state of consciousness via hypnotism and or meditation.

A practical way of acting "mediumship", says Edgar Allan Poe, (1809-1849), is: "When I wish to find out how wise, or how stupid, or how good, or how wicked is anyone, or what are his 'thoughts' at the moment, I fashion the expression of my face, as accurately as possible, in accordance with the expression of his, and then wait to see what thoughts or sentiments arise in my mind or heart, as if to match or correspond with the expression."

All of us are profoundly in love with ourselves. The Narcissus Effect plays on this universal narcissism: You look deep into the souls of other people; fathom their innermost desires, their values, their tastes, their spirit; and you reflect it back to them, making yourself into a kind of mirror image. Your ability to reflect their psyche gives you great power over them; they may even feel a tinge of love.

Automatic writings are words, texts, paintings (penned and or sketched) by mediums in trance. Sometimes complex and beyond the understanding of the writer (sketcher, painter) in usual state of consciousness, the words are thought by someone to be dictated by spirits (of dead geniuses and world fame artists, writers, poets, philosophers). However, a more popular theory is that they come from writer's subconsciousness, either telepathically received or buried information.

Ouija boards have been used for automatic writings, divination, trance-mediumship, where the user and a seeker take down messages, texts, and guidelines dictated by spirits on the other side.

To channelize communication from the 'other side', the mediums have spirit guides and it is this that distinguishes them from psychics and magicians. Some expectants are said to have received a highly personal and relevant message from their respective mediums. It is claimed, the British medium Leslie Flint had contacted with the spirits of some extremely famous personalities, such as Oscar Wilde, Queen Victoria, Winston Churchill and Mahatma Gandhi.

Some good spirits possess the power of foretelling, clairvoyance and clairaudience. They have love and affection for their friends and relatives. They try to help them in times of their distress, misfortunes, dangers and calamities. They give a warning message to avert dangers.

The Vedantic view is that the spirits have no knowledge of the highest truth. They cannot help others in attaining self-realization. Some are foolish, deceitful and ignorant. These earth-bound spirits control the mediums and pretend to know everything regarding the planes beyond death. They speak falsehood. They put on the appearance of some other spirit and deceive the audience. The poor innocent mediums are not aware of the tricks played by their dishonest spirit-guides.

Such mediums would have lost the power of self-control. Their vital energy, life-force and intellectual powers are used by the spirits which control them. These mediums, in turn do not gain any useful information. These spirits are not angels as the mediums claim. They are really earth-bound spirits.

Nevertheless, there are spirits who do portrait-painting and typing. Such spirits materialize in the seances. They melt away in mist-like white substance and disappear. You can hear the noise of the pencil during automatic slate writing. You may feel a gentle shock while the spirit writes on the slate. The spirits may place their hands on you and catch hold of your shirt, tie, etc.

Seances became a popular pastime in Victorian England. A small group of expectant people link hands in silence in a darkened room. All eyes turn to the presiding medium (trance-medium). The low lights flicker and the closed curtains rustle as her (mediums used to be females mostly) wavering voice splinters the night. “Is there anybody here?” A call for physical-cum-mental spirit-guide.

Many a time diviners, dowsers, pendulum healers, Ouija board operators, automatic text writers, and psychic artists are clubbed in the category of trance-mediumship. However, an American top psychic, Edgar Cayce termed Ouija board as a “dangerous toy” and suggested not to use it.

Some people believe the Ouija board reveals the hidden quarters of mind, leading to problems in mental health. Others worry that it is a gateway to possession by negative or evil spirits. There have been many reports of the pointers flying from the board and an apparent invasion by spirits, some of them hostile. If that is the case, it is similar to the planchette.

Mediumship is not limited to magical or mystical feats as those of Daniel Dunglas Home and Jose Arigo.[15] Arigo, a humble Brazilian, performed many psychic surgeries during 1950s and 1960s under the spiritual guidance of a German, Dr Adolphus Fritz, who had died in 1918.

---

15. Blitz Editions, *The Unexplained Mysteries of Mind, Space and Time*, Orbis Publishing, England, 1992, p. 138.

According to Dr Susan Phoenix,[16] an acknowledged aura photographer, "Everything in our life is an energetic force of some form — all those vibrating molecules that we learned about in school are now coming into their own. The Universe is definitely trying to communicate with this New Age and is ready to bypass the traditional channels of mediums and psychics by allowing us all to feel and eventually to see ourselves."

3.8 Psychotronics

Psychotronics is a process of mental manipulation through 'telepathic command' — spontaneous telepathy[17] (thought radiation, reception, and action) resulting in instant hypnotism and hypnotic behaving. It is the way of gaining another person's compliance. So, the psychotronics is the study of telephathically hypontizing a person to act according to your bidding — imposed will-power. The other form of the imposed will-power is through 'Brainwashing'.

Soviet military leaders and politicians are believed to have planned use of psychotronics as a weapon of war against the West. A report suggests that Joseph Stalin himself was interested in the use of telepathy for military purposes. He was assisted by Dr. Leonid I. Vasiliev, (1891-1966), a soviet parapsychologist, who had been using hypnotized subjects to carry out instructions by telepathic order.

A highly sensitized and intensive research was conducted in the Soviet Union during 1920-1960. The research terminology was vivid — 'distance influence', 'mental-suggestion', and 'transfer of motor impulses'. The telepathic messages were found to be effective with the objective to make people act and think according to instructions of which they were not consciously aware.

Birds following human commands, is well known. Even animals follow, and could be trained to be team members in the psychotronic

---

16. www.Phoenixplanes.com
17. Blitz Editions, *The Unexplained Mysteries of Mind, Space and Time*, Orbis Publishing, Hungary, 1993, p. 374.

war theatre. A Russian circus manager Vladimir Durov[18] trained a fox terrier bitch named Pikky, who could sense silent mental commands and follow them. Lately, dolphins are being trained all over the world, to be part of high-sea warfare.

A leading Czechoslovakian researcher Dr Zdenek Rajdak has equated psychotronics with parapsychology and defined it as: "The science which, in an interdisciplinary fashion, studies the distant interactions between living organisms and their environments, internal and external, and the energetic processes underlying these manifestations in order to supplement and widen man's understanding the laws of nature."

East Euopean researchers have assigned yet another dimension to psychotronics, and have found that certain structures, shapes and materials are capable of generating and storing high levels of psychic energy. The square-based pyramid, constructed according to the ratios of the Great Pyramid and similarly aligned, has been found to be amogst the most efficient psychotronic shapes. This suggests, probably the Great Pyramid at Gizah, Egypt, which was constructed around 8000 BCE, is a gigantic psychic energy accumulator. Further, simple experiments have revealed that foodstuff stored under such a pyramid shape are inexplicably preserved for a longer time period than similar food left in the open or beneath another shape.

Jain scriptures also talk about *leshya* (aura) and psychic powers and their use in warfare and peace. Some details have been given about psychic powers of *tejaleshya*, which can act like a missile and can cause extensive damage, and about *sheetaleshya* which can counter such damages and psychic violence.

Many parallels have been drawn between "psychotronic attacks" and "psychic attacks — having symptoms, said to include extreme fear, anxiety and mental distress, bruises on the body — sometimes in the form of goat's hoof or an ace of clubs — broad smears of slime, sometimes with footprints in them, the smell of decomposing flesh,

18. Vladimir Durov, *My Four-footed and Feathered Friends*, Mir Publishing, Moscow.

poltergeist phenomena and inexplicable outbreaks of fire and a curious and sinister sound called 'the astral bell', which may vary from a clear bell-like note to a faint click". But, both are transparent to clairvoyant vision.

In a psychic attack launched by a magician, the magician forms in his mind a clear picture of a creature he intends to attack with. By concentrated imagination and will-power, and by feeding into the mental picture his own violent emotional forces — his hatred, cruelty, lust, or expansionism — he can endow the creature with life and send it out to attack an enemy. It may appear in animal form — as a toad or snake or a wolf perhaps — or as something which is part human and part animal (or weapons of mass destruction released as psychotronic worms). It will not be visible to ordinary sight, but the person attacked by it will see it and so anyone else who is clairvoyant.

3.9 Psychokinesis

Poltergeists have been known to cause psychokinetic activity — objects to fall and break. Demonic entities specialize in levitating and displacing physical matter to induce fear in their victims. Other examples of poltergeist incidents[19] are cases of table-tripping during mediumistic seances, furniture being moved across the room, and the acceleration of objects from a position of rest to a high velocity.

The word "poltergeist" is derived from two German words — a folklore term, polter, meaning 'noisy' and the word for spirit, geist. Thus, the activity incorporates mysterious bangs, loud crashes, objectionable smells, and furniture that moves about on its own; sudden cold spells, inexplicable voices, objects that appear and disappear, and the uncontrolled levitation of victims. Poltergeists, unlike ghosts, 'hunt' by causing commotions, making noises, throwing things around and creating chaos. Are they malevolent spirits, or merely projections, perhaps, of the unconscious mind? Nevertheless, these psychokinetic phenomena have been reported since antiquity.

---

19. Osborn, A. W., *The Superphysical*, Ivor Nicholson and Watson, London, 1937.

Based on these reports, material objects were moved in space by the power of thought, and have since been demonstrated under scientific scrutiny.[20]

Scientists use the term 'psycho-kinesis — PK' to refer to the movement of a physical object without any known physical means being applied. This motion is due entirely to mental (telepathic) mechanism — the action of the human mind at (the mind of) matter.

The phenomenon of PK involves a force exerted by a psychic moving an object by telekinesis. It was reported as early as 1930-31, when a well-known psychic Rudi Schneider moved a handerkerchief from some distance that he could not touch, but it was within his view.

This moving of the handkerchief was repeated in an experiment conducted by the director of the Paris Institute of Metapsychology, Eugene Ostys[21] with the help of his son Marcel Ostys. When the handkerchief moved, no visible object had approached it, but the galvanometer recording showed that some type of palpable force[22] (which was known as "ectoplasma" to researchers) had broken through the infrared beam at the time of its displacement.

During the experiments, the rate of breathing of Rudi Schneider got accelerated to 200-300 per minute, or about eighteen times the normal rate! There are, besides, innumerable examples of accidental ejection of the astral substance to varying extents, the type of incident in which a person is scared by nocturnal "spirit rappings". Nevertheless, Rudi Schneider's demonstration shows us how close to the material level an astral substance can be.

In a different experiment conducted in the laboratory of the medical department of the Leningrad University on March 10, 1970, in the presence of Dr. Grenady Sergeyev and D. Sergei Sarichev, a

20. A.R.G. Owen, *Demonstration of Voluntary Psychokinesis*, New Horizons, vol. I, No. 1, 1972, p. 25.

21. Ostys, Eugene et al., *Revue Metapsychique*, Paris, No. 6, 1931 and No. 1 & 2, 1932.

22. Sonia Volochova, translator, *Human Psyche*, University Books, New York, 1965.

frog was dissected for testing the PK ability of 50-year-old Nina Kulagina, a Czechoslovakian. The Frog's heart was taken out. The heart was still pulsating slowly in spite of its being taken out of the frog's body. Nina commanded the heart to beat at a rapid pace, and it started beating rapidly, and it stopped beating only after Nina removed her gaze. The experiment was repeated many times, using hearts of different frogs, to confirm the force of her command.

Nina had revealed her remarkable ability of moving solid objects through will-power alone. She could move objects weighing upto 200 grams. In a test experiment lasting half an hour, she separated the yolk and white of an egg cracked into a saline solution. The electrostatic field around Nina increased when she worked, acting like the vibrations of magnetic waves.

In the second case, Dr. Grenady Sergeyev of A.A. Utkomskii Physiological Institue (a Leningrad Military Laboratory), took readings of the brainwaves, heartbeats and pulse-rates of Neyla Mikhailova during her numerous demonstrations of psychokinesis.[23] He found that while Mikhailova was causing objects to move without touching them, his instruments recorded a tremendous vibration throughout her body and its surrounding force-field which pulsated in the direction of her gaze. Her heart and brainwaves also pulsated in unison with this energy vibration, indicating that the energy Mikhailova used in her psychic feats was intimately connected with her whole body.

Reports go on to state that: "After doing these experiments, Mrs Mikhailova was utterly exhausted. There was almost no pulse. She had lost close to four pounds (≈1.8 Kgs) in half an hour. The EEG showed intense emotional excitement. There was high blood-sugar and the endocrine system was disturbed. The whole organism was weakened as if from a tremendous stress reaction. She had lost the sensation of taste, had pains in her arms and legs, couldn't coordinate and felt dizzy." At one time, after making a seven hour film of her abilities, Mikhailova was temporarily blind.

23. Ostrander, S. and Schroeder, L., *PSI–Psychic Discoveries behind the Iron Curtain*, Abacus London, 1977, pp. 88, 398.

Arther Koestler[24] writes:

> Karl Gustar Jung had experimented in parapsychology and spiritualism from his early days as a student of medicine to the end of his life. In his early twenties he organized regular spiritualistic seances; in the course of one of these, a heavy walnutwood table, an old heirloom, split with a loud report, and soon afterwards a bread knife in a drawer inexplicably snapped into four parts, again with a sound like a pistol shot. The four pieces of the knife are still in possession of the Jung family.

Was it a psycho-kinetic force of someone or another case of poltergeist activity?

Another of the most talked about practitioners of PK was Uri Geller, from Tel Ariv, Israel. In 1969, he earned himself a worldwide reputation for moving the hands of watches and clocks, and bending spoons/forks with just a rub. The rubbing of steel metal by his fingers was enough to transform the strength of the solid implements into dangling limpness.

Pschokinesis has been studied in the laboratory with the attempts to influence the fall of a group of rolling dice[25]. In other words, the mind tries to interact with moving mechanical system and tries to get certain dice numbers to appear face up. Such experiments have been conducted at Duke University, Columbia University, and at Pittsburg University, and the results indicate that dice can be controlled far beyond the expectations of chance. This kind of evidence from dice experiments shows that the mind can influence the behaviour of inanimate objects in motion.

This PK faculty, if at all developed in future course of time, will give rise to RSPK (Recurrent Spontaneous Psycho-Kinesis). A football professional, Jack Nicklaus is said to have RSPK power that he can influence the ball in flight. Similarly, a golfing professional Arnold Palmer is reported to have claimed that he could visualize the line his ball

24. Arther Koestler, *The Roots of Coincidence*, Hutchinson and Co., London, 1972.
25. J.B. Rhine, *The Reach of the Mind*, Faber & Faber, London, 1948.

should take on the golfing green. Some professionals, who have practised moving meditation, state that as they develop their skills, the intuitive aspects of the mind take over and direct their actions so that they become observer and enjoyer of the sport.

However, every gambler dreams of being able to direct the skittish roulette ball into a particular slot with nothing more than a moment's concentration. In theory it is possible. Those who have mastered mind over matter, or psychokinesis experts, would be able to determine the movements of a roulette ball. As casinos are still gleefully opening their doors across the globe and depriving punters of large amounts of hard-earned cash, we can easily assume the art of PK or RSPK is yet to be comprehensively learned.

RSPK is a continuonus process in the human brain. It has been lucidly pictured in the words of Sir John Eccless, Neurologist and Nobel Laureate: "If you want to see real psychokinesis, then consider the facts of mind-over-matter performed in the brain. It is quite astonishing that with every thought, the mind manages to move the atoms of hydrogen, carbon, oxygen and the other particles in the brain's cells."

3.10 Telekinesis and Teleportation

The telekinesis is the art of moving objects without using physical means. It is the advanced stage of psychokinesis because the kinetic action is at much more extended distances.

The telekinetic energy is somewhat of a mystery, yet to be solved, but it is very much in nature, and has been acquired by a few. To have it, the basic requirement is an absolute integrity, which cannot be violated. The telekinetic energy connot be used for any wrong purpose. Only on the terms of its own nature is this intelligent power consigned to the individual.

Telekinesis is a phenomenon which is responsible for the act of teleportation — a phenomenon where a mysterious force can transport objects from place to place without traversing the intervening distance.

The term "teleportation" is used when an object passes through matter, or materializes at a place from nowhere. In the former case it is supposed that the object first dematerializes before entry into matter and then rematerializes after its passage through the matter. In the latter case, the object (or person) disappears from one place and reappears (without much loss of time, irrespective of the distance) at another.

There are many reported instances where saints and psychics have produced apports from thin air; there are stories of material things and human beings vanishing into thin air, like those of ships and aircraft disappearing in Bermuda Triangle. To explain teleportation of human beings, some theorize that time may 'slip', enabling events and distances to be telescoped together. Others believe that the universe may contain strange whirlpools which draw people irresistibly, into them and move them at will, to anywhere on different or the same planet. Or possibly that these whirlpools whisk them away into another dimension altogether — scientists have perceived a four dimensional geometry and occultists have gone to twenty-four dimensions. Typically of paranormal instances, the proof is perplexingly vague.

Scientists are working to have hold of teleportation. A team of physicists,[26] Ping Kog Lam and his associates, at the Australian National University (ANU), have successfully disembodied a laser beam at one location and rebuilt it at a different spot about one meter away at the blink of an eye — using a process known as quantum entanglement. These scientists claim that science was not too far from being able to teleport solid matter from one location to another. However, teleportation of humans faces a near impossible task as we are made up of zillions of atoms — quantified by one with twenty-seven zeros.

3.11 Tulpa

A *tulpa* is an extremely powerful example of what occultists term a 'thought form'. It has been claimed that Tibetan adepts are capable

26. Belinala Goldsmith, *Get ready for Laser Travel Now*, The Times of India, New Delhi, 18 June, 2002.

of making their thought forms materialize so strongly that they can be seen by other people. Scientifically it is very logical to think it as a mystic reality — as it has already been enumerated that matter-energy-emotion-thought-Consciousness (meet-C) chain is possible; so why not the reverse chain C-teem be feasible!

An ideological extension of the above school of thinking is *tulpa* — a phantom form born solely from the imagination, and yet so strongly vitalized by the adept's will that it actually becomes visible to other people.

The tradition of the *tulpa* was a lot more eerie. The belief was intense visualization and concentration on, for example, a religious image could eventually make the mental picture visible to others. Indeed, in certain circumstances the image could take on a life of its own and behave in many respects like a ghost. Madame David-Neel, (CE 1868-1969), a prolific writer on Tibetan mysteries saw her first *tulpa* when a young painter entered her camp. The man had a special devotion to a particular Tibetan deity, which he had painted many times and visualized even more often in the course of his meditations. Madame David-Neel saw the etherical but perfectly visible figure of the god looming behind the painter.

To understand the nature of the *tulpa*, one has to appreciate that, as far as Tibetan Buddhists (and most Western occultists) are concerned, thought is far more than an intellectual function. Every thought, they believe, affects the 'mind-stuff' that permeates the world of matter, in very much the same way as a stone thrown into a lake makes ripples upon the water's surface. A thought, in other words, produces a 'thought ripple'.

Usually thought ripples have only a short life. A parallel in the scientific term is plasma (C-teem chain of nucleonic-plasma-vapour-water-ice) in a controlled thermo-nuclear power reactor. Thought ripples decay almost as soon as they are created and make no lasting impression. If, however, the thought is particularly intense, the product of deep passion or fear, or if it is of long duration, the subject of much brooding and/or meditation, the thought ripple builds into a more permanent thought form, one that has a longer and more intense life.

Tulpas and other thought forms are not considered by Tibetan Buddhists to be 'real' — but neither, according to them, is the world of matter that seemingly surrounds us and appears solid enough. Both are illusory. As a Buddhist classic from the first century CE expresses this firm belief: "All phenomena are originally in the mind and have really no outward form; therefore, as there is no form, it is an error to think that anything is there. All phenomena merely arise from false notions in mind. If the mind is independent of these false ideas, then all phenomena disappear."

If the beliefs about the thought forms held by Tibetan Buddhists, mystics and magicians are justified, then many ghostly happenings, hauntings, and cases of localities endowed with a strong 'psychic atmosphere' are easily explained. It seems plausible, for example, that thought forms created by the violent and passionate mental processes of murder, supplementated by the terror-stricken emotions of a victim, could linger around the scene of the crime for months, years, or even centuries. This could produce intense depression and anxiety in those who visited the 'haunted' spot and, if the thought forms were sufficiently powerful, 'apparitions', such as a re-enactment of crime, might at times be witnessed by people possessed of psychic sensitivity.

Sometimes, it is even claimed by students of occult, that those 'spirits' that haunt a particular spot are in fact *tulpas*, thought forms that have been deliberately created by a sorcerer for his own purposes.

The existence of extremely potent thought forms that re-enact the past would, of course, also explain the worldwide reports of visitors to old battlefields 'witnessing' military encounters that took place long before.

The word "*tulpa*" is a Tibetan one, but there are adepts in almost every part of the world who believe they are able to manufacture these beings by first drawing together and coagulating some of the mind-stuff of the universe, and then transferring to it some of their own vitality.

In Bengal, home of much Indian occultism, the technique is called *Kritya Shakti* (creative power), and is studied and practised by the adepts of Tantrism. As there is very strong resamblance between the physical, mental and spiritual exercises used by Tantric yogis of Bengal and the secret inner desciplines of Tibetan Buddhism, it is very likely that theories about *tulpas* coincided with the techniques of the practitioners of *Kritya Shakti*.

> We are what we think.
> All that we are arises with our thoughts.
> With our thoughts, we make our world.
> — Lord Buddha

In Bengal, there was a Gandha Baba,[27] who could produce scents (=Gandha). His proper name was Swami Vishuddhananda. He had learned many astonishing yoga secrets from a master, who lived for a thousand years in Tibet.

Gandha Baba, attuning himself with the pranic force by certain yoga practices, was able to guide the 'lifetrons' to rearrange their vibratory structure and to objectify the desired result. His perfume, fruit and other miracles were actual materializations of mundane vibrations.

We know, a fully God-realized master's thoughts are so powerful that he is able to resurrect his body and to appear in it before the eyes of earth dwellers. Materializing the atoms of a physical body can scarcely strain the powers of one who is united with the Lord — Him whose solar systems defy computation!

"I lay down my life that I might take it again," Christ proclaimed. "No man take it from me, but I lay it down of myself. I have power to lay it down, and I have power to take it again." — John 10:17-18, Bible.

The infinite potencies of vibrations derive from the creative word. AUM, the cosmic vibratory power behind all atomic energies. Any

27. Parmahamsa Yogananda, *Autobiography of a Yogi*, Yogada Satsanga Society of India, Kolkata, 2006 edn., p. 46.

word spoken with clear realization and deep concentration has a materializing value and assuming the thought-form. Loud or silent repetition of inspiring words has been found effective in Couéism and similar systems of psychotherapy; the secret lies in the stepping-up of the mind's vibratory rate.[28]

3.12 Thoughtography

Telepathy is not only confined to verbal thoughts; it can also communicate in picturesque thoughts. In March, 1992, Tanjag-Pool from Belgrade reported that a person with extrasensory powers from Novosibirsk, Russia, transmitted five images: the sun, eye, mountain, cross and a circle containing three smaller circles. The mental images received here by about 400 participants sitting 4000 km away at "Sara" centre, Belgrade.

Tele-picturesque-spots and picturesque-thoughts have been photographed directly even on polaroid films. It is a paranormal photography in which images match on photographic film through thought process.

Ted Serros — a chainsmoking, alcoholic Chicago bell-hop-psychic photographer filmed many thoughtographs during 1960s. The Eiffel Tower, Big Ben, the White House and the orbitting satellites all featured in his album of thoughtographs.

Dr Jule Eisebhul, an associate professor of psychiatry at the University of Colorado Medical School examined some impressive demonstrations of paranormal powers by Serros, from April 1964 to May 1967. Two eminent American psychical researchers, Dr. J.G. Pratt and Dr. Jan Stevenson observed Ted Serros in approximately 800 trials. Serros, even, invited investigators to bring with them target pictures concealed in envelops, which he tried to reproduce paranormally on polaroid film.

Soon after an experimental session on 27 May 1967, Serros'

---

28. Parmahamsa Yogananda, *Autobiography of a Yogi*, Yogada Satsanga Society of India, Kolkata, 2006 edn., p. 10.

psychic powers waned for a while and, within a year, although he continued to submit to experiments, all he could produce were 'blackies' or 'whities' without discernible images leaving psychical researchers still baffled about just what paranormal forces had been at work to produce his former astonishing pictures.

Peter Hurkos, who worked with Andrija Puharich, a leading American neurologist, on research investigations in the field of parapsychology during 1950s, is the other example of a thoughtographer. Hurkos' mind was able to mimic the effects of light on photosensitive surface; though the human mind can consciously activate on photoemulsion even when no light is striking the film.

The human mind could activate orthochromatic process film. This mental "something" which activates film must be that which also registers a personal meeting pattern on an object which is later recoverable by the technique of psychometry as intelligence.[29]

Psi-plasma is that "something" which expands outward from the telepathic person, and that which imprints a personal memory pattern on an object and thoughtograph on a negative as well as a polaroid film.

Now, of course, a question arises, do we need these psychic feats — like thoughtography, when all sorts of secure communication systems are available at the drop of a hat? Anyway, thoughtography continues to remain a fantasy, though a reality for rare souls and inspiration for many more.

3.13 U.F.O.

Unidentified Flying Objects (UFOs) were first sighted[30] in June 1947. And in 1976, U.S. President Jimmy Carter claimed: "I am convinced that UFOs exist because I have seen one . . .. It was big, it was very bright, it changed colours, and it was about the size of moon. We watched it for ten minutes, but none of us could figure out what it was."

---

29. T. Fukari, *Clairvoyance and Thoughtography*, Rider and Co., London, 1951.
30. Kenneth Arnold and Ray Palmer, *The Coming of the Saucers*, U.S.A, 1952.

UFOs are certainly not confined to the telepathic visions, because ufologists think that as we are exploring existence of worlds beyond, it seems reasonable that other civilizations might have similar interest[31] in us.

The para-psychologists have reported that UFO sightings are frequently accompanied by psychic manifestations, such as precognition or poltergeist activity, while the anthropologists often detect parallels with myths and traditional beliefs.

Everything from ghosts to bending of keys to UFO sightings are attested to by people who have no trouble passing lie-detector tests, yet when the time comes to photograph these phenomena, they don't show up. Positive clues come from experiments like the classic ones performed at the Princeton engineering department in 1970s, where subjects were asked to stare at a machine that randomly spit out zeros and ones (known as a random number generator). Their task was to use their minds to sway the machine to generate more ones than zeros, or vice versa. No one touched the machine or changed its software programme.

The results were surprising. Using nothing but focused attention, most people could, in fact, significantly influence the outcome. Instead of spewing out exactly equal number of zeros and ones, the machine skewed five per cent or more away from randomness. This establishes "everything around us is the product of the telepathic thought-impressions."

Whatever may be the reflections in mind, the question arises, are UFOs real — or are they some kind of mass psychotic images? A great number of people would probably agree that UFOs exist on both the psychological and physical level. But even though they may be real enough, the likelihood is that they are not what they seem. This is the paradox that lies at the heart of all UFO mysteries.

---

31. João Martins, *Experiences of Antönio Villas Boas*, Rio de Janeiro Sunday Review; Domingo, Illustrad, 10 Oct, 1971.

3.14 Telepathic Voices of the Dead

Thousands of voices — purporting to be those of the dead — have been recorded without rational explanation of their origin. Receiving, listening and recording voices of the dead, is an example of communication from dead, a telepathic link.

Thomas Alva Edison (CE 1847-1931), who invented the phonograph and the electric light bulb, in 1920 worked on a device that would, he believed, make possible a form of telepathic contact with the dead. What he proposed, was no less than the instrument for communicating with the dead. Edison wrote:

> If our personality survives, then it is strictly logical and scientific to assume that it retains memory, intellect and other faculties and knowledge that we acquire on this earth. Therefore, if personality exists after what we call death, it is reasonable to conclude that those who leave this earth would like to communicate with those they have left here . . .. I am inclined to believe that our personality hereafter will be able to affect matter. If this reasoning be correct, then, if we can evolve an instrument so delicate as to be affected, or moved, or manipulated . . . by our personality as it survives in the next life, such an instrument, when made available, ought to record something.[32]

Edison worked on the development of such an instrument, but was unsuccessful in his attempts to record voices from the dead. However, in the opinion of many modern scientific researchers, his views were vindicated in 1959, apparently, when, a celebrated Swedish painter, musician and film producer, Friedrich Jurgenson[33] captured the voice of his dead relatives as well as friends, in his battery-operated tape recorder, first by chance and then on trial.

A former student of Carl Gustar Jung, Dr. Konstantin Raudive, born in Lativia and living in Germany, recorded over 1,00,000 tapes

---

32. T.A. Edison, *The Scientific American*, 30 October, 1920.
33. Fredrich Jurgenson, *Voices from the Universe*, Stockholm, 1964.

between 1965 and till his death in 1974, under stringent laboratory conditions with the 'goniometer', an instrument that was designed for him by Theodor Rudolph of Telefunken to record 'spirit' voices. His work and an exhaustive analysis, generated strong attention among researchers in the fields of depth psychology, anthropology and parapsychology. How much more likely was it that the sophisticated recorders carried in spacecraft would pick up the voices?

All over the world, in some form or the other, there is belief that the living persons are a continuation of the life stream of the first beings. Ancestors watch over the living and act as intermediaries between them and the invisible world which is remote from men. Men can communicate with the spirits of their ancestors through prayers, chants, magical rituals and sacrifices — the blood (whether of animal or of human) setting in motion certain latent spiritual force facilitating the communication.

Cornelius Agrippa (CE 1485-1535), the great German soldier, astrologer and a well-known magician, gives the following ancient presription to talk with the dead: "Make the powder of supermaceti, aloe wood, musk, saffron and thyme, sprinkle it with the blood of a hoopoo (crested bird). If this powder is burnt upon the graves of the dead (of course, there are no graves of Hindus) the ethereal forms of the dead will approach, answer questions and may even become visible."

Cornelius Agrippa[34] was himself empowered — he could speak with the dead. In the last years of his life, he was accompanied everywhere by two great black dogs wearing spiked collars; these he openly referred to as 'my devil's watchdogs.' Hell's price to Agrippa was a 'Magic-glass' in which he could see 'objects distant in time and space.'

"If ghosts (astral bodies of the dead) lived in the fourth dimension, and if you have the capability of manipulating the fourth dimension, then you will be able to mentally commune with ghosts and spirits of

34. F.D. Colaabavala, *Witchcraft, the Forbidden World of the Devil*, Orient Paperbacks, New Delhi, 1977, pp. 128, 153.

long-dead ancestors," says Michio Kaku, who founded String Field Theory in 1974.

According to Sri Sri Ravi Shankar, an enlightened master, "There is possibility to contact people who have gone, but it is not of much use. Because, trying to contact them, you usually just ask them, 'What did you feel about me?' and other such things, and many times you get back mixed information." If the person who is the medium is not fully clear, they can put their own mind stuff into the answer also. This happens often, that people say, "Oh, I am channeling Mother Divine, I'm channeling this god, or that person, or something. Then a lot of their own stuff comes through, and you don't really know what is what."

However, a Hindu mystic Swami Shivananda[35] says, "No one should allow himself to become a medium, as communication with the spirits will mar their soul-psychic march on the path of evolution. Therefore, give up the idle curiosity of talking to the dead on everything regarding the spirit-world. You will not get anything tangible and substantial. You will disturb the peace of the dead."

Do not allow yourself to be fascinated by mediumship, and similar quests like crystal gazing, mirror magic, etc. They will lead you astray. Specially communication with the dead and talking with the dead are all facts which have no connection with real telepathy — the telepathy with God. Purpose of life is different. The final goal is to realize the essential imperishability of your Self. This alone will confer perfect bliss and peace.

3.15 Telepathy of Rebirth

Rebirth phenomenon is about the reported cases where a person, usually very young, 'recalls' events from his 'previous life' which are then found to closely correlate with the life of a deceased person. People often jump to the conclusion that this is an evidence of 'transmigration' of 'soul'.

---

35. Swami Sivananda, *What Becomes of the Soul after Death*, A Divine Life Society Publication, Shivanandanagar, 2004, pp. 167, 196.

Hundreds of such instances of alleged rebirth, around the world have been investigated, ascertained, and testified, but still questions keep arising, whether the rebirth phenomenon is:

(1) trans-time telepathy?
(2) temporal-cum-teleological transference of information?
(3) a clairvoyant vision of the past?
(4) an early-age dream-vision phenomenon?
(5) multi-mediumship transference of information?
(6) multiple re-relay psychic phenomenon?
(7) that reborn person encountered the dead person's 'ghost' subsequently in his/her childhood?
(8) autonomous past-life regression taking place?

"Actually all that has happened here is that a person possesses information about another person, which should not normally be available to him. That is, this is at the best evidence of 'information transfer'. In other words, it is no different from telepathy, only the other person (the thought or information 'donor') is not alive. If both persons were alive, we would call it telepathy and would not invoke explanations involving 'souls'. This is then telepathy 'out of sync' in time. If information can flow across the 'barrier' of space, there is no reason why it cannot flow across time. After all we do recollect our own past experiences across time", says Nitin Trasi,[36] and he hypothesizes: "Very young person would be expected to naturally have a better developed sense of ESP as their sense of individuality is not yet fully developed. In most such reported cases, the recollections pass off as the person grows into an adult."

Another view is; aclaimed re-birth cases. These most probably, are instances of autonomous past life regression phenomenon. There is perception of the previous-life taking place of its own without the help of a hypnotherepist or any other technique.

Past-life regression — or deep-memory process — explains rebirth

36. Nitin Trasi, *The Science of Enlightenment*, D.K. Printworld, New Delhi, 2004, p. 258.

phenomenon and has continually proved itself to be a powerful and empowering tool for those who journey into self-discovery. Not only can it release us from fear, paralysing patterns, relationships, phobias and sometimes psysical symptoms, but it also gives us a chance to realize and know that we are souls having human experiences. Our unfinished business — *karma* — from previous life dramas, creates the situations, mind-sets and meetings with particular people that occur in this present life.

Part of the deal, as the soul inhabits its present form, is to forget the details of its past experiences. These are held, like our own personal websites, waiting for unfinished business to be cleared or edited by the current computer operator. "There are always clues as to what needs to be addressed, remembered, healed or released. These clues are all around us," says Sue Minns, lecturer, College of Psychic Studies, London.

There is a wealth of science on how reincarnation, telepathy, and many miracles are possible from scientists such as Professor Emeritus Bill Tiller[37] at Stanford University, USA.

Indian sages and seers consider the rebirth as subsequent-birth phenomenon only. According to Nisargadatta Maharaj (CE 1897-1981), a spiritual teacher from Bombay:

> The memory of the unfulfilled desires traps energy, which manifests itself as a person; when its charge gets exhausted, the person dies. Unfulfilled desires are carried over into the next birth. Self-identification with the body creates ever fresh desires and there is no end to them, unless this mechanism of bondage is clearly seen. It is clarity that is liberating, for you cannot abandon desire, unless its causes and effects are clearly seen. I do not say that the same person is reborn. It dies and dies for good. But its memories remain and its desires and fears. They supply the energy for a new person. The real takes no part in it, but makes it possible by giving it light.[38]

---

37. Bill Tiller # www.tiller.org
38. Sri Nisargadatta Maharaj, *I AM That*, Chetana Pvt Ltd, Mumbai, 2008, p .364.

How do the boundaries of birth and death become so thin as it appears in rebirth. People who spend time with geniuses and prodigies often find them unearthly, somehow preternatural as if a very old soul has been confined to a new body and yet brings in experience far beyond what that body could have known. It is easy to credit that some kind of former life is casting its influence on the present. Speaking of his own experience, one music prodigy stated, "It is as if I am playing from outside of my own consciousness. The music comes through me. I am the conduit, not the source." Geniuses, prodigies and some mystics have a hue of rebirth.

Paramahamsa Yogananda, (CE 1893-1952), an incarnation of Love, says, "My far-reaching memories are not unique. Many *yogis* are known to have retained their self-consciousness without interruption by the dramatic transition to and from 'Life' and 'Death'. If man be solely a body, its loss indeed ends his identity. But if prophets down the millenniums spake with truth, man is essentially a soul, incorporeal and telepathic."

3.16 Telepathic Networks

Telepathy is never as simple a process as dialling a land-line telephone, wireless-loop (WLL) or a cellphone, because the electromagnetic radiation/transmission is not the means but thought-waves or thoughtons are — which traverse much faster.

However, it is simple enough to see a one-to-one relationship between a telepathic sender and a telepathic receiver when the intelligence transmission and reception is contemporaneous. It is perhaps puzzling to include a third person (or an object, as in psychometry, discussed in the chapter five) into this simple telepathic relationship and look upon him either as an unconscious relay, or an unconscious tuning mechanism, or an amplifier of the telepathic signal.

Telepathy can exist between more than two people at a time even though some of the members of this network may be totally unconscious of their participation in the phenomenon. A telepathic network involving three persons, has one of them as sender, the other is receiver, whereas the third does not have a well-defined role. In most of such networks, the third person has assumed the role of an unconscious relay — the relay agent is tense, concentrated and perhaps even worried, a state fitting that of a sender (adrenergia — beta brainwaves); of course, the receiver is relaxed and in the state of Cholinergia (approaching alpha brainwaves).

Let us look beyond the three-member telepathic network, and the question naturally arises as to how large such network can become? In cases of many persons, two distinct possibilities are: (1) one sender and multiple receivers — as in the 'Indian Rope Trick', mass hypnotization; (2) multiple senders and single receiver — as is the case with lone cop looking for grouped criminals (here the guilt-conscious thoughts are involved, which are being radiated/suppressed by the culprits).

The Indian Rope Trick hallucination, assuming that it is telepathically inspired, can extend to several hundred people present as receivers of the delusion, at one time. This gives us an idea of the large network that telepathic interaction can assume. However, it is hard to say as to how large a number of people can be embraced by one telepathic situation. The second option of telepathic networks is from opposite point of view, namely where there are multiple senders (attracters?) and a single receiver.

When we look at a large broadcasting effect emanating from a single telepathic sender as in the case of the Indian Rope Trick (or some other trick being demonstrated by a stage magician), or look at the converse phenomenon of a large number of telepathic senders focusing on a single receiver, we indeed begin to get into the deeper complexities of telepathy.

3.17 Telepathic Sense

Telepathic sense is high with the human life as compared to the animal and plant lives. A human is born with a telepathic command of God, and dies after receiving and reading a telegram from Him.

Man is born with high telepathic ratings and dies with high ratings, though it is not yet established which of the two ratings is higher. A newborn child has frequent telepathic conversations/communions with God, as is evident from his blissful smiles and gigglings. These communions keep on declining as ageing takes place and, intelligence and indulgence grow.

A human being is born to accomplish a goal. As s/he grows, s/he gets coordination between her/his brain and sensory organs. Then coordination between the brain and the mind arises. S/he begins thinking systematically, and her/his pscho-physical activities become goal-oriented.

Towards the end of life, we again start remembering God, inclining our outlook towards spiritualism, resulting in telepathic sense enhancement.

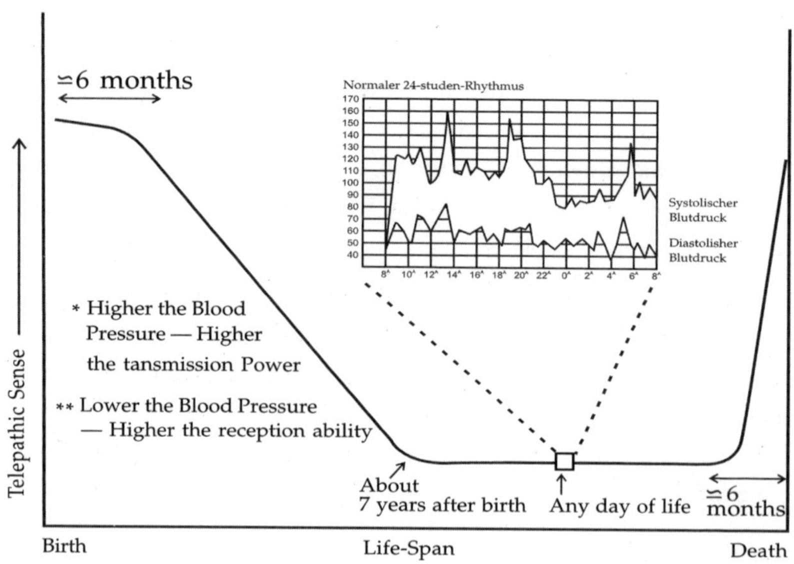

Fig. 3.1 Telepathic Sense during Life

It is not possible to draw any curve for telepathic sense, however, a crude attempt has been made. It is just possible that the telepathic sense from about seven years of age upto about 5 to 6 months before the death (in case of natural death), for a materialistic person, may keep on fluctuating randomly. It may almost fluctuate in a fashion as human blood pressure fluctuates during 24 hours of a day, during this period of life. A syndetic pictogram is given in Figure 3.1

This pictogram, however, is based on intuitive insight of the author. It is not result of any research, and is not based on Francis Kinsman's[39] TAROT (Trend Analysis by Relative Opinion Testing) system. Nevertheless, La Croix Mystique, Confucius' eye and psychic phenomenon may have had their effect or maybe goose-flushes of the automatic writing!!

Gravitational fields between various planets may be the factor responsible for fluctuations of the telepathic sense. For, during full moon, the gravitational field potential decreases, which leads to an expansion of the psychic (also called Psi-plasma) field of an individual who has telepathic sensitivity — amounting to increase of telepathic receptivity.

It may be noted that a couple of months, very often even only a couple of days, before death, reviewing your actions, interactions, transactions retrospectively for the lived life can be taken as telepathic conversations between your conscious mind on the one hand and subconscious/unconscious on the other. During this period, the telepathic sense is not as rough as shown in the figure 3.1 for 24 hours. Their retrospective thinking is the most scintillating part of soul-psychic sleuthing. It may provide a panoramaic viewing as in the case of 'Near-Death-Experiences (NDEs)'.

If you read scriptures and folklores, you will discover that our ancestors were endowed with more telepathic sense, which has come to very low ratings as we are tuning to the Western cultures and their

39. Francis Kinsman, *Future Tense — A Prophetic Consensus for Eighties*, Pendum Publishing Co., London, Feb, 1980.

ways of living. However, it must be accepted as a fact that the West is giving many more telepaths to the world, presently.

Our ancestors, especially our savants, sages, saints and shamans were very near to nature. We can even say that they were almost one with it. They could commune with each other and every particle of it. They could intercept their messages and convey their own messages to them. Even without seeing the charts they could say many things about the native and be precise with the vagaries of the nature. This was so, perhaps, because they could talk not only to his body, but also to all who have had their influence on her/him anyway.

It would still be better if we project the telepathic sense in terms of spiritualism. The spiritual intelligence is the most important attribute of a human being and the foundation of both IQ (intelligence quotient) and EQ (emotional quotient). The three, IQ, EQ and SQ (spiritual quotient) are being integrated by the modern psychology experts.

In multi-cultural and multi-ethnic societies like ours, where people have to constantly interact with people from across the world, there are several cross-cultural problems which can crop up. This, in turn, could lead to disillusionment. It is at times like this that spiritual strength, gained through soul-psychic sleuthing techniques, comes to the rescue of a person. In fact, spiritual awakening among the masses has led to remarkable growth in the productivity, and in turn lust and love for the laws of nature.

According to the Scottish theologian, Henry Drummond — who claimed so in 1894 — "Telepathy was the electricity, and would one day be widely used. . . ."

3.18 Telepathy's Truths

Telepathy is a form of extra-sensory perception through which one can introspect the minds of others. It is also one of the possibilities of establishing the knowledge of other minds including that of God. However, telepathy has its own defects in establishing the knowledge of other minds in the sense of it being dubbed as the telepathic poaching.

Nevertheless, no means can be discarded to know the truth —worldly or absolute — or achieve 'Telos', the Greek word meaning 'the fulfilment of an activity — 'aim', 'goal', 'purpose', 'result' and 'Thee'.

A radio microscope divised in CE 1939 revealed a new world of hitherto unknown rays. "Man himself as well as all kinds of supposedly inert matter constantly emit the rays that this instrument 'sees'," reported the Associated Press. "Those who believe in telepathy, second sight, and clairvoyance, have in this announcement the first scientific proof of the existence of invisible rays that really travel from one person to another. The radio device is actually a radio-frequency spectroscope. It does the same thing for cool, non-glowing matter that the spectroscope does when it discloses the kinds of atoms that make the stars . . .. The existence of such rays coming from man and all living things have been suspected by scientists for many years. The discovery shows that every atom and every molecule in nature is a continuous radio-broadcasting station . . .. Thus even after death the substance that was man continues to send out its 'delicate rays.'[40]

The search for the worldly truth is such a false affair, as though by searching for it telepathically, asking others the way to it, reading about it in affidavits and investigation reports, trying this or that system, you will be able to find it. To find it as if it were something there, fixed, motionless, and all you do to recognize it, grasp it, and say you have found it.

The absolute truth isn't far away: there is no path to it. It is not something you can capture, hold, treasure and verbally convey to another. Search implies a seeker and in that there is division, the everlasting fragmentation that man has made within himself and in all his activities. It is not that there must be an end to seeking but rather the beginning of learning. Learning is far more important than finding. To find one must have lost. Losing and recognizing is the pattern of search.

No one can teach you about it, so you need not follow anybody. All that one can do is to understand by careful observation the intricate

40. Parmahamsa Yogananda, *Autobiography of a Yogi*, Yogada Satsanga Society of India, Kolkata, 2006, p. 150.

movement of thought: how thought divides itself, how it creates its own opposites and thereby brings contradiction and conflict. Thought is so restless and in its restlessness it will attract itself to anything it thinks is essential, permanent, completely satisfying and truth becomes its final attachment of satisfaction. You can never invite truth by any means. It is not an end; but it is there when the visual observation is very clear and when there is the perception of understanding. Understanding can take place only when there is complete freedom from all one's conditioning. It is this conditioning that is prejudice. So do not bother about truth but rather let the mind be aware of its own prison. Freedom is not in the prison. The beauty of emptiness is freedom. And freedom of thought brings in the true telepathic signals.

'It's a plausible guess', said the Oxford Philosopher H.H. Price, 'that many of our everyday thoughts and emotions are telepathic or partly telepathic in origin.'

Swami Vivekananda had expressed the same view three quarters of a century earlier. Just as light-waves from distant stars travel for years before they reach our planet, he asked, could not thought-waves travel the atmosphere till a properly-tuned human antenna could pick them up? There are men "who really know the power of thought; they are sure that, even if they go into a cave and close the door and simply think about five true thoughts and then pass away, these five thoughts of theirs will live through eternity. Indeed, such thoughts will penetrate through the mountains, cross the oceans, and travel through the world. They will enter deep into human hearts and brains and raise up men and women who will give them practical expression in the working of human life . . .. Many of the greatest men in the world have passed away unknown."

In the phenomenological approach, consciousness and the production of meaning are portrayed as a result of intersubjective relations between actors engaged in mutual telepathy. Alfred Schutz[41]

41. A. Schutz, *The Phenomenology of the Social World*, North Western University Press, Evaston Il, 1932, p. 112.

argues that it is the condition of intersubjectivity through which the individual actors are able to grasp each other's consciousness and construct their life world. By sharing time and space, individual actors can engage in a process of understanding which involves the discovery of what is going on in the other person's mind.

Sometimes the concept of spiritual being is brought to the aid of explaining the process of telepathy. The spiritual being or astral body is not subject to earth's gravitational froce. This is the state in which one can float about and move easily anywhere without the use of legs or feet. In this spiritual state of being, it can go at high velocity to any part of the globe or anywhere in outer space too. Beyond the three dimensions of length, breadth and height, this is a new existence in which other dimensions also would be experienced, as expressed by those who have returned from it to the life in this world. However, there is the record of the witness of a woman (in fact of many humans) who came back to life, in which she felt as if her spiritual being was in the very same form as she was previously in her temporal physical body. She felt that it was possible to think more clearly and distinctly and to effortlessly understanding and very many things than she could in the physical body. There was no feeling of heat or cold, but feeling perfectly happy. There was no sensual feeling of the five senses of the physical body, of smell, touch, etc. related to earthly substances. But the ability to see very far was beyond imagination. The power of understanding and capability to read exactly the thoughts of anyone far from view was quite wonderful. Mutual understanding of thoughts of others, whether they are physical beings or spiritual beings, if they are thinking anything with the intention of communicating with other at the same instance, the soul can understand.

Therefore, telepathic communications are possible when out-of-body experiences are recorded as astral travels (AT) or out-of-body experiences are recorded as Near-Death-Experiences (NDEs).

Man has in his soul the ability to converse with the God at any time and at any place, as the soul is the part of God. This is the birthright of any human being in the world, irrespective of caste, creed, nationality or language or even spiritual-quotient. And, this conversation takes place telepathically. However, the telepathic conversations are more frequent for people having high spiritual-quotients.

Understand your thoughts, because every thought makes an impression on the whole field of intelligence. This physical world is just a mirror of a deeper intelligence. Intelligence is the invisible organizer of all matter and energy, and since a portion of this intelligence resides in you, you share in the organizing power of the cosmos.

Therefore, you organize your thoughts and brainwaves to heal your future and the future of the world. Scientists have also shown that if sufficient people — one in every 100 — can send out consistent, concentrated, positive, loving thougths to their loved ones and our world, then the accumulation of loving thoughts begins to create an invisible lattice grid all around us — which can eventually manifest into our physical world. Our thoughts can literally help to stop wars, reduce violence and stress — and they can heal people.

Swami Pranabananda says, "The subtle unity of the phenomenal world is not hidden from true yogis. I instantly see and converse with my disciples in distant Calcutta. They can similarly transcend at will every obstacle of gross matter."[42]

Experience it yourself. When a scientist describes an experiment and its results, usually you accept his statements on trust and repeat his experiment as he describes it. Once you get the same or similar results, you need not trust him anymore; you trust your own experience. Encouraged, you proceed and arrive in the end at substantially identical results. Similarly, you need to 'Trust-test-taste' telepathy.

Many a time telepathic communications have been classified as hunches and intuitions. The "hunches" is the universal language that deals with the past and the present of all people. Nearly everyone has had the experience of an inexplicably correct "hunch". And, "intuition" is really a sudden immersion of the soul into the universal current of

42. Parmahamsa Yogananda, *Autobiography of a Yogi*, Yogada Satsanga Society of India, Kolkata, 2006, p. 22.

life, where the histories of all people are connected; we are able to know everything, because it's all written there. Intuition appears naturally in a man during those instants when his mind is calm.

Almost everyone has transferred his/her thougths accurately to another person. Even the dead continue to transfer their thoughts. The telepathic signals of the dead have been captured with the aid of modern instruments. Thank God that no receiver has been developed to detect and decode telepathic signals from the living humans in spite of leap frogging development of instrumentation and innovative nano-technology. What would happen, if it was? Just imagine for example, a situation in the presently perverted environment of human emotional curry, where your wife is thinking about other man!

Just as a quantum of energy can leap between two points without crossing the space in between, so apparently can a thought. A field of awareness flows in around, and through each of us. Some of this awareness is localized. We say "my" memory and "my" thought but that isn't the whole story. A neuron can't claim "this is my idea" until millions of cells have come together to form each image or thought.

Thus, subtle field of awareness is the medium for telepathy. For example, old married couples seem to merge in both personality and thought. Twins can have uncanny similarities in the way their lives unfold. Extensive studies of identical twins, however, show that no stereo-type covers all cases. At one extreme, a pair of identical twins can be so completely merged that they never live apart and, when questioned, speak with one voice and apparently think with one mind. In the unfortunate instance that one twin dies prematurely, the other mourns for life. At the other end of the spectrum, a pair of identical twins can be almost total strangers, sharing no experience or thoughts. Many studies have been conducted of twins separated at birth and raised apart by totally different sets of parents. Generally, in these cases, the twins still exhibit about fifty per cent strong resemblance in behaviour and thought waves. When reunited, they also can form strong bonds, and then it is likely that some kind of mental sharing, whether it is the ESP or not, will take place. Even when the empathy is intense, though, the twins do not divide into a sender and receiver of thought, telepathy is in operation.

What this implies is that in the mind field, any boundary can be tenuous. If necessary, your mind can merge and communicate with another mind. A thought that, properly speaking, should belong to one of you becomes a joint experience. In general, momentous events will act as a trigger, causing a spouse to intuit her dying partner's last wishes or one twin to know that his brother had suddenly been struck by lightning. The twin to whom this actually happened felt the shock of the lightning passing through his own body at the instant his sibling was killed.

We all assume that we are the authors of our thoughts. They don't simply appear as messages in our heads; we actively think them. But ESP thinks to contradict this assumption. If two people vividly share the same thought it may be that neither one is the author; there is simply the simultaneous reception of an idea and/or concept. We can cite instances where two philosophers or scientists had the identical inspiration without knowing each other. The simultaneous invention of the calculus by Leibniz and Newton is one famous example.

Sometimes the telepathic network covers a vivid philosophical phenomenon. Deepak Chopra gives an example: "I met a lawyer who was pulled from an afternoon meeting by a wrenching pain in his abdomen. He had never had such an experience and departed for home immediatly. When he got there police were waiting with the tragic news. His mother had been stabbed and killed by an act of random violence at exactly the moment he had felt the pain. By what a mysterious stroke to synchronous timing were mother-son and murderer tied in a karmic dance?"[43]

Two intimately connected minds can be united at the level of awareness.[44] You may have cried out for help or solace from someone

43. Deepak Chopra, *How to know God: The Soul's Journey into Mystery of Mysteries*, Rider, London, 2000, p. 238.

44. Ibid., p. 239.

miles away, and sometimes they respond by showing up or calling. In war time it is not uncommon for parents to know with certainty the exact moment that a son is killed on the battlefield.

Awareness doesn't have to be human; it seems to pervade all life-forms. In a forest where trees are being heavily foraged by animals, individual trees can protect themselves with a chemical defense. They start to exude indigestible tars into their leaves before they are even touched — having been warned by neighbouring trees via chemical signals in the air or through their roots. In a similar act of communal awareness, the cells of a sea cucumber are arranged to give a mouth and digestive tract to this primitive animal, which is little more than a giant feeding tube. You can puree a sea cucumber in a blender, pour the solution of brine and cells into a bucket, and after a while the entire animal will regroup itself from the unformed biological sludge.

These are all examples of awareness as a field beyond the body. These examples help us to shift away from a strictly private, isolated mind to universal, shared mind whose body is universe. Isolation is matarial fact but not a quantum fact. The boundaries dividing "me" and "you" are much thinner than we realize. There is reason to believe the personal identity is just another convenience, useful for everyday living but ultimately too flimsy to be taken as real.

> All things are possible to him that believeth.
>
> — Mark

Everything is a vibration. Quantum physics and superstring theory — and now the latest articulation of this, called M-theory — tells us that everything in existence is composed not of points, or "dots", of energy, but of smaller-than-minuscule circular "strings" that vibrate constantly, at differing rates. These strings have the ability to interconnect, or interwine, with each other, creating a "superstring."

It is possible that "superstring" vibrations can be created with the mind? When we walk into a room where people have been having an argument, even though the argument may have stopped the moment we entered, we know we have walked into a room with bad vibes. We can feel it. Did those arguing people create those vibes?

All of us create variations in the energy flow around us. We produce fluctuations. We, ourselves, are fluctuations. We are ever-changing alterations in the energy field that swirls about us. Our fluctuations in turn create other fluctuations, or "disturbances", in the energy field adjacent to our energy field, and those affect the field around that, and those around that, and so on — outward and ever outward in an eternal distribution of energy that touches bigger and bigger fields of influence the farther it radiates from the originating source, but with smaller and smaller impact the greater the distance from that source.

In this way every thought affects the whole world — indeed to some degree, the universe. How much? Probably not very significantly, given the lack of pure focus and consistency in the energy that most people emanate. Yet if that energy is focused and consistent, if it becomes a pinpoint of laser sharp and unremitting clarity, it can cut through virtually an obstacle in the surrounding energy field, reshaping that field in the form that we, as individuals, choose.

It is in this way that many peole have learned to deeply affect and dramatically impact their personal reality. They live the lives they choose — being in the continuous telepathic contact with nature. And when many individuals make the same choice collectively, the combined energy of collective consciousness can have an immediate and detectable effect on the larger reality in any environment. Ultimately, this can influence life on earth itself.

So the trick here is focus and consistency, the fuel here is feeling, and the tool is thought. How do we focus? How do we maintain consistency? Here, too, we have been given an easy-to-understand, easy-to-use mechanism. That mechanism is "intention".

We are affecting our creative energy with our intentions in every movement. we either do this consciously or unconsciously, but we do it all the time. To the degree to which our intentions are clear to us, to that degree we become consciously creative — telepathists.

Thus, telepathy with others, nature and God, plays an important role throughout the life of man.

4

Clairvoyance

In French, clairvoyance stands for 'clear seeing' and refers to both internal and external visions and images. It is a 'third-eye sight', also termed as a 'paroptic vision' — a vision of mind and soul.

What we understand by clairvoyance is actually the spiritual vision and insight, the gradual unfolding of consciousness exemplified in the lives of the world's great mystics.

However, the clairvoyance has been brandied about in pseudo-occult groups and is stretched to mean everything from crystal gazing to seeing auras and astral bodies and conversing with spirits. If the clairvoyance involved only this, it would justifiably be but a nine-days wonder, undeserving of the occultist's attention.

The meaning of clairvoyance is "extrasensory knowledge about material objects or events which is not obtained from another person's mind" — in other words, not simple telepathy. It can take many different forms, range from a vague awareness of a distant event to a vision in which scenes unfold vividly before the eyes of the clairvoyant. Or simply, clairvoyance is an ability of seeing an event taking place far away from the subject through perception of mind, without the aid of any physical means.

In time dimension, clairvoyance is unfolding of consciousness of quietened minds and progressive souls, along the path of 'time-travel'. There the boundary of time dissolves completely, then it is possible to experience a kind of mental time-travel called clairvoyance. Thus, clairvoyance is the 'clear-seeing' of the future, and it is the ability to see from the past while on backward time-travel.

For ordinary people, clairvoyance is most likely to occur in stressful situations or when people or places connected with them are in danger.

In normal course, opening up to your clairvoyance can bring a powerful new intimacy, effectiveness, compassion and playfulness to all that you do. For many of us, our natural intuitive and perceptive abilities, so intrinsically a part of who we are, have been misunderstood, closed down and in some unfortunate cases, declared perverse. In some ways, denying this aspect of ourselves is denying ourselves at the very heart of who we are. It could be said that, in opening our clairvoyance, we open up a view from our heart, a view of our profound interconnectedness with each other and All That Is.

It is an unfortunate truth that, psychologically speaking, we live in a "closed" society. "The mass of men lead lives of quiet desperation," as Thoreau noted and this "quietness" extends quite often even to close friends, for we've been told for so long that there is something dishonourable or weak in showing our emotions, in reaching out to others for help even when we need it desperately.

Therefore, often the only way we can learn what is happening to someone we love or care about is to employ methods like clairvoyance and psychometry, which some might feel are devious — and so they are, if our motives are unworthy. But, then you may not be in a position to apply and retain these faculties for a long time.

A clairvoyant can transgress infinite space-time continuum, and therefore, development of clairvoyance ability will be of great help for the sleuthing purpose.

Indian scriptures suggest that clairvoyance is gained through the soul. According to the Jaina way of thinking, there are five varieties of knowledge, viz.

1. Empirical Knowledge (*mati-jnana*)
2. Articulate Knowledge (*sruta-jnana*)
3. Clairvoyance (*avadhi-jnana*)
4. Mind-reading (*manah paryaya-jnana*)
5. Omniscience (*kevala-jnana*)

The empirical knowledge is achieved through senses and mind. The articulate knowledge is gained through the sacred scriptures. The remaining three are obtained through soul. These are independent of senses.[1]

Optimum opening of the third-eye is by the reliving method of single or multiple senses — eyes, ears, nose, touch, taste, mind; the individual himself remaining in present time. In other words, some people, when they think of rose, see one, smell one, feel one. They see in full colour, vividly — with the "mind's eye" to use on old colloquialism. They smell it vividly. And they can feel it even to the thorns. They are thinking about roses by actually recalling a rose in reality.

Those who are more visual can see clairvoyantly. If you are somewhat clairaudient, you may hear the pictures "pop". If you are more kinesthetic (feeling-oriented), you will feel the pictures (rose, of last example), and be able to develop clairsentience talent more easily as compared to the other two faculties of clairvoyance and clairaudience.

There is a concept of "mobile centre of consciousness" getting into action in the case of clairvoyance. That is "when the cellular consciousness is no longer caught and imprisoned in the net of a body, what happens at that point of time, it is in perfect continuity with the entire terrestrial body, scatters? It's a strange thing . . . the eyesight is absolutely different from physical sight: you see thousands of miles away and very near the same time."

The brain cannot construct the clairvoyant state, as far as we know, since its visual centres are preoccupied with present sensations. Dreams are kind of false vision, in that they are not really happening before our eyes yet appear to be. The clairvoyant is also experiencing an "unreal" visual state, yet these visions happen to come true.

Clairvoyance, though not always reliable, has sometimes provided

---

1. Baidyanath, Saraswati, *Voices of Senses, Traditional Thought and Modern Science*, D.K. Printworld, New Delhi, 2007, p. 51.

startling and unexpected clues in cases of crime. Psychics often volunteer their services to the police, and there are countless stories of people whose extrasensory powers have given glimpses of crimes. But all too often the accuracy of their statements cannot be verified until after the criminals have been caught by conventional means. In other words, clairvoyance and ESP seldom lead the police directly to a culprit.

Nonetheless, physical science is affirming the validity of laws discovered by occult science. For example, a demonstration that man has televisional powers, was given on Nov 26, 1934, at the Royal University of Rome. Dr. Gluseppe Calligaris, professor of neuro-psychology, pressed certain parts of a subject's body and the subject responded with minute descriptions of persons and objects on the opposite side of a wall. Dr. Calligaris told the professors that if certain areas on the skin are agitated, the subject gets supersensorial impressions enabling him to see objects that he could not otherwise perceive. To enable his subject to discern things on other side of a wall, Professor Calligaris pressed a spot to the right of the thorax for fifteen minutes. Dr. Calligaris said that when certain spots of the body are agitated, the subjects can see objects at any distance, regardless of whether they have ever before seen those objects.

All men are born clairvoyants — as you may have noticed — newborns are seeing God and playing with him. However, they do not sustain the capability and/or drawn away by their upbringing and conditioning. Only a teensy-weensy percentage either retains it or develops it on the journey of life.

> Thou seest Him, yet thou knowest not that thou seest.
>
> — Mohyaddin Ibn Arabi

Nevertheless, you develop the ESP and clairvoyance, and offer your soul-psychic sleuthing ability for establishing peace, harmony and welfare of society you live in.

4.1 Types and Orders of Clairvoyance

It is not easy to give a definition of 'clairvoyance' which shall be at once succinct and accurate. Simply, it is the power to see what is hidden from ordinary physical sight. It will be as well to premise that it is very frequently (though by no means always) accompanied by clairaudience.

We may group instances of clairvoyance under the following headings:

1. Simple clairvoyance
2. Clairvoyance in space
3. Clairvoyance in time

Simple clairvoyance — is to say, a mere opening of sight, enabling its possesor to see whatever astral or etheric entities happen to be present around him, but not including the power of observing either distant places or scenes belonging to any other time than the present.

Clairvoyance in space — is the capacity to see scenes or events removed from the seer in space, and either too far distant for ordinary observation or concealed by intermediate objects. The space is confined to surface of this world and the air-space around it; in case subject or object is in space-shuttle, reaching them. Space clairvoyants have not yet visited Mars or other planets.

Clairvoyants in time — that is to say, the capacity to see objects or events which are removed from the seer in time, or, in other words, the power of looking into the past or the future.

A clairvoyant's higher order visions are:

(1) Etheric sight,
(2) Astral sight,
(3) Prophetic vision,
(4) Spiritual vision, and his lowest order is called:
(5) Prevision or second sight.

There is distinct difference between the etheric sight and the astral sight, and it is the latter which seems to correspond to the fourth dimension of substance (here 4th dimension is not 'time' as is the case in Einstein's theory of relativity).

The easiest way to understand the difference is to take an example if you were looking etherically at a wooden cube with writings on all its sides, it would be as though the cube were glass, so that you could see through it, and you would see the writing on the opposite side all backwards, while that on the right and left sides would not be clear to you at all unless you moved, because you would see it edgewise. But if you looked at it 'astrally' you would see all the sides at once, and all the right way up, as though the whole cube had been flattened out before you and you would see every particle of the inside as well — not through the others, but all flalttened out.

Astral vision offers to the clairvoyant additional information in case of animate objects. He will be able to see the etheric double, the aura and the astral body. His capacity of examining the etheric double will give him considerable advantage in locating and classifying any defect or diseases of the nervous system, while from the appearance of the astral body he will be at once aware of all the emotions, passions, desires and tendencies of the person before him, and even of very many of his thoughts also.

As he looks at a person he will see him surrounded by the luminous mist of the astral aura, flashing with all sorts of brilliant colours and constantly changing in hue and brilliance with every variation in the person's thoughts and feelings. He will see this aura flooded with the beautiful rose-colour of pure affection, the rich blue of devotional feeling, the hard, dull brown of selfishness, the deep scarlet of anger, the horrible lurid of sensuality, the livid grey of fear, the black clouds of hatred and malice, or any of the hundredfold indications so easily to be read in it by a clairvoyant eye; and thus it will be impossible for any person to conceal from him the real state of his feelings on any subject.

Another wonderful result which the full enjoyment of astral clairvoyance brings to a man is that he has no longer any break in consciousness. When he lies down at night he leaves his physical body to rest which it requires, while he himself goes about his business in the far more comfortable astral vehicle. In the morning he returns to and re-enters his physical body, but without any loss of consciousness or memory between the two states, and thus is able to live, as it were, a double life which yet is one, and at the same time is usefully employed during the whole of it, instead of losing one-third of his existence in blank unconsciousness.

Prophetic vision gives ability in blank unconsciousness of the future and assumes importance in guiding and directing the destiny of men, cultures and nations.

Spiritual vision is a marvellous faculty having its ineffable bliss. with spiritual vision a clairvoyant sees a world in which all that we can imagine of utmost glory and splendour is commonplace of existence.

Spiritul vision gives ability of magnifying at will the minutest physical or astral particle to any desired size, as if by a microscope — though no microscope ever made or is ever likely to be made shall possess even a thousandth part of this psychic magnifying power. By its means the molecule and atom postulated by science become visible and living realities to the occult student, and on their closer examination he finds them to be much more complex in their structure than the scientific man has yet realized them to be. It also enables him to follow with the closest attention and the most lively interest all kinds of electrical, magnetic, and other etheric action; and when some of the specialists in these branches of science are able to develop the power to see those things whereof they write so facilely, some very wonderful and beautiful revelations may be expected.

Spiritual sight development needs almost superhuman qualifications in the way of lofty spiritual aspiration and absolute purity of thought and intention.

A person having spiritual sight has the ability which is referred to as "the power of making oneself large or small at will," and of levitating.

Short of these perfect visions we find, that all degrees of 'prevision' type of clairvoyance exist, from the occasional vague premonitions which cannot in any true sense be called sight at all, up to frequent and fairly complete 'second-sight.'

Second-sight is that awful faculty which foretells in vision calamities that are shortly to occur. The faculty has always been commonest among mountaineers and men of lonely life. Persons gifted with second-sight bear on their palm two islands forming the figure of 8 at the starting point of the line of fate.

Sometimes the second-sight consists of a picture clearly fore-showing some coming events: more frequently, perhaps, the glimpse of the future is given by some symbolical appearance. It is noteworthy that the events foreseen are invariably unpleasent ones — death being the commonest of all. It has a ghostly symbolism. In some cases it appears to be, to certain extent, dependent on locality, for it is stated that inhabitants of such locality lose it when they leave the place and move only by a few miles. The gift of such sight is sometimes hereditary in a family for generations, but this is not an invariable rule, or it often appears sporadically in one member of a family otherwise free from its lugubrious influence.

Recently (in 1970s), a paranormal investigator named Marilyn Schlitz[2] wanted to test if anything like second-sight was real. Schlitz chose the phenomenon of just turning around to discover that you were being watched from behind, which she called "covert observation." She took a group of subjects and looked at them through a video camera in another room. By turning the camera off and on, she could test whether each person was aware of being watched, even with the observer not physically present. Rather than relying upon subjective guesses, she used an instrument resembling a lie detector; it measured even the faintest changes in the skin's response to electrical current.

The experiment was a success — up to two-thirds of the subjects showed changes in skin conductivity while being observed from a distance. Schlitz announced the success of her experiment, only to find that another researcher who tried to duplicate it failed miserably.

---

2. Deepak Chopra, *How to know God, The Soul's Journey into Mystery of Mysteries*, Rider, London, 2001, p. 157.

He used exactly the same methods, but in his laboratory almost no one responded with second sight; they couldn't tell the difference between being watched and not being watched. Schlitz was baffled but confident enough to invite the other researcher to come to her lab. The two of them ran the experiment again, choosing subjects at the last moment to ensure that there was no tampering.

Again Schlitz obtained her desired results, but her colleague had obtained nothing. This was an extraordinary moment. How could two people run the same objective test with such dramatically different results? The only viable answer, as Schlitz saw it, must lie in the researcher himself/herself. The outcome depended on 'who you are.' As far as we know, this is as close as anyone has come to verifying that observer and observation can collapse into one (seer, seen and seeing is one — Advaita). This fusion lies at the heart of the sacred response, because in unity all separation ends.

4.2 Mystic Clairvoyance

Is clairvoyance useful or not? Should one try to develop it or ignore it out of respect for boundaries of time? Here no fixed answer can be given. Our DNA has to be clairvoyant; we could not survive if our genes did not know the future; the unfolding of an embryo in the womb, as it evolves from a single cell to billions, requires that DNA precisely foresees when neurons, heart cells, muscle tissue, and every other specialized mutation needs to develop. If neurons grew on the wrong day, the day when fingers needed to emerge, for example, havoc would result. So that first fertilized ovum contains a map of the future imprinted in invisible ink.

Other situations are not so clear. In general, the highest purpose of clairvoyance may be to give us a glimpse into the mind of God, because a divine mind could not be constrained by time and does not recognize past, present, or future. If you decide to soften the boundary of time, you must take responsibility for all that comes with such a decision. Science fiction is rife with stories of reckless time travellers who met with disaster when they broke into the future or the past. At the very least, one runs the risk of getting present time and vision time hopelessly confused. The spiritual masters keep teaching us that living in the present moment is the ideal, if only we can reach it. The Jewish philospher Philo, who was a follower of Plato, writes: "'Today' means boundless and inexhaustible eternity. Periods of months and years and of time in general are ideas of man, who calculates by number; but the true name of eternity is Today." This is the ultimate mystery of clairvoyance — any moment, whether now or later, is the doorway into same eternity.

> Thyself stimulate and direct thyself; thus self-protected and clairvoyant thou shalt live happy. — *Dhammapada*

Thus, in developing this ability, you would take away quite a bit of the mystique that has been built around clairvoyance.

4.3 Clairvoyance Development Techniques

The clairvoyant ability cannot be easily developed by all of us just as not all can attain mastery in music or painting though the ability lies latent in everyone. Children remain natural recipients of ESPs up to an age of six to seven years. ESP being the basis of clairvoyance, remote visions, and precognition, they must be brought up with due care, and be initiated to clairvoyance development at that early age.

Also, we can all awaken slowly to a greater measure of the mastery of life and circumstances by increasing our clairvoyant receptivity at all levels, by widening our consciousness and cultivating a telepathic rapport with all creations. This can be done by developing an attitude of kindness and love.

> Kindness is a language which deaf can hear and blind can read.
> — Mark Twain

> Love conquers all things, let us, too give in to love.
> — Virgil

Further, if you wish to grow receptive to the finer forces of the universe you will have to discard the junk food and drinks — meat, tobacco and alcohol (non-judicial consumption). The junk of negative emotions — anger, lust, self-pity, envy, intolerance, vanity, etc., lowers the pace of the advancement of clairvoyant faculty. Be at peace: "Peace is not absence of war, it is virtue, a state of mind, a disposition for benevolence, confidence, justice," says Spinoza.

Keep in mind, the prime requisite for any occult development is secrecy. If you go on gabbling about your occult practice you will not go far.

There are extrasensorial centres in the human brain, which are known as suprasonic circuits. These circuits are inherent in every man. They need to be activated in order to develop clairvoyance ability. Our eyes are the main activators.

The working of our eyes is not like an ordinary camera but more like the most sophisticated electronic automatic camera. To adjust the focus, the pupils of eyes open up. Accordingly the muscles of the eyes expand or contract to allow proper light inside. Colours are identified and proper picture develops in our mind. All these processes are automatic. But for clairvoyant view, some extra means are to be activated.

Now, in all electronic cameras there is a battery so that all the working of camera becomes automatic. If this battery becomes weak, the recharging of flash light becomes slower and when the battery becomes very weak, all the functions stop and so we have to replace the battery. Such a battery is created in our body at the time of conception. And the electricity created from this battery, gives power to all the organs and also to the eyes so that they work automatically.

The human foetus develops eyes in the third month. And if at that time, there is neglect and lack of proper nutrition, child's eyes do not develop properly. Therefore, in order to have more clairvoyants in future generations, expecting mothers are to be fed appropriately.

Further, in our brain, the cerebrospinal fluid is being extracted from the blood. This fluid rotates in the most vital organs through the central nervous system. And flow of this fluid is the source of nutrition to the eyes via optic nerves. Moreover, optic nerves are controlled by our most important endocrine glands — the pituitary and pineal glands. Therefore, to develop the clairvoyant vision, one has to sensitize his eyes.

Some of the methods for developing clairvoyance are given below:

4.3.1 OCCULAR FATIGUE TECHNIQUE

It has been discovered that one of the surest ways of developing clairvoyance is by inducing occular fatigue[3] by staring fixedly at certain objects such as crystal balls, diamond stones on your rings, lighted candles, etc. This is very helpful, but if not practised intelligently it is apt to lead only to eye-strain and self-deception.

An alternate and useful way of development of this faculty, is through a Hermetic exercise of the magnetic eye-bath. Dip your face completely in a basin of water. Then open your eyes while your face is immersed in the water and slowly roll your eyes in all directions.

Do this seven times. The water should have been previously boiled and filtered and then allowed to cool till it is tepid.

Initially you will feel a stinging sensation in the eyes but this will disappear as the eyes get gradually accustomed to the exercise.

This will strengthen your eyes and make them more receptive to the subsequent clairvoyant exercise. It reduces eye-strain, strengthens weak eyesight, makes the eyes resistant to change of light and weather and brings a lustre to them which is unmistakable.

If desired a thin decoction of eyebright euphray (herbaleuphrasia) can be added to the basin of water.

4.3.2 BATES TECHNIQUE

An excellent exercise as proposed by Bates for development of psychic

3. W.E. Butler, *How to Develop Clairvoyance*, The Aquarian Press, London.

sight is that of palming. This involves closing one's eyes and covering them with one's palms in such a way that the left palm and fingers are over the left eye and right palm and fingers are over the right eye and partly over the left hand. Thus, the eyes are cupped in darkness. It is helpful to rest the elbows on arms of a chair.

The induced darkness is a wonderful exercise for relaxing the eye muscles and removing eye fatigue, as well. After half an hour of such a steady palming one will notice a definite improvement in one's vision even without glasses.

Once the eyes have been relaxed and rejuvenated by these daily palmings, one will notice that the induced pitch darkness behind our eyes will graduatly lift up and lessen.

Curtains of different colours will move before the closed eyes without any outside stimuli of light. You must sit relaxed and watchful and slowly try to pierce this shifting veil of darkness. Geometric forms and flashes of coloured light will rise and subside.

You will feel yourself passing as if through a series of sliding doors that open before the concentrated penetration of your gaze. Persevere in this effort and learn the results for yourself someday.

4.3.3 LEWIS TECHNIQUES

According to Dr. H. Spencer Lewis,[4] "The faculty of psychic seeing is not an unusual or an extraordinary function of some mysterious centre but a normal one — in other words, the inability to see psychically is an abnormal condition of the human ego."

Dr. Lewis has suggested a few exercises, and asks us to practise daily and even hourly. He tells us to close the eyelids for two to three minutes at a time, remain relaxed and wait for sight impressions.

Another exercise is to sit in an absolutely dark or deeply shaded place and wait for the impressions of colour or light.

---

4. H. Spencer Lewis, *Development of Psychic Sight*, Rosicrucian Digest, December, 1951.

For the third exercise, says Dr. Lewis, "Sit in a comfortable relaxed position, with eyes turned away from all bright lights; close your eyelids and press lightly upon the eyeballs with the tips of right forefinger and thumb until colours appear on the dark field before the eyes."

Yet another is to sit in softly lit place and pick out a bright point of light (such as reflexion on a piece of silver or glass) at some little distance from you; concentrate your gaze on it until you no longer see its proper colour but notice its colour changing.

The fifth exercise: Lie down in a relaxed condition (at night) in a dark or softly lit room; close the eyes as for sleep but select a distant city, or locality or room as the thing you desire to see and wait until you see some part of it. Repeated tests for the same 'vision' will eventually bring clearer and more distant pictures to your consciousness.

Then, try this last step of Dr. Lewis, by selecting a person at a distant place at an hour you want to know what he or she is doing. Eventually, you will be able to 'reach' persons with your psychic 'sight' and know what they are doing almost any hour of the day.

Spencer Lewis reminds us that better the physical health the better will be the ability to see by any means. He cautions us to drink plenty of water, keep the body well and strong, and in case we wear glasses, to remove them during these exercises.

Your physical eyes improve as your psychic sight develops. The results do not depend upon faith, but the mind must be open to conviction or at least free from the false conviction that all 'seeing' is through the carnal eyes. "Practice alone will bring the gradual development," says Dr. Lewis.

4.3.4 PUHARICH TECHNIQUE

Andrija Puharich[5] had developed the technique basically for testing the ESP-cognition scores, but it is good for developing clairvoyant sight if practised regularly.

---

5. Andrija Puharich, *Beyond Telepathy*, Pan Books Ltd, London, 1975, p. 123.

A practitioner (telepathic receiver, clairvoyance learner and psychometric reader) looks through his closed eyelids, at a distance of about nine inches, into a million candle power stroboscopic light. The light could be controlled to flash within a frequency range of two times per second to forty-eight times per second. The trainee while looking into the light controls the frequency of the flash with a knob and adjusts it to that point which pleases him/her the most.

As soon as the frequency adjustment is reached, the trainee's whole mental field becomes illuminated with a multiplex geometrical pattern. Very often it would be like looking at a brilliantly coloured mosaic made up of small regular geometrical figures. The coloured geometrical pattern in the trainee's mind will start revolving first slowly and then rapidly resulting in a feeling of being whirled outward, in other words, a centrifugal mental effect. By sharply turning the frequency adjustment, the practitioner will be able to ignore the sense of being whirled outward and concentrate on the centre of the pattern finally being tunnelled to a distant vision. While gazing into, s/he could accuratley describe by extrasensory perception physical scenes going on thousand of miles away.

A constant and regular practice will finally eliminate the use of stroboscopic light, and verifiable heightened telepathy and/or clairvoyance would be available with peace, relaxation and concentration.

4.3.5 CANDLE TECHNIQUE

This is the most commonly used method to develop the clairvoyance talent. The beginner assumes one of the traditional sitting postures or a comfortable posture on a chair with vertical back, placing a candle before him/her, then attempts to gaze at the flame with fixity and steadfastness. S/he seeks to keep her/his attention unwaveringly fixed upon the lit candle as long as possible. This develops control of the tides and fluxes of the mental stream of associations. The trainee may dispense with an external object to exercise the power of concentration, s/he may, in fact, simply pick a point between her/his eyes, an imaginary point, and concentrate upon it just as s/he would upon the candle.

Basic to the exercise of mental tranquility is the act of visual concentration.

The lighting required in the practice room is of very low order. Burning of lavender incense and/or camphor is helpful. With fresh air available, and room temperature maintained at a pleasant level, cool and collected you fix your eyes on the flame. Do not jerk. After some time you will begin to see many sights. And, you may better select the sights which you are familiar with in the physical world.

You should rather better keep doing this practice regularly and try to see sights and places situated faraway. Your eyes will not help in this practice. When you close your eyes, the mind's *eye* opens up. It is this eye which succeeds to see clairvoyantly.

The initial stage needs a long, protracted practice and after a few verifiable sightings, the practitioner begins to see all such sights and locations as he might want to see, the moment s/he takes the position in a calm environment with a tranquil mind.

4.3.6 CHAKRA TECHNIQUE

While the whole body and aura are ultimately involved in the deveolpment of your clairvoyance, two areas stand out: the heart (Heart charkra – 4th *chakra*) and the head (Third eye – 6th *chakra*). By concentrating on one or the other *chakra*, you can probably succeed in developing your clairvoyance. But an easy, accurate clairvoyance requires both. A very important aspect of clairvoyance is the harmony between the heart and head *chakras*. Different people, however, may find one or the other an easier place to start with, charging it up with the desired images, as in the candle technique.

There has been a mix-up about the two *chakras* in our skull, viz. the 6th and the 7th *chakras* in the minds of occultists. Some of them identifying the 6th, i.e. third-eye or eyebrow *chakra* with the pineal gland; while others identifying it with the pituitary gland, and vice versa the crown *chakra* — the seventh *chakra*. Therefore, allowing the fields of your pineal and pituitary glands to "charge up" simultaneouly will stimulate your clairvoyance considerably.

Further, it is said that the pineal gland begins to calcify and become rigid in most of us by about the age of six to seven years — allowing us to be a natural clairvoyant till that time. Therefore, clairvoyance practice of stimulation of your pineal gland needs to begin from an early age of five to six years; it would lead to a quicker and powerful development of the faculty.

Our attitude is an important parameter during our psychic practice. People who are genuinely non-judgemental seem to have an easier time achieving clairvoyance.

Being non-judgemental requires knowing our own feelings and opinions, and acting on them, while suspending the tendency to assume we know another's heart. Thus, we can be responsible for our own emotions and opinions and act on them, and meanwhile honour the unknowable uniqueness of the other person.

4.3.7 YOGIC TECHINQUE

Focusing the eyes on the tip of nose — nosetip gazing creates different sensations in the *nadis* which are connected with each other in the forehead region as well as *ida*, *pingala* and *sushumna*, which in turn creates a certain stimulus at the base *chakra* (*chakra* one) and helps to awaken the different psychic centres.

There is a lot of emphasis during concentration on being observant, and this observation faculty is gradually made subtle. Through observations it is possible to reduce the distraction which arises with the interaction of the senses and the outside environment. So when the mind is removed from a state of 'at tension' (attention), then psychic awareness, which is more natural and spontaneous, dawns. Being aware is the last stage of the concentration practice.

Imagination is the process through which we direct our mind from one type of experience to another. If we try to visualize a flower with our eyes closed, there is no clarity. The image is not seen; there is just a mental idea that, "I am seeing a flower." However, when there is intensity of thought, that flower can be seen in the form of a vague, shadowy outline. So, imagination is used in order to pass through the first two stages of concentration — gazing and observing. Then when the psychic awareness dawns, the process of seeing becomes a glimpse or sight or vision or sequentially moving scenes.

With the dawn of psychic awareness, attained through the meditative practice of nose-gazing coupled with sleuthing fortitude we can maintain our peace, harmony and integrity.

4.3.8 SURYA-TRADITION TECHINQUE

The Surya tradition teaches that by focusing the sight on a flame which is radiating light, it is possible to change the whole visual structure and concept, so the matter is not perceived as matter but as energy — the foundation for clairvoyant experiences.

To increase the faculty of sight, this tradition has evolved certain techniques which are related to the third-eye. The third-eye is a concept to describe a process that happens in the realm of the consciousness. In this process, the vision which sees matter, name and form is changed into extrasensorial vision which sees the energy beyond matter, name and form. In order to achieve this extrasensorial faculty of vision, one has to control the faculty arising through carnal eyes.

The Surya tradition emphasizes gazing on something luminous like the sun or flame. The awakening of heart *chakra* or of the third-eye are the two techniques used to bring about a change in the sighting faculty, while maintaining awareness and control of the mind.

The information gained clairvoyantly — or the knowledge, as the old saying goes, is power — and knowledge about people can be used to help them or to destroy them. Therefore, you must keep in mind the responsibilities that go with the power your knowledge gives you — the clairvoyance ability will, only then, stay with you.

"When one does meditation (including practices for development of clairvoyance) it is constantly seen that so long as there is an important defect somewhere, circumstances so happen that the occasion comes for the defect to rise until it is thrown out of the being. If one can take coming of these circumstances clairvoyantly as a call and an opportunity for conquering the defect, then one can progress very quickly," says Sri Aurobindo.

4.4 Clairvoyants

Expert clairvoyants can see anything they decide to see; the past, present, and the future of any person, or of a person present before them (called a sitter). They can see what all transpired in his/her past, and what actually took place on certain occasions and what is in store.

In case the person (subject) is not present, the clairvoyant needs to see his/her/its (animal's, material object's) picture. Then, in meditiation distance does not count for the clairvoyant, let it be hundreds of thousands of miles. Flitting from the past to the future is no problem.

The occult scientists have claimed that the children are all clairvoyants for a longer or shorter time after birth; they converse with God in their sleepy dreams and have often been found smiling, in a blissful state of ecstasy — a state of 'unification of consciousness'.

A gifted clairvoyant contemplates, when his mind is calm and in response and acts only as a screen to receive clear and true images. But when he consciously thinks of something or tries to change the course of the flow of thought or tries to answer a question suddenly flung at him, his own effort comes into play. He now takes upon himself to change the course, to lift the wheel and put it in the right groove. Unless there is a perfect mastery, there is every chance of positioning the wheel in a slightly off-the-course orbit. As this is the task of precision of untold perfection and the system is delicate and highly sensitive, every possibility of error, however small, looms ahead. That is why, no matter how advanced a seer, he can sometimes foretell wrongly or give a wrong opinion or answer; and, if he grants a boon, it might fail; or, if he tries to achieve something, it might not fructify. All this is because he has failed to put the wheel in the right orbit due to his personal involvement.

All clairvoyants are not gifted with the same abilities. Inner vision can be clear or blurred; it can come and go, which makes it often unreliable; and its accuracy is always open to question, since no one knows to what extent the future is predetermined or open to change.

There are clairvoyants who live in backstreets and make money therefrom. More women are talented at calirvoyance than men. It is, also a fact that many women have calirvoyant ability off-and-on, that is, it is not constant, it cannot be switched on at their will. There is frequently the case that a woman who is most talented at clairvoyance in brief flashes will astound her friends with true prophecies. She should never take money for the service rendered, as she is most likely to lose the ability sooner than later.

Oftentimes it is better not to talk how much you know clairvoyantly. The more normal, the more natural you appear, the more you will pick up. You should never try to prove, because if you try to give proof you will be really inundated by doubt-waves from others, which can cause great harm to your ability.

Many of the greatest clairvoyants have some physical affliction, which enhances and confers the talent. You cannot know of person's spirituality by just looking at him/her. Don't judge a person to be an evil clairvoyant because s/he is diseased/disabled; disease or disablement may have been taken on deliberately in order that the person can increase her/his rate of vibration required for ESP-cognition.

A clairvoyant has soft hands, with short smooth fingers and often a small thumb. The mounts of Saturn, Mercury and especially the Moon, are quite prominent or raised with a good many small crosslines. A drooping and often fragmented line of head and a poor line of heart. A clear line of intuition, often islanded at the start, is read in the same way in the absence of a line of intuition proper.

Gerard Croiset (1909-1980), a Dutch clairvoyant, rendered his services to International Police Forces to locate missing people and things.

Jean Dixon (1918-1997), an American clairvoyant, saw the death of John F. Kennedy, eleven years before the tragedy; the assassination of Robert Kennedy a week before the incidence; and even predictated the assassination of civil rights leader, Martin Luther King.

4.5 Clairaudience

Clairaudience is the perception of sounds inaudible to normal human ears (the audible range is 20 cycles per second to 20,000 cycles per second). Even the deaf persons have been reported to be clairaudient.

Put in other words, the clairaudience is a psychic ability of hearing voices, music, or sounds of the past, the present, but organically non-audible, and those to be generated in the future.

There are various kinds of sounds that a clairaudient perceives; it could be the roaring of a lion, sound of waterfall, tinkling of bells, buzzing of bees, a single note of flute, sound of musical instruments at a distance, sound of wood-winds, vibration of a high tension wire or cool breeze, banshee's mournful wail, a train moving on rails saying "I told you so . . .", etc. Different sounds correspond to different levels of evolutionary prefection. In the highest state one hears the sounds of gods and messages of prophecies.

One form of clairaudient prophecy is the inner-voice which should not be encouraged, as it can mislead one in the day-to-day happenings. It can also lead one back to ego and the gross mind. It likes to prattle on and bestow favours and boons. It should be respected rather as a showerer of blessings than as a foreteller of events. It tends to exaggerate and use hyperbole. All that it prattles need not come true. The validity of this voice depends upon the purity of an individual mind. Finally, it gets dissolved though it can be invoked at any time, which is dangerous as it often tells you what you want to hear. In such a case of even unconscious wishfulness, the voice is tainted and ruled by the wants of the gross mind. Only in a state of total purity is this inner-voice reliable, honest and educative.

People may recognise clairaudient voices as those of a dead relative or a friend or their spiritual guide. Socrates used to hear a spirit speaking to him, especially at the times of some crisis. Shamans do receive clairaudient information.

Invariably, a clairaudient's/shaman's body becomes so sensitive that any sound, loud or gentle, like the rustling of leaves, the whirring of a fan, the drone of a plane, the swish of a sweeping broom, the whisper of a caressing breeze, an auto-rickshaw noisily passing by, sets even the insides of the bones dancing. These pleasurable inner vibrations vary in intensity with the fluctuating decible and volume of sound. It feels as if one has become an extremely responsive oscillator. The whole atmosphere seems to gently vibrate with this softly reverberating music.

The availability of clairaudience faculty is a mystery. There are no known techniques of developing it. It is most of the time a god-given gift. However, various meditations — transcendental meditation, Tabor meditation, hypno-meditation, etc. do lead to the development of this psychic ability. Sometimes, clairaudience ability also gets developed along with the developmental practices for clairvoyance.

Certain sages and yogis are clairaudient and can understand the language of animals, birds, bees and plants. When the faculties of individual consciousness are raised, the raised consciousness intuitively transforms sounds and vibrations into words, into a language known to that individual. This is how the sages were adept at understanding animal and bird communication — sages and saints have always been close to nature.

Also, the founder-sages of the Ayurveda could understand even plants who would envision them how to use each herb and for which ailments.

It is not that the plants or birds or beasts are reaching out to humans, they are being themselves. It is the transcended individual consciousness that becomes so sensitive and receptive to auras, vibrations, sounds and other modes of transmission, and acquires the rare ability to metamorphose these modes of communication into human communication.

> Thou shalt hear what no ear has heard, thou shalt see what no eye has seen.
> — Ahmed Halif

Organically as well as aberrationally, hearing can become remarkably extended or closely inhibited so that one person may hear footsteps a block away as a normal activity and another would not hear a bass drum thundering on the porch. Clairaudience is not about the cases of such persons.

Quinine makes a man's ears ring, so he hears sounds that are not there (no man can hear sounds above 20,000 cycles/second when they are there; above 20,000 c/s is ultrasound — detected by big bats and dolphins). Thus, quinine sets in hallucinatory clairaudience.

4.6 Clairsentience

Clairsentience is a word from the French for 'clear sensing', it is the sensory detection of psychic information. Such as aura sensing or 'astral body' detection or the detection of symptoms due to 'psychic attacks'. It is the psychic sense of feeling.

Let us first examine in detail what is sentience. Not even a rank materialist can deny that sentience, whether in an animal or plant, is a part of biological evolution. It is not only the physical structure, but the state of sentience also which changed with every change brought about in living forms, during the course of evolutionary climb that continued for millions of years. Sudden radical change in climate and upheavels of the Earth caused the extinction of thousands of forms of life that had survived for colossal epochs of time in conditions favourable to them. Even gigantic creatures like dinosaurs vanished away clean after millions of years of undisputed sway over certain parts of the Earth. Their disappearance is still a mystery and the only probable explanation is lethal change in the environment. The dinosaur as a sentient creature would not survive in the changed conditions and hence disappeared from the arena of the Earth. Other creatures existing then survived because the life in them could adapt themselves to the change.

The entire resources of a living organism are pressed into service to keep the flame of life alive. This applies to every form of life from man to rudimentary cell, when due to an adverse change in environment disease or decay in organism is not capable of maintaining the stream of life, it ceases to struggle and dies. The carcass of the higher form of life may then become the food or abode of other lower forms, such as worms or bacteria, but its own existence in the intrinsic form comes to an end. Since survival is the main objective of the struggle put up by a living organism, it follows that it is life or sentience which is the chief actor in the drama and every other incident is woven round it. This is true of the evolutionary movement also.

The concept of evolution can be traced to the earliest stages of the Greek thought. Aristotle's knowledge of animal life, it is said, was remarkable. He distinguished some five hundred species of vertebrates. "Nature is always striving after the most beautiful that is possible, . . . by degrees from the lower to higher types", he wrote centuries before Darwin. Among the Greeks the idea of evolution can be traced even to the earlier time of Thales and Anaximander. The latter had the idea that man had risen directly from a fish-like form. According to Lucrelius:

> The earth first attempted to produce a host of monsters, grotesque in build and aspect — hermaphrodites, halfway between the sexes, yet cut off from either, creatures bereft of feet, or dispossessed of hands . . .. They could not gain the coveted flower of maturity nor procure food, nor could copulate for procreation. In those days, many of these species must have died out altogether and failed to reproduce their kind. The species that survived must have been protected and preserved from the beginning of the world either by cunning or by prowess or by speed.

It is thus clear that the idea of growth from a lower to a higher or from a cruder to a perfect form is not entirely new. The Indian view, current from the Vedic times, makes evolution a spiritual progress. It is the spirit/soul that rises to higher and higher states of self-awareness, from the lowest to the highest form of life, until it culminates in man.

Now it is a curious thing that although "everybody knows" it is "human to err", the sentient portion of the mind which computes answers to problems and which makes man a Man is utterly incapable of error.

The more sentient the man, the less he is a "push-button" instrument. Aberrated and reduced he can, of course, in a limited degree, be made to perform like a marionette, but then it is understood that the more aberrated a person is, the closer he approaches the intelligence quotient of an animal.

Man is to be regarded as a sentient being. His sentience depends upon his ability to resolve problems by perceiving or creating or understanding situations. This rationality is the primary, high echelon function of that part of mind which makes him a Man, not just another animal. Remembering, perceiving, imagining, he has the singular ability of resolving conclusions and of using conclusions resolved to resolve further conclusions. This is a rational Man.

Men having kinesthetic (feeling) sensitivity are high clairsentients. The kinesthetic people perceive by how their aura layers feel. Is the layer hot? Is it cold? Is it rough? Is it smooth? Is it flowing? Is it sticky? Is it weak? Is it strong? Allow your layers to flow and feel comfortable in whatever way you would like them to feel before making clairsentient excursion.

Ganzfield stimulation (restricted sensory deprivation) is used to encourage the reception of a perception — restricted deprivation of kinesthetic sense leads to clairsentience, of ears to clairaudience, and of the eyes to clairvoyance.

Clairsentience capability is possible, also, when man has acquired vivid wisdom approaching the eternal-wisdom. Fo-shu-hing-tsan-king says: "As the light of a torch illumines the objects in a dark room, even so the light of wisdom illumines all men, whosoever they be, if they turn towards it."

Clairsentience turns a person 'ominiscient'. It comes through self-realization, when the person is endowed with the 'omniscience'. To lose entirely all interest in knowledge, also, results in omniscience. It is but the gift of knowing what needs to be known, at the right moment, for error-free action. After all, knowledge is needed for action and if you act rightly, spontaneously, without bringing in the conscious, so much the better.

> Equal in heart, equal in thought, thou hast won for thyself omniscience.
> — *Lalitavistara*

4.7 Crystal-gazing and Clairvoyance

As crystal-gazing and mirror magic are simple extensions of the range of techniques used in the development of psychic-sight or clairvoyance, they find a place here to be described.

For thousands of years there has existed an art known to seers and diviners, fortune-tellers and mystics, to aid in the production of visions — or, if you prefer, hallucinations; to the initiated it is known as scurrying, although most people would call it crystal-gazing.

Here we're going to approach it not as "telepathic TV" or "astral-projection" but as a method of seeing images of the inner-mind (somewhat similar to 'mobile' centre of consciousness going on clairvoyant excursion). It is one of the traditional systems by which information from deep levels of the psyche can be made conscious.

Crystal-gazing is intertwined with thought transference, mind reading, visualization and automatism. The crystal or speculum is the medium. Speculum or a crystal ball has no direct power of its own but has the characteristic of tuning the mind of the person gazing at it, and driving his unconscious mind to surfy realm so that the veil is lifted from the problem to be solved.

The list of speculums used is endless — sheeps shoulder blade, embers of fire, blade of a sword, blobs of ink and/or blood, opaque mirrors, bowls of water and or wine, bowl of molasses, diamond jewels, crystal balls of quartz or beryl, glass balls, plastic balls, etc.

The consulting room should be noise free, at comfortable temperature, full of fresh air, dimly lit and serene.

The gazer ought to have great powers of concentration and its application. In earlier times the practitioners wore protective talismans and indulged in rituals in order to safegurad themselves of psychic attacks and enhance the ability to gather the unknown information.

The crystal gazing technique is simple — almost too simple; you seat yourself comfortably, relax, and gaze into the depths of a ball or any other speculum which you find suitable, with your question firmly in mind. Don't stare fixedly at it, or consciously try to avoid blinking; doing that will only cause eye strain which will distract you.

In a successful questioning session, the ball will first begin to appear milky, as though a cloud had drifted into it. After a time this cloud will take on the appearance of a curtain, and still later this curtain will begin to lift and roll away. What you see then will have some bearing on your question.

Of course nothing actually appears in the device being gazed at; it's merely a "screen" on which you project the picture in your mind's eye. You have to be constantly on the alert not to let your imagination distort what is there. Sometimes being able to differentiate between what you think you see, and what you imagine you see, can be an extremely difficult proposition.

Sharply focused images will appear only with psychic skill and practice. Gazer may see the picture with his "mind's eye" and provide interpretation of the composite imagery with commanded wisdom.

Similarly, scurrying is divination by allowing the eyes to rest on a plain suface so that the mind becomes stilled and receptive to imagery that arises from the unconscious in the form of swirling mist, wispy clouds and sharply defined signs, symbols, scenes, etc.

Mirror magic is a technique which was once used to foresee and manipulate future events by using mirrors. A sorcerer directs his gaze into the mirror, using it in much the same way as one uses a crystal ball or any other speculum as a point of concentration. The initial images were blurred forms, but later, the more the magician concentrated his attention into the mirror, the more he could see — the past, present and the future events.

In case of event manipulation,the magician projects the person into the mirror. The subject would then experience some fortune or misfortune. For example, the black magician would see his victim standing at the top of a flight of stairs. At that point, if he wanted to make his victim fall down the stairs and break an arm, all he had to do was desire to see it happen. Working this kind of magic, the magician would actually see his spiteful justice occur in the mirror just the way he planned it — something like watching an instant replay before the action takes place.

These malicious actions wouldn't happen just on the magician's direction; they would be carried out by inhuman demonic spirits that he commanded as a part of the ritual process. In order to make the victim fall down the stairs, an inhuman spirit would either momentarily disorient the person, apport some grease on the step, or go as far as to even give the victim a psychokinetic push.

On the other hand, a white magician will use the technique as a *modus operandi* for psychic healing and/or as a solution for the sitter's benefit.

4.8 Dream Clairvoyance

Dreams put us in touch with our own imaginations, essentially, which in turn create most of our dreams. Dreams offer us fantastical visions that complement our existence, and keep tabs on our actions. Dreams are mystic experiences for evolved souls.

> Dreams are displays of images, symbols, scenes for clairvoyant seeing.
> — N. Vanvari

The images and symbols of a dream may be mysterious at the first glance, but since the dreams are wholly drawn from past experience, like old wine in new bottles, they are subject to interpretation. A clairvoyant, however, sees something new. But dreams and clairvoyance do have one strong link; they seem to depend on a person's belief or the belief of system of a whole society.

This implies that there is more than one way for the future to flow into the present. It can send messages ahead or keep itself completely veiled; it can choose those who will see and those who will be blind. Much more than we realize, our own awareness may be creating the boundaries of the past, present and the future. In other words, we may be choosing not to be clairvoyant so that our belief in a hidden future is confirmed. When Cassandra foresaw the fall of Troy in the Iliad, her vision might have been believed, since the belief system of the ancient world included clairvoyant knowledge. (as it happened, the gods had cursed her always to be right and yet never to be believed; we call such person a Cassandra to this day).

Dreams are crazy-house mirrors by which our psychic imprints of thoughts, emotions and feelings are screened. Dreams find application in the field of mapping the unknown and unfolded terrain of our minds and have been used considerably by various schools of mental healing.

Changing the dream for good or ill, during lucid dreaming[6] — desired mode for purpose of healing, is a great temptation, but it is a fool's game. The world's most powerful sorcerer, whether a saint or a sinner, comes inevitably to face the futility of his or her existence at the moment of death. Implicitly suggesting the futility of soul-psychic sleuthing!

Dreams or nightmares, we have to live our experiences as it is, and we have to live it awake. We live in a world which is penetrated through and through by science, and which is both whole and real. We cannot turn the experience into a game simply by taking sides. However, remember:

---

6. Nandlal Vanvari, *Dreams as foreshadows of the Future, mirrored in fantasies of the Present, and fixations of the Past*, D.K. Printworld, New Delhi, 2009, p. 59.

> Beware, dreams (nightmares) could be deadly and dreams can turn you into a dare-devil. — N. Vanvari

What we can do is to develop scientifically soul-psychic sleuthing temper for healing our future.

A Christian, Father Jertullin (CE 160-240) held the view that dreams were natural revelations about medical treatment, hidden treasures, stolen goods, or future honours, demons might cause impure, frivolous or turbulent dreams; and visions containing sacred prophecy, might proceed from holy angels.

Dreams of prophetic or telepathic nature have been recorded, wherein dreamers have "witnessed" accidents, "read" headlines pertaining to disasters or have been "told" the name of a horse that turned out to be the winner. These are often few and far between to be judged accurately, but they constitute an intriguing phase of dream experience. When a day-dream or sleep-dream is telepathic in nature, i.e. in which a relative/friend is seeking some sort of help directly or implicitly, need to be heeded with a sense of urgency. Because, most of the reported and recorded stories of telepathic dreams have validated and vindicated the action taken.

> Dreams featuring mental telepathy forecast an exciting good news.
> — N. Vanvari

The spiritual dreams are brought about by the higher-self penetrating the soul realm, and reflecting upon the waking-mind approaching events. When we put our animal mind and soul in harmony with our higher-self we become one with it, and, therefore, one with the universal mind or will by becoming part of it. It is through the higher-self that we reach the infinite. It is through the lower-self we fall into the whirlpool of matter. These dreams are a part of the universal-mind until they transpire in the life of a man. After this they go to make a part of the person's soul.

Physical dreams are more or less unimportant. They are usually superinduced by the anxious waking mind, and when this is so they possess no prophetic significance. Dreams induced by opiates, fevers, mesmerism and ill-health come under this class. A man who gambles is liable to dream of cards; if he dreams them in deep sleep the warning is to be heeded; but if it comes as a reverie while he sleeps lightly, he should regard it as worthless. Such dreams reflect only the present condition of the body and the mind of the dreamer; but as the past and present enter into shaping the future, the reflections thus left on the waking mind should not go unheeded.

During the sleep the 'will' is suspended leaving the mind often prey to its own fancy. The slightest attack of an enemy may be foretold by the unbridled imagination exaggerating the mental picture into a monstrous shark or snake, when indeed, a much less portentous sign was cast from the dream mold.

The mind loses its reason or will in sleep, but a supersensitive perception is awakened, and, as it regains consciousness from sleep, the sound of knock on the door may be magnified into a pistol shot.

Since it is impossible to find the man twice in exactly the same mental state, it is equally impossible for him to dream the same dream twice; though there are many instances of repetition.

When man sleeps, he dreams. His mind, thought, intellect are also sleeping or are suspended: he is, in short, in a state of meditation. Yet he dreams. So what is this dream? A projection of a sleeping man . . . in meditation! Without his active participation, his senses, thought, body, intellect, are in meditative suspension — a world projected around him, which he can feel and see. There is time and space, and matter in this world, much like the world he lives in. There are people in it, moving, living, communicating. This is a world alive, a duplicate of the world we live in. And the sleeping man lends his own life to this dream and makes it come alive. He experiences everything that the dream participants experience. He sees his dream, experiences it, but neither controls it, nor interferes in it. The dream is him, but he is not the dream, and he is not bound by that dream. As is his mental state, so the dream.

Dreams are usually forgotten, but powerful dreams are recalled.

These are sometimes clairvoyant, telepathic or shared, lucid, gifted, etc. although no one can explain why?

It may be because our unconscious uses the language of symbols, which includes myth and legend. Yet this unconscious, as we know from Jungian psychology, is not merely our repressed desires or instinctual patterns, it also contains within itself the deeper levels of our soul and cosmic mind. The most primary symbols, or the archetypes of the psyche, are those of time, as in the riddle of the Sphinx. Our most primary issue in life is that of birth and death and the meaning of our transient existence. As our myths and symbols are naturally of time, they are of the planets. They reflect the dialogue between our soul and the cosmic energies and archetypes transmitted through the planets. The language of symbols, the language of the deeper unconscious, which also contains hidden within it our higher consciousness is essentially the language of dreams.

At night when we sleep, our mind expands to include the whole universe. We move into our astral or dream body which encompasses our whole field of waking experience, and finally into our causal or deep sleep body, which encompasses both our waking and dream experiences. We are each physically just a point projection of the cosmic circle of light that is cosmic soul; we are merely one of its rays, which projects the dream images.

Thus, when you go to sleep, dream and out-of-body experiences take place, which are nothing but simulations of the 'akashic' records of your Karmic Cycle inscribed on your soul. That is during dreaming state, an imaginary series of events, having some association with your present, or past or future life occur.

When the senses are cut off from the external world, as in a dream state, the dreamer creates its own empire, its own world, and it acts in the world which it has created. The information used to create this subtle world, with its subtle images and ideas, is received from the external world. The empire, the drama, the enactment of dreamer is experienced in the form of dream.

Normally, we are caught in a limited view of life, however, our soul sends us a dream to give us a deeper view — the soul's view — of our situation. Dreams, thus, illustrate the whispers of the soul that nudge and guide us to live a spiritually informed life.

In dreams, alter-ego or its clinical extreme multiple-personality syndrome formed under psychological pressure, plays an important role. The stress that one personally cannot contain spills over into another (a dream personality). If you feel unfairly treated at work, you may have a dream in which you are a lion-tamer whipping a big cat to do your will, and these may be symbols of stress. You are not able to handle when you are awake. The lion is your boss or that your fear of him is being acted out here.

Therefore, it is believed that during sleep the brain discharges its pent-up potentials which have built up during the day. This flow of electricity in the brain serves to restore the brain to its resting equilibrium. This has been likened to the 'Rezeroing' of electronic analogue computers which is required after their prolonged use. And one simple explanation of why people dream is that dreams are the images perceived when the brain discharges these pent-up electric potentials.

It seems logical to postulate that the potentials which build up are merely caused by unnecessary thinking. If that is so, then it would also be logical that a liberated person's brain would always be more or less at equilibrium, and hence very little of such discharge would occur in his case.

Of course, it is possible that dreams may occur and may not be remembered, as it happens in the case of deeper sleep dreams. But it is probably the remembered dreams that are indicative of restive mind, and which are really significant.

You take a journey into the unmanifested every night when you enter the phase of deep dreamless sleep. You merge with the Source. You draw from it the vital energy that sustains you for a while when you return to the manifested, the world of separate forms. This energy is much more vital than food: "Man does not live by bread alone". But in dreamless sleep, you don't go into it consciously. Although the bodily functions are still operating, "you" no longer exist in that state. Can you imagine what it would be like to go into dreamless sleep with full consciousness? It is impossible to imagine it, because that state has no content.

But don't ever attempt to stay conscious in dreamless sleep. It is highly unlikely that you will succeed. At the most, you may remain conscious during the dream phase, but not beyond that. This is called lucid dreaming, which may be interesting and fascinating and healing, but it is not liberating.

After the occurrence of enlightenment and liberation a remarkable development is that dreams begin to intrude less and less upon sleep, till finally (on liberation), they cease altogether.

"I rarely dream. I had dreamt only three or four times in my life, and all of my dreams had come true," says Swami Rama[7] (1925-1996).

Just as we live out our emotions and episodes in dreams and till such times as a dream lasts, it is reality, and we allow the dream to take its course, trying to come out of it only if it turns into a nightmare; so is the case with our lives. Just as, only after we wake up and gauge our past, persent and future life, do we find the dream was not our true life but was a minuscule experience of our mind (real all the same), apart from our true life and with only a momentary repercussion on it. So also, at a very highly developed stage, when we can perceive the past, the present and the future lives, do we realize that this life is also like a dream, a tiny episode in long cycle of lives, leaving only a momentary repercussion on it. Till then, this life is reality, to be endured, just as the dream was reality and had to be gone through.

Nothing that the mind of a man can conceive is impossible. The dreamers of today are achievers of tomorrow. "And forever they are

---

7. Swami Rama, *Living with the Himalayan Masters*, The Himalayan Institute Press, Honesdale, Pennsylvania, 2007, p. 135.

dreamers who make their dreams come true," says Orison Swett Marden, a wise man of America.

In sleep man dreams the future by intuitive perception of invisible signs or influences, while in waking state he reasons out by cause and effect. The former seems to be the law of the spiritual world, while the latter would appear to be the law of the material world. Man should not depend alone upon either. Together, they proclaim the male and female principle of existence should find harmonious consumation.

The dreams which weave consciously (upon soul-psychic sleuthing) or subconsciously for our bright and prosperous future, must be acted upon by suitable efforts. The same is suggested by Yiddish axiom: "If you want your dreams come true, do not oversleep."

Think of what the world owes to our forefathers' dreams and specifically the dream of democracy. That mighty dream which crumbled thrones and toppled monarchies in the past has gone on increasing in vividness and strength until today when mankind is actually talking of a World Republic. And, that is possible only when each one of us indulges in soul-psychic sleuthing sincerely.

4.9 Witchcraft Clairvoyance

The witchcraft has inveigled common run of people as well as individuals. The greatest attraction of it has been the lure of the unknown future and the lure of hidden things, which have long intrigued the human mind. On top of it is the veil of secrecy.

In a report submitted to UNESCO in 1963 by Professor Krush, it was stated that France had 60,000 practising witches, Germany more than 70,000 and Rome 500. There are regular meetings of registered witches; in the Soviet Union a village milkmaid was charged with witchcraft; about 10,000 Italian witches were fighting for social security benefits and state pensions.

In 1965, the king of witches, Alex Sanders[8] said: "Witches (female

8. Captain F.D. Colaabavala, *Witchcraft, The Forbidden World of the Devil,* Orient Paperbacks, New Delhi, 1997, p. 62.

and male) learn to think about everything, and they train their eyes to look as they think about the things they look at. With training it can bare the soul of any problem."

According to Sanders it is also possible to have astral sex with incubi (male) and succubi (female) evil spirits and sexual intercourse intellectually through projections.

Witches can attain second-sight — one of the clairvoyance abilities. According to Sanders, it takes time — perhaps nine months — before a practitioner of witchcraft can see his/her first vision, either in a crystal or a bowl of ink, or in magic mirror or tarot cards or in tea cups; divinations, intuitions and by many techniques and strange ways in which the human race has tried to discover what lies beyond the normal range of perception. From personal experience I can state, says Sanders: "I have never known a witch who fails to achieve clairvoyance wihin two years. Their power of vision is uncanny — they never seem to lie, although the witches are not able to interpret the time factor correctly."

Witchcraft is mostly put to use in healing, or cursing besides looking into future — often for the other people; discovering new methods for industry, art and commercial purposes; bringing opportunities of success or money or position; for captivation of person(s); for power; for sexual gratification; finding runaway husbands, wives and children; and various other uses, too numerous to mention here.

Armed forces personnel, artists, businessmen, criminals, doctors, lawyers, politicians, preventive and law enforcing agencies, even writers and people in other walks of life ask for help from the witches, frequently. Witches develop the powers of clairvoyance and some of them do set down as professional seers.

4.10 Dzogchen

The Dzogchen practitioners are highly visioned — good clairvoyants/ seers. They render their services to society and the system through astral projections and travels and not as psychic readers.

Dzogchen is the great knowledge of space and light.[9] Space is the empty Great Mother from which all things arise as a luminous display in which all things have their existence, and into which all things dissolve. The luminous display is the play of five pure lights, the essence of the five elements — earth, water, fire, air and space. The manifestation of all things, all beings and all elements is a matter of experience.

Dzogchen does not attempt to overcome problems or correct their causes, nor does it renounce problems or attempt to transform them. In the pure Dzogchen view, there is no such thing as a problem. When a thought or feeling or sensation arises it is left as it is. It does not cause a reaction. And if there is reaction, the reaction is not further engaged. The practitioner does not relate to what arises as an object of subject who must deal with it. It just is — and then it is not. Because there is no engagement on the part of practitioner whatever could be a problem dissolves into empty luminosity and then has no effect. Because there is no reaction, there is no new karmic trace.

In Dzogchen, rather than work on problems, the practitioner works on recognizing and abiding in the natural state of mind. That is the actual resolution to problems, not in their particulars but as an end to "problems" as a category of experience. In Dzogchen it is said that to know one is to know all. To really know the nature of any problem is to know the nature of all problems — they are all empty luminosity.

The point of the practice is to stop being the person who has problems, and instead to abide fully in the nature of mind where there are neither problems nor a separate individual to struggle with them.

4.11 Seers and Mystics

Seers are supersensitive clairvoyants. They have uninterrupted clairvoyance ability. However, the term 'seer' is freely used for

9. Tenzin Wangyal Rinpoche, *Healing with Form, Energy and Light*, New Age Books, New Delhi, 2003, pp. 112-22.

clairvoyants, crystal gazers, mirror magic conjurers working for welfare of human and other forms of life, dream visionaries, clairvoyant witches, Dzogchen practitioners, psychic readers, etc.

The words 'saint', 'sage', 'mystic' are often used synonymously, to mean seers of the Truth. Seers are the ones who have delved into high-flown philosophy. They are awakened, enlightened or liberated persons.

> The seer does good and makes not much of it. He accomplishes great things and is not attached to them. He does not wish to let his wisdom appear.
>
> — Lao Tse

According to *Narada Purana*, "From Brahma's thoughts came seven seers, the Sapta Rishis — Gotama, Bharadvaja, Vishvamitra, Jamadagni, Vasishtha, Kashyapa and Atri. One of these seven seers had a son called Kashyapa who fathered Devas (gods), Asuras (demons), Garuda (half-man, half-bird, on which Vishnu rides) and Nagas (serpants). Kashyapa was also the father of Manu, from whom came humans."

Seers, saints, mystics, prophets, yogis or other categories of holy men, are looked at by a sense of reverence justifiably as is due towards purer and more elevated human beings. The idea behind this has been that the chaste aspirants to the vision of God, who renounce the world and comforts of flesh, deserve our homage and those who obtain the vision not only homage but even our worship.

The penance, self-torture and sufferings which they inflict on themselves, and the extreme forms of privation and hardship which they voluntarily undergo, appear natural in the context of the idea that they resorted to these extreme measures to show their love of God.

Such great souls, broadly, fall into three classes:

(1) Meditating monks
(2) Mediumistic monks
(3) Mystics

The mediumistic monks hold that a finer body of some mystic/genius/savant, separated into billions of atoms, comes to them, which they take into their body; and perform psychically like them.

Mystic is simply the one gifted with spiritual sight and vision. He is a man "who transcends all categorical framework in the quest of the ultimate reality." Taken in this sense the Upanishadic seers as well as Shankara and Nagarjuna are mystics.

The mystic is not a peculiar person, nor is he necessarily psychic. He does not consort with spirits, nor does he interpret dreams. The thing that distinguishes him is that he "intuitively perceives truth, and without conscious mental processes, arrives at spiritual realization." He has learned that God is within him, and he has learned to withdraw from the haranguing voices of men from their false notions, their sheep-like following of commonly accepted ideas, and has gone into the deepest part of himself, there to contact the Divine. In a sense he has looked into the face of God, has heard things which he instinctively knows are basic truths, and has come forth to speak that which he knows of as certainty. He has awakened his superconscious mind.

The state of superconscious mind, of *samadhi*, is actually when the three areas of conscious, subconscious and unconscious are experienced together with equal intensity of awareness. Rather than separate experiences of awakeness, dream and sleep there is only one homogenous experience, only one state of perception. So, superconscious mind, or state of *samadhi*, is in no way influenced by the intellect or the analytical and comparative mind. This final state is experienced with the awakening of the "knower" aspect of the self. In yoga this knower aspect of the self is known as the drashta, 'the seer'. It is the witness, the seer behind the action, behind the scenes of life and living. Further, the idea of seers being wielders of strange and exotic powers of the unknown and hidden things have long intrigued the human mind.

The lives of seers often abound in miracles. Many of these reported events are hearsay, matters of faith, lucky coincidences, and generous exaggerations. The stories grow as they are handed down from generation to generation. But a few of these events may be genuine 'paranormal' phenomena. The saint may have a heightened sense of ESP because of which he may be liable to have flashes of telepathy, clairvoyance, precognition and the like. The heightened ESP may be explained by his 'oneness' with the Universal Consciousness and by the fact that in his case the blocking effect of individualistic thinking is absent. But this is not proof of his 'all-knowing' nature — 'seership', or miracle man.

The ancient seers of India, the Vedic *rishi*s were great men of spiritual realization and occult perception who lived in the legendary ages of light and truth at the beginning of this cycle of human civilization. Perhaps the greatest or most famous of the ancient seers was the Rishi Vasishtha, and his grandson Parashara Shakti. Parashara was considered knowledge incarnate.

Vedvyasa, son of Parashara, was a *rishi* of the Mahabharata times — about 3200 BCE. His epic the *Mahabharata* remains a marvel in world literature. He gave the world a storehouse of wisdom via the eternal Vedas in the form of Shastras or written documents. Till this time, Vedic knowledge was in the form of Shrutis (memorized and unwritten).

The other seers finding a place in the Hindu lore are Narada, Jaimini, Garga, Sushruta, Bharata, Patanjali, Chanakya, etc.

The knowledge of *rishi*s has been passed down through the millennia, largely through oral traditions. Gradually, it has been lost, distorted, or made rigid but the core of it still remains. It is accessible on the deeper levels of the mind as the heritage of the spiritual humanity from which we have come. We, too, can be seers.

The legendary sage and guru of Lord Rama, Vasishtha epitomised the force of spiritual knowledge. He is the central figure of *Yogavasishtha*, one of the most detailed scriptures on the nature of the mind and the way to free it from illusion.

The liberated one is, in many ways, comparable to a very young child or even an animal, in the sense that he can remain without thought, without concept of (psychological) time, living spontaneously in the present, reacting to the moment. But he is different from them in the sense that he can use thought where necessary, he can be consciously aware of the world around — a perfect clairvoyant, a miracle man; he can feel the sense of wonder and joy, beautitude and benediction which the animal cannot.

Any man of divine realization could perform miracle because, like Christ, he understands the subtle laws of creation; but not all masters choose to exercise phenomenal powers. Each saint reflects God in his own way; the expression of individuality is basic in a world where no two grains of sand are exactly alike.

It is believed that the seventh son, born to the seventh son, is to be a clairvoyant, with natural healing powers. Throughout the Middle Ages, the seventh son usually predicted future events, practised magic and administered the laying on of the hands to the sick.

Gypsies seem to be the only people who give equal credit to the seventh daughter of the seventh daughter. They say she always tells an accurate future.

A seer has transparent hands, almond shaped nails, very pointed and smooth fingers, specially the first finger. The seers have a high mount of the Moon, clear line of intuition and Mystique Cross in both hands.

Sometimes, it is too difficult to differentiate a seer's hands from that of a clairvoyant's hands, though a seer's hands are more softer and thus assume a level of transparency. The sensitivity of seer's is higher than those of clairvoyant's in general. Clairvoyants can only reach any part of this world, where as seers can reach the whole universe(s).

Seers need to be distinguished from prophets, though distinction invariably becomes blurred. Prophet Elizabeth Claire could see several thousand years back in the past and has given the voluminous and intricate details of the lost civilization of Atlantis and the Mayan culture.

Nostradamus (CE 1503-1566), the sixteenth century seer — a mediumistic monk, is credited with having prophesied many major world events, including the Gulf War of 1990s. His predictions are described as lucky shots in the dark, by some authors. But he was certainly a gifted crystal gazer and clairvoyant.

Lahiri Mahashay (CE 1828-1895), an incarnation of yoga, was a great seer. He was no bookish interpreter of the scriptures. Effortlessly he could dip into the 'divine library.' Foam of words and spray of thoughts gushed from the fountain of his omniscience. He had the wondrous clavis that unlocked the profound philosphical science hidden ages ago in the Vedas.

Madame Helena Petrovna Blavatsky (CE 1831-1891), a Russian-born psychic, travelled the world, giving displays of mediumship, levitation, clairvoyance, clairaudience and clairsentience. To promote her hermetic beliefs she helped to found the Theosophical Society which became most famous for its headquarters in India. Tainted by a fraud scandal, she retired to Germany to write. Her death on 8 May 1891 is still commemorated by Theosophists as White Lotus Day.

One of the best known seers of the last century, Edgar Cayee (CE 1877-1945), born in Kentucky, U.S.A, gave about 30,000 successful readings and psychic healings. He disliked taking money for readings, and until 1923, he carried out his psychic work in tandem with his day job as a photographer.

Another seer, Wolf Messing (CE 1899-1972), born in Poland, impressed the Russian dictator Joseph Stalin, with his predictions and hypnotizing powers. He was best at clairvoyance as compared to clairaudience.

His Holiness the Dalai Lama is a great living seer, scholar, author, mystic and saint. He is revered by Buddhists as the incarnation of Avalokiteshvara, the Buddha of Infinite Compassion. He has taken interest in all aspects of contemporary physics, neurobiology, psychology, and politics, and his views and messages of universal responsibility are embraced not only by the Buddhists but by people of all persuasions, all over the world. His dedication to non-violence in the forty-year-long agonizing struggle, has won him the Nobel Peace Prize in 1989. Dalai Lama admits: "The leading edge of the Tibetan spiritual practice produced some of the most remarkable insights into nature of reality and nature of mind that the world has ever known. Generations of Tibetan lamas, mystics, hermits, and magicians embarked on an investigation of the human mind unmatched anywhere on the Earth. Personal experience was everything. They became 'psychonauts' exploring the deepest reaches of inner space — soul and psyche composite."

Invariable rules may not be formulated about God — illumined saints: some perform miracles, others do not; some are inactive, while others (like King Janaka of ancient India and St. Teresa of Avila) are concerned with large affairs; some teach, travel, and accept disciples while others pass their lives as silently and unobtrusively as shadow. No worldly critic can read the secret scroll of *karma* (past actions) that unrolls for each seer a different script. However, consult some available seer, to be on the right-path of soul-psychic sleuthing:

> Follow the great man and you will see what the world has at heart in these ages. There is no omen like that. — Emerson

4.12 Seen

Clairvoyance is a paranormal event, a manifestation of 'Advaita' (non-duality), where seer-seen-and-seeing is one entity.

Most Indians, understandably proud of Advaita, believe that the Vedas have no beginning, no end, and required no human touch in their creation, but were clairvoyant/telepathic manifestations. Just as Jews and Christians believe that the writing in the Bible is sacred and has come from the Lord, Indians believe that the Vedas have orginated directly from God. They existed eternally in space, and the seers and visionaries (*rishis*), in their superior state of consciousness, saw them vividly and clairvoyantly. It was their '*darshan*.'[10]

A form that takes shape in front of the internal visionary organs and thus becomes 'visible' is *darshan*. This *darshan* could be of a specific subject or an overwhelming, all-encompassing principle, like Vedanta *darshan*, yoga *darshan* or *darshan* of the existence of the omniscient power that controls everything (*Tat Tvam Asi* — Thou art That). By this difinition, the knowledge that dawned upon Buddha was a *darshan* (Buddha *darshan*). Similarly, there could be various darshans like Mastana Mansur's *darshan* (*Ana'l Haqq* — I am God), Nanak *darshan* of unity (*Tu hi Nirankara* — Thou art the only one; *Sat sri akala* — Truth is beyond time), Gandhi *darshan* (of non-violence). One can even stretch this link further to add Newton's gravity *darshan*, Rutherford's atomic *darshan*, Einstein's relativity *darshan*, Bill Gates' DNA (Digital Network Architecture) *darshan*, Ramanujan's hyperspace *darshan*, Hawking's wormholes (ten to the minus 33 centimeters) *darshan*, Michio Kaku's superstring theory *darshan*, and physicists' challenge *darshan* ("Did God have a mother?"), and so on.

These examples unify, the matter-centric approach of scientists with the spirit-centric belief of philosophers. The scientific approach uses matter, particles, atoms and the structure of matter to understand the universe. The other follows the subtle path, using the mind, intellect, senses, etc. to reach extrasensory perception (ESP).

---

10. Sannyasi Gyanshruti, Sannyasi Srividyananda, *Yajna: A Comprehensive Survey*, Yoga Publication Trust, Munger, Bihar, India, 2006, p. 27.

5

Psychometry

THE psychometry can be termed as "seeing through the fingers" — the third sensitive centre associated with the mind. Everyone has had some form of this experience. For instance, take a heap of coins and get some other person to hold just one of the coins for a few minutes. When that coin is put back with the others you will be able to identify and pick up the coin, because it will be warmer than the rest — here you are picking up the heat energy because of higher heat sensitivity of your fingers; but if you are able to pick up the coin after some time when the coin has attained the same temperature — then your fingers are able to pick up subtler energies — your are entering the realm of psychometry. And, if you can know the coin's origin, what has happened to it, whether it was lying for a long time at some place or it was in circulation, you are well trenched into the art of psychometry.

A psychometrist fingers an object to tap into the energies not just of the object itself, but of the energies which have been placed upon it by others — animate or inanimate. The psychometry is founded on the remarkable fact that any exchange of physical energy between an object and the perceiving hand results in a memory record both for the seer of the object and the object itself.

From various investigations, it appears as though 'something is transferred from a human being to an inanimate object and that thing is carried for long periods by the object. This suggests that memory and intelligence can also exist outside of biological organisms. And, this something is, thought impressions, auric imprints, astral records, etc. . . .

The impressions, imprints and records can, as a sort of intelligence network extending from a living individual, reach not only into other minds and cause them to respond, but register on physical objects which serve as reservoirs of discrete intelligence that can be recovered in the future.

During psychometry you are working with the astral vibrations of the object you psychometrize. It is held in your hands, and while you are psychometrizing it you cradle it, pass it from one hand to the other, and from time to time turn it about; this contact aids your awareness of the object, besides helping to settle your mind into tranquility.

The ability to pick up intelligence from objects was investigated as early as CE 1949 by Joseph Rhodes Buchanan, a physician in Ohio, U.S.A. He found that some people he tested were able, for example, to identify medicines hidden in sealed envelopes or to give accurate descriptions of the writers of letters. He then went on to coin the word psychometry — which means, in Greek, 'measure of the soul' — to describe this ability.

Raynor Johnson[1] has presented an outline of a telepathic theory of psychometry. According to him, an "aetheric structure" provides the linking mechanism between the object, the owner of the object, and the psychometrist's mind. The sensitive person sharply focuses upon the object, which is placed in his hands, or in his vicinity at watchable place. He is able to glean verifiable intelligence, as found in the test experiments[2] by Hans Bender.

Psychometry in exceedance involves clairvoyance for which a very ingenious hypothesis has been offered. It suggests that every object is perpetually throwing off radiation in all directions, similar in some respect to, though infinitely finer than, rays of light. The akashic records

1. Raynor, Johnson, *The Imprisoned Splendour*, Harper and Brothers, New York, 1953, pp. 185-189.
2. Hans, Bender, and W.H.C, Tenhaeff, *The Croiset Experiments: Tommorrow*, 1953, vol. II, no. 1.

and impressions seem to be formed by these radiations. Clairvoyance being the power to see through by means of these finer radiations, distance would be no bar to the sight, all intervening objects would be penetrable by these rays, and they would be able to cross one another to infinity in all directions without entanglement. Also, time factor is no problem to read the record and impressions, for infinite spread of time.

For example, says a British occultist Leadbeater:

> I once brought from Stonehenge a tiny fragment of stone, not larger than a pin's head, and putting this into an envelope and handing it to a psychometerist who had no idea what it was. She at once began to describe that wonderful ruin and the desolate country surrounding it, and then went on to picture vividly what were evidently scenes from its early history, showing that infinitesimal fragement had been sufficient to put her into communication with the records connected with the spot from which it came.

The scenes through which we pass in the course of our life seem to act in the same manner upon the cells of our brain as did the history of Stonehenge upon that particle of stone; they establish a connection with those cells by means of which our mind is put in rapport with that particular portion of the records, and so we "remember" what we have seen.

Psychometry can also be confusing, because an object may have been subject to a variety of energies and you have to learn to focus and really concentrate to pick up coherent information regarding different people and areas into which that object has been placed.

The Tibetan monks have made an intriguing observation that psychometry phenomenon was weather dependent and was adversely affected by rain. The psychical phenomenon worked perfectly well at ten thousand feet but would not work at all at thirteen thousand feet above the sea level.

Psychometry is a curious form of general extrasensory perception in which the sensitive person uses an object as the primary inductor of intelligence. However, psychometry cannot be classified as a pure ESP talent. The term extrasensory is a misnomer as the process is indeed fortified by the sensory modality of touch.

5.1 Psychometry Talent Development

Man possesses an astral and a mental body, each of which can, in process of time, be aroused into activity, and will respond in turn to the vibrations of the matter of its own plane, thus opening up before the Ego, as he learns to function through these vehicles, two entirely new and far wider worlds of knowledge and power. Now these new worlds, though they are all around us and freely interpenetrate one another, are not to be thought of as distinct and entirely unconnected in substance, but rather as melting into each other; the lowest astral forming a direct series with the highest physical, just as the lowest mental in its turn forms a direct series with the highest astral.

It is not then difficult for us to grasp the possibility of a steady and progressive extension of our senses, so that we may be able to appreciate vibrations far higher and far lower than those which are ordinarily recognized and picked through our fingers.

Our hands can easily sense energy changes and differences. We have all experienced some aspects of this. When we touch someone or shake their hand, we get definite impressions about them. Our sense of touch helps us to attune to that individual's energy.

Thought impressions, auric showers, ectoplasma sprays, odic forces and or psi-plasma fields leave permanent traces on inanimate objects in use and in close surroundings of every human. These recordings constitute intelligence for all psychometric, clairvoyant and telepathic readings.

As psychometry is so much about the sensation of touch and also about focusing your mind in a more disciplined way, there are several exercises to sensitize your fingers, but you may begin with the one given below:

There are energy lines or meridians, as they are called in psychic terminology, terminating at fingertips. Rub the fingertips of both of your hands face-to-face mildly for a minute or so. Take them apart by about twelve inches, while facing each other. During the period you take deep breath, sustain it, and release; inhale, hold; exhale ratio being 1:2:3 or 2:4:7, whichever is convenient for you. Now bring fingertips too close, repeating the breathing cycle. You can continue to turn on the whole exercise. Within ten minutes or so you will have tingling sensation in your finger tips, signalling your readiness for reading work — psychometric reading. Regular practice of the exercise will in long run, say two to five months, prepare you signally as fast as an electric switch.

After this short exercise, you will have energized as also sensitized your touching abilities. Then you can initiate psychometric reading ability by enlisting the help of a sympathetic friend. This is how you set out on a learning journey.

Assuming that your chosen friend wants to see you progress, you get him to wash his hands and then pick up a stone or a pebble. That also should be washed with soap and water and should be well rinsed. Then your friend should carefully dry his hands and the stone, and then, holding the stone in his left hand, he should think strongly for about a minute, he should think of just one thing — it can be of colour black or white, or good temper, or bad temper, it does not matter what he thinks as long as he thinks strongly of one subject for about a minute. Having done that, he should wrap the stone in a clean handkerchief or paper handkerchief, and hand it to you. You should not unwrap it then and there, but wait until you are alone in your "contemplation room."

As said "with the left hand" and let us first explain the reason. Under the esoteric love the right hand is supposed to be the practical hand, the hand devoted to the things of the world. The left hand is spiritual hand, that which is devoted to metaphysical things. Provided that you are normally right handed, then you will get greater results by using your left hand for psychometry. If you are one of those who are left handed, then you will use your right hand in the psychic work. It is to be observed that you can often get better results with the left hand.

When you are in your room of contemplation, wash your hands, rinse and dry them suitably. Then lie down, make yourself comfortable, in a well-lit or partially lit environment. Thereafter, unwrap the stone or whatever it was, in your left hand, see that it rolls into the centre of your left palm. Do not think about it, do not bother about it. Just try to let your mind go blank, think about nothing, though a difficult task, but certainly possible. Having made your mind noise free, you will start experiencing a very light tingling in the left hand, and next you will get an impression, probably of what your friend was trying to put over to you — thought transference through an inanimate object. You might also pick up the impression that he really thinks you are engaging in a crackpot stunt! If you practise with tranquil mind you will pick up only most rewarding impressions.

After your friend is tired of assisting you, do it on your own, and practise psychometry alone, free from any distraction. In a state of calm relaxation, allow your reflective faculties to function, unimpeded by analytical processes, so that your consciousness is free to receive the information that your emotional–instinctual nature will transmit to it from the astral vibrations of the object being psychometrized.

For the object, go out somewhere, get hold of a pebble which has not been touched by any person so far as you can imagine. This is easy if you are by seashore, or you can dig up a small stone from the earth. By regularly experimenting, you will have truly remarkable results. You can, for example, pick up a pebble and know about the time when it was part of a mountain, how it was swept down by a river and out into the sea. The information that one can pick up through psychometry is truly amazing.

It is possible to pick up a letter which is still in an envelope and to be aware of the general trend of the contents. It is also possible to pick up a letter written in a foreign language, and by running the finger tips of the left hand lightly over the surface you will pick up the meaning of the letter even though you do not understand the individual words. This is quite infallible with regular practice, but never do it just to prove that you can do such a thing. Do it only for the benefit of other people.

As you advance, choose an object that won't have too many outside influences on it. A piece of modern jewellery that has been worn only by one person is a good choice. Antique jewellery can cause difficulties, even if it has been owned by the 'subject' for thirty or forty years. Some people wear chains, bracelets or rings that are never taken off their body; obviously they are then well imbued with that person and no one else. Even a pen makes a good object.

A good procedure is to psychometrize, on different occasions, items with certain features in common and certain contrasted differences, so that you may gain ability and confidence in discerning the vibrations involved in each case. You could, for example, buy a second-hand prayer book and psychometrize it, then an old, well-thumbed novel; or you could acquire an old piece of jewellery and a newly tumbled gemstone, or an old and a new piece of craftwork.

Don't rush through this collecting and psychometrizing of different materials; it is a fascinating and rewarding phase of your self-training. When, however, you feel you have developed real confidence in your abilities, you can proceed to work with complicated items.

Let us consider, as an example, a gemstone mounted as a piece of jewellery, which has passed, maybe, through the hands of several possessors and has been worn on many uneventful occasions as well as a few eventful ones.

You might in certain circumstances receive a panoramic view of all that. If you might — but this would be very advanced psychometry — get behind all that to the making of the stone itself: its volcanic or meteoric origin in vast fires when no life was yet present, and the long ages of slow cooling and pressure in the Earth's curst. Or you might receive something of the drama and fascination of the gemstone market, the deliberation of the lapidary over the stone's form and structure, its cutting and setting. A variety of impressions are possible.

When you have practised on different objects, you will gain a better understading of how psychometry works for you, and you will gradually be able to focus more astutely and take on more challenging objects. You will soon learn if it's a useful tool to get a good connection with different objects.

The process of psychometry has been likened to the growing of water-lilies. The concept is of a lake, whose serene and placid water represents the mind; the lilies represent material gathered in psychometry that arises from the deep waters to blossom in consciousness.

You should always verbalize the information that comes to your consciousness; this is good procedure in psychometry, even when you are alone. Have a tape recorder in action for these sessions; not only will you then have a record of your utterances for later reference, but, more importantly, it will relieve your mind of the possible stress and concern of trying to remember the impressions you receive.

As you progress further in the practice of psychometry, your conscious mind will become more proficienct in grasping the impression proportionately as you give more heed to it. You, too, as a person, will become more skilled in psychometry as you gain more practice in it.

Another of the most effective ways of developing and testing your hand sensitivity is through the use of colour flashcards.

We know that every colour is an expression of energy and has its own unique qualities and characteristics:

1. Take a set of 3x5 index cards and on one side colour it, using a marker, crayon, etc. Use one card for each colour. On the other side, you can list some of the qualities of the colour like frequency, wavelength, etc. Begin with just the rainbow colours

of VIBGYOR — violet, indigo, blue, green, yellow, orange, red.

2. Relax and quieten your mind. Perform a progressive relaxation and techniques for tranquility of the mind. Take a moment to study the cards one by one. Focus on the colour, and visualize the characteristics to yourself.
3. With eyes closed, shuffle the coloured cards after making sure that the coloured surface of the cards are facing upwards. Pull one card from the set, and hold either one or both hands over it. Stay relaxed. Allow your hand to do the sensing. Does it have a warm feel or a cool feel? If warm, it is in the red and orange spectrum. If cool, it is in the blue spectrum.
4. What else do you feel or sense as you hold your hand over the coloured card? Do you think you know what colour it may be? Is there any kind of tingling? Do you notice anything in any particular part of your body? Pay attention to every impression — no matter how odd it may seem. These little details will eventually help you in becoming more knowledgeable of the colour and its possible effects and applications.
5. With practice you will be able to identify colour by its feel. Remember that you are working with subtle vibrational energies casting the impressions.

Do not look for rewards in the midst of your efforts. You will be rewarded when you have practised with desire, determination and dexterity:

> God does not pay weekly. But HE always pays at the end.
>
> — Dutch Proverb

The practitioner has to be in good health in order to withstand adversary psychic impressions, should be animated by pure intentions in mind, and be full of perfection of purity in heart and soul.

Let the practitioner choose a certain time everyday — a time that he can rely upon being quiet and undisturbing — though preferably in the daytime rather than at night — and see himself at that time to keep his mind entirely free for a few minutes from all earthly thoughts of any kind whatsoever and when that is achieved, to direct the whole force of his being towards the highest spiritual ideal that he happens to know. He will find that to gain such perfect control of thought is enormously more difficult than he supposes, but when he attains it, it cannot but be in every way most beneficial to him, and as he grows more and more able to elevate and concentrate his thought he may gradually find that new worlds are opening before him.

A practitioner should also realize that the sin and suffering are there, whether he is able to perceive them or not, and that when he can see them he is after all better able to give efficient help than he would be if he were working in the dark. The moral side of his nature should be sufficiently developed to stand the strain which it imposes. Put briefly, the restrictions are that there shall be no business, no selfish use of the power.

One can develop the skill to trace the misplaced things by concentrating on the person who has lost the object, or on his picture. The faculty can be extended into the realm of finding lost people. Psychometry also goes into the world of police working, when psychometrists are asked for help to trace escaped criminals or to descirbe murderers.

The faculty of psychometry brings clairvoyance and telepathy skills along, but you can learn how to use them realiably and to the best advantage only by increasing sensitivity and fidelity for psychometric investigation.

5.2 Investigation Technique

Certain objects are difinitely a good idea to accept as investigation items. Stones, gems, and crystals have strong energies of their own and you are better-off avoiding them until you've sufficient expertise.

There's a good example to demonstrate this. A psychic held a lump of rock that was from a previously active volcano. As the psychic tuned in, he was overcome by a sensation of burning heat and suffocation. It was overwhelming in its intensity and it took considerable control to release the image and wipe it away. A less experienced psychic could have ended up traumatized for a period of time. Avoid coins and keys because of their tendency of being haunted by so many people. Anything antique will also make 'reading' harder.

Metals of all kinds, linen, silk, gems, crystals and glass hold psychic energies well. Stone is a fair retainer of psychometric vibrations. Therefore, these objects are good for psychic investigation. Whereas, wool, cotton, artificial fabrics, paper wood and earthenware objects are practically useless. Book, though mainly product of paper, retains psychic energies because of being in use with concentration.

Be careful when you are preserving test objects for investigation by an expert psychometrist/psychometer. Your own thoughts may contaminate these specimens, as may the materials with which you pack them. Since wood retains little energy, it is wise to pack your items in a container made of wood, and alternatively in paper, wrap them in some padding material which is new and hasn't been touched by others. Handle these specimens as little as possible.

Before reading, always wash your hands thoroughly and dry them well. This is to cleanse yourself of energies that you would have picked up from other objects. Also, always cleanse after every psychometry reading.

After necessary initial preparation, ask your sitter, the one who has brought the object for investigation, to hand you over the object. You may ask your sitter about the object before s/he hands it over to you, as to how long the object has been with the subject, or object's back record if any which is known, as this information certainly helps you to discern the unknown facts.

Having received the object, unwrap it into your left hand and finger feel the object with a relaxed, focused and benign mind. Then see, what is the first feeling or emotion that comes into you as you hold the object? Peace? or do you feel worried? Begin your enquiry (within your mind) and work on it. Why are they (subjects who have had the object with them) feeling good? or what is worrying them? Start with a basic emotion or feeling and then work at a deeper level.

If you receive a mish-mash of cross-currents of impressions and can't distinguish any one feeling or image, then cleanse everything away and start again. Ask your higher-self to help you tune in to that which is relevant and which will best benefit your sitter.

You might in certain instances receive a panoramic view of circumstances related to the object itself and particulars about the person who touched the object. Generally speaking, more recent impressions associated with an object will be read first — but it is also true that a more powerful impression, even if earlier takes precedence over a later, weaker one.

You might, also in certain investigations, come across deliberations regarding the future actions in the mind of the subject, and even foreshadows of events yet to unfold.

If the outcome of the investigation does not fit with the facts of psychometrized object (or it's subject), then the investigation needs a re-look research:

> If the facts don't fit the theory, change the facts.
>
> — Albert Einstein

Alternatively, the object ought to be psychometrized by another psychometer.

> Better to ask twice than to lose your way once.
>
> — Danish Proverb

Anyway, it is always better to get at least two opinions for any item from different psychometerists.

Don't ever offer false hopes to your sitters because it will leave them in a more vulnerable and unhappy situation than everbefore.

They will appreciate your honesty and concern if you explain the position from the beginning — your level of expertise, skill, ability, talent, faculty, etc.

Another word of warning — people often think of psychometry as a means of contacting people who are dead. You may find someone turning up with their mother's wedding ring or their grandfather's spectacle case. You won't be able to work at the learning level yet and, if you try, you'll only end up with disappointing results that may cause further distress to your sitter. Consistent, controlled communication with spirits can only happen after years of practice; whatever you might achieve before then would be spasmodic and most likely inaccurate.

5.3 Predictive Psychometry

We have seen that psychometric investigation leads us to the impressions left with an object and the circumstances and stages through which the object has come up to the present status. For example, if we investigate a pair of glasses of a person, then a psychometer may come to certain personality tracts of the person, strong ups and downs through which the person may have passed while using the glasses, may receive faint images of the factory where the glasses were given shape, etc. This all is coming from the inner mind and the sensitivity of fingers of the psychometrist. But all this relates to the past and closest present. Then, in order to extrapolate it to future, we ought to have some more data.

Again, we all know palmistry, numerology and astrology have their own limitations, for they use the services of only outer mind in ninety-five per cent cases. And the outer mind being faced by various difficult situations of the present living, cannot be fully relied upon for making the correct and objective predictions.

Further, the canvas of these three predictive systems is limitless and is prone to uncertainties and widely differing formulations. Suppose as many as ten astrologers study a particular horoscope, they are likely to make ten sets of predictions. Possibly one or two might come true while the rest might go wrong. It is claimed that these one or two astrologers had chanced to receive the cooperation of their inner-mind also.

Hence, such predictions, coupled with the powers of the inner mind — ESP, psychometry, telepathic thoughts, clairvoyant sights, clairaudient sound-bits, prophetic visions, are bound to be more accurate and reliable.

It is, therefore, appropriate that psychometrists, clairvoyants study object(s), photograph of the subject having used the object(s), his/her horoscope, birth data, and an impression of the palms, and even a bunch of hair.

They may give their observations, but should never discuss the impressions they gathered while psychometrizing and sighted the scenes clairvoyantly along with, if that is to upset their sitter.

> Give your decision, never your reason; Your decisions may be right,
> Your reasons are sure to be wrong. — Lord Mansfield

> No man can justly censure or condemn another, because indeed
> no man truly knows another. — Thomas Browne

Finally, while making any kind of predictions, it is needless to remind that all the occult formulations have to be followed in word as well as in spirit — like noble cause, mitigation of troubles and traumas launched injustifiably, and social service for the deserving. This will enhance the effectiveness of soul-psychic sleuthing.

5.4 Telegnosis

The telegnosis is an art and ability of psychic reading of history (history is little more than register of the crimes, follies and misfortunes of mankind, according to Gibbon) and assoication of objects. The psychic reading is possible through application of thought transference from cosmic consciousness.

When thought transference is via surroundings it is telegnosis, when thought transference is via material objects which we can hold with our hands it is psychometry and when thought transference is from one mind to other mind it is telepathy.

By now, we know a psychometrist can know the histroy of an object and of persons who have had any association with the object by holding it in his/her hands.

In case of a telepath to indulge in telegnosis, s/he will have to work on the prémise that the thought waves of the powerful personalities, be it kings, ministers, celebrities or scientists get embedded in the objects around them, like palaces, battlefields, theatres, laboratories and/or alien objects. These objects continue to emit telepathic signals all the time, which when received by telepathic experts result in telegnosis. Here, as in psychometry, one need not hold the object in hands, the object may be before the telepath, or even could be away, as is the case of a telepathic transmitter.

It is well known, almost all clairvoyants can travel back in time and be experts in the faculty of telegnosis.

The lure of the unknown and the lore of hidden things have long intrigued the human mind. Even an occult art of tephramancy — seeking of messages in ashes of the dead, and tombs built over the buried dead, has been indexed as a part of telegnosis.

Telegnosis is one aspect of "time" and teleology is the other side of the coin of "time". So far we talked of "past to present" — history, and now we shall discuss the other side "future to present" — causation.

According to "teleological causation," the future determines the present, or at least influences it, like the legendary carrot held in front of the donkey's nose. If a student is working hard in the hope of passing an examination, it is argued that the present spell of hardwork is the effect of a future cause, namely an examination which is to be held at some future date. But, it is surely more true to say that the cause is not examination — which after all may never take place, and so can hardly be the cause of something which has already taken place — but the hope of passing the examination. This hope is not in future; a man will not be working for an examination at this moment unless the hope of passing it has been in his mind at some previous moment, so that the proximate cause of his hardwork is in the past, and not in the future. To some extent, the whole matter is one of juggling with words, but in whatever sense words are used, ideas such as teleological causation can throw no new light on the ultimate problem.

The universe is teleological. Social justice is given in the nature of things. It has been ordained by the Divine. Therefore, it is bound to be there, the sooner the better. God himself has prescribed a moral order in the universe — the prescription to be brought to light by soul-psychic sleuthing techniques.

5.5 Psychic Readings

Though psychic-reading has very little in common with psychometry as far as the process of reading is involved, it finds a place here to supplement the inputs required for sleuthing.

Let us, once again, highlight the term "psychic", which comes from the Greek word psychike (psyche), meaning mind. The psychic refers to aspects of our being beyond the known physical world of our five senses. The psychic data requires an understading of invisible forces that do not register on our scientific laboratory equipment, or any search machine except for bringing momentary changes in the chemical laboratory of a living organism.

Sleuthing exercises and practices for telepathy, clairvoyance, psychometry, Raja yoga, Kundalini-awakening can lead you from mere flashes of sudden insight, rudiments of ESP, premonitary dreams, dim thresholds of prophetic visions at one end, to a perennial contact with cosmic Consciousness at the other. The seer and the seen now appear to be the two different facets of one underlying Reality.

There is, no doubt that human ingenuity will one day discover how this physiological speciality in the systems of such individual can be determined and measured. And also, the method to know exactly the attainment of the "transhuman state of consciousness."

A psychic is sensitive to non-physical forces. S/he can receive ideas, thoughts, or impressions from some distance in proximity (e.g. aura readings), crystal-gazing, telepathic poaching, clairsentience, clairaudience, clairvoyance, psychometry, related to the past or the future, or be aware of things through or around other people without any method of physical perception. Planchet Ouija-board, tarot-cards, dowsing, pendulum swing, hypnotic regression and progression, super-conscious mind-lap, are some of the other techniques available to psychics.

Psychic readers are advised to give an honest, open and unbiased picture of the impressions so gathered.

There are sensitives who are three-in-one type: telepathist, clairvoyant and psychometrist. Andrija Puharich[3] has claimed of Peter Hurkos, who worked with him. The example is cited in his words:

"Two businessmen, Mr. C.L. Wood and Mr. Tom Slick, visited Hurkos in Miami in May 1959. They had arranged to have Mr. Wood's secretary, in Los Angeles, California mail them a sealed package whose contents were not to be revealed to them until after the 'psychic reading' was completed. Hurkos was not allowed to touch the sealed package. Furthermore, it was held by another gentleman who went into the next room so that Hurkos could not even see the shape of it. Hurkos' statement about the contents of this package was as follows:

"I see in this package some brown hair from a dog. I see a leather collar from a dog with brass trimmings on it. This package is about a small dog, brown in colour. The dog has a lame left hind leg. The owner of the dog does not know what is wrong with it. The doctor is not sure what is wrong with it. The doctor thinks that it is some sort of an arthritis. I think that this is not an arthritis but is due to neuritis. I believe this dog will be cured by some sort of a shock."

---

3. Andrija Puharich, *Beyond Telepathy*, Picadore edn., Pan Books Ltd, London, 1975, p. 41.

"The facts in the case are that the sealed package contained some brown dog hairs, and it contained a metal chain from a dog. There was no leather brass-trimmed dog-collar in the box; in this respect Hurkos was wrong. The other statements were remarkable in their knowledge of the situation. The dog in question was a brownish poodle called Cocoa. The dog had been sick for several weeks, limping and favoring his left hind leg. No definite diagnosis had been established by the veterinarian in charge. The most curious aspect of this case is that a week after the reading by Hurkos, the dog was hit by a car but merely rolled over, and after this accident the limp disappeared and the dog has been well since that time."

"Apparently Hurkos received intelligence about a situation several thousand miles away which was not known by the owner of the dog. I'm referring, of course, to the actual diagnosis of the dog's malady and the suggestion of a cure by shock. I think it is fair to assume that the dog suffered some shock when hit by the car."

"Here we have a case where Hurkos not only got knowlege that was in the mind of the owner of the dog, but knowledge that was privy to the dog in the sense that the dog had the affliction connected with the limping. But no one at the time of the reading had any knowledge of how the dog would be cured. Certainly not the two businessmen who were with Hurkos in Florida, nor the owner, nor the veterinarian. In this instance we have some evidence that Hurkos' mind was focused on the far-off dog through the mediation of the chain and the hairs sealed in the package. We have reason to believe that the intelligence that he gained from this object was outside of that of the human beings concerned in the case, therefore pure clairvoyance."

The three-in-one or to say highly sensitive psychics are able to read much more than what is apparent in a photograph of a person under scanner. Let us look at this phenomenon a little more closely. A photograph is being taken of a person. Light from some source strikes the individual being photographed, is reflected from his surface, and enters a camera box. Here the reflected light falls upon a photo emulsion. The photo emulsion is made of tiny grains of silver-halide. The photonic energy activates discrete specks on the silver-halide crystal, and the distribution of these specks of activated silver form what is called the latent image. The latent image is amplified by a subsequent chemical developing process which reveals an image that has a one-to-one correspondence with the person originally photographed.

What is there in this purely physical process of light reflection from an individual as registered on film emulsion that allows sensitives, to gain intelligence other than that physically recorded on the film. Much of the intelligence that sensitives get comes from other segments of time and space than the one in which the picture was taken. This means that whatever it is that is transferred from the person to the film remains on the film as permanent record ready to be read by a sensitive mind, and is of the nature quite similar to psychometric recording. It almost seems as if the film captured a good deal of the life history of the subject latently stored away for many years. At the time that much of the subject's past history is transferred to the film, some bits of his future history are also added to this record. This process has absolutely no analogy in any of the known dynamics associated with matter or energy.

If you wish to develop all the three faculties of telepathy, clairvoyance, and psychometry, you better awaken "Kundalini" with ability to move *kundalini* upward to the crown *chakra*, you will have under your control, a wide specturm of paranormal/supernatural skills — ESP, telepathy, clairvoyance, psychometry, astral travel, lucid dreaming, levitation, etc.

The faculties of telepathy, clairvoyance and psychometry will no doubt manifest themselves, as the man evolves, but you can learn how to use them reliably to the best advantage of humanity.

Psychic readers are advised to give an honest, open, unbiased and professional reading, which should be providing the best solution. For example, a surgeon would not ampute a limb to show that he knew how, but he should do so if the limb needed amputating and the operation would help the patient. All ESP perceivers should proceed upon this idea. Do what is necessary for the help or guidance of the client, but nothing merely to exhibit skill. A strict adherence to this principle will win in the long run.

The study of moods of your sitter may be helpful during psychic readings and narration. Man has different shades of mood in life, all depending on the circusmstances. It may be cheerful, worrisome, enthusiastic, depressive, pragmatic, sentimental, philosophical, mystic, peaceful, merciful, indifferent, composed or the like. Try to access it before giving your readings.

Let us be careful lest in the pursuit of knowledge we despise what may seem to be beneath us — there is nothing beneath us; there is nothing common, for all fulfil the purpose of humanity. Let us not think there is no truth because we do not know, or that we possess the mysteries of the sun becuase we see its light. Let us be humble, that knowledge may raise us; let us be seekers that we may find truth.

> Millions, misconduct and might of the wrong melts before the truth like snow melts before the sun. — N. Vanvari

Every cell in your body emits its own unique rain of vibrations/ frequencies (information) which are as unique to you as your DNA. And people who know this are able to 'hear', 'sense' and interpret these frequencies, hence psychics can know so much about you, and when a psychic's sensitivity is high enough, he can know about you even without ever having met you.

The fact of matter is that there are no high priests in the field of soul-psychic sleuthing, in the market, whatever, you come across, whether three-in-one or a telepathist, or a clairvoyant or a psychometerist, they make an observation only because it appeals to their intrinsic sense of logic and the practice.

5.6 Psychic Tracking

The Nature's system that directs all 'psychic-tracking' and 'human approach to a problem', is as much a science as are chemistry and physics, governed by predictable laws and patterns of action and reaction. You can think of your own system — the five components that determine how you evaluate everything that happens in your life — as a kind of Periodic Table, detailing the elements of human behaviour. Just as all physical matter breaks down to the same basic units, so does the process of human behaviour to one who knows what to look for. It is the combination and structure — how we use these elements — that makes each of us unique. Some mixtures are volatile and produce explosive results. Other combinations neutralize, some catalyze, and some paralyse.

Anthony Robbins[4] writes:

> Several years ago, I began to hear about the incredible success of a man named Dwayne Chapman in tracking down and capturing felons who had eluded the law for years. Known to most as 'Dog', he has become known as the top bounty hunter in the country (U.S.A). I was fascinated and wanted to meet him and discover what makes him so effective. Dog is a deeply spiritual man whose goal is not only to catch the felon, but also to help him make changes in his life. Where this desire came from? It came from his own pains.
>
> As a young man, Dog made poor evaluations about whom he chose as his friends. Out of his desire to belong to a group, he joined a motorcycle gang, the Devil's Disciples. One day in the midst of a drug deal gone bad, a gang-member shot and mortally wounded a man at the scene. Panic ensued; the members immediately fled. Although Dog did not commit the murder, in that state there was no line drawn between being an accessory to murder and being the man who actually pulled the trigger. He ended up serving years of hard time, working on a chain gang, in the Texas prison system. This gave him so much pain that he re-

4. Anthony Robbins, *Awaken the Giant Within*, Pocket Books, London, 2001, p. 332.

> evaluated his entire philosophy of life. He began to realize that his core beliefs, values, and rules had created his pain. He began to ask himself new questions and to focus on his prison experiences as being the effect of choices he'd made with his previous life philosophy. This got him to the point where he believed he must change his life once for all.
>
> In the years following his release, Dog pursued a number of colourful careers and finally settled on starting a private investigation business. When he was brought before a judge for back child-support payments (payments he'd been unable to make while in prison and in the financially unstable period following his release), the judge offered Dog a money-making opportunity in lieu of a payment he would never materialize. He suggested that Dog track down a rapist who had victimized many women in Denver area. The judge suggested Dog use the distinction he'd made in prison to assist him in figuring out what this criminal might be doing and where he might be hiding. Although law-enforcement officials had tried unsuccessfully to find this rapist for over a year, Dog discovered him in three days!
>
> To say the least, the judge was impressed. This was the start of a brilliant career, and today, more than three thousand arrests later, Dog has one of the best records in the country, if not the best. He has averaged over 360 arrests a year — essentially one arrest a day. What is the key to his success? Certainly, a critical factor is the evaluations he makes. Dog interviews his quarry's relatives or loved ones, and in a variety of ways he elicits the information he needs. He discovers some of the beliefs, values, and habitual rules of the man or woman he is pursuing. He now understands their life experiences, which enables him to think the same way they would and anticipate their moves with uncanny precision. He understands their 'system' and his results speak for themselves.

The knowledge of psychology and human behaviour, helped the Dog to track down the criminals. He was a self-developed sleuth-hound. Similar, but gifted 'psychic-trackers' have been picturized in the Hollywood films: "The Day of Jackal," "Outrageous Fortune," and some more films; psychometry does help in 'psychic-tracking.'

The modern psychology is concerned with the mind (the conditioned entity of memory), whereas the Vedic psychology is concerned with the soul (the unconditioned entity of pure consciousness). Methods of modern psychology aim at understanding and healing the conditions of mind, the Yoga psychology aims at going beyond the mind.

According to the Vedic psychology, psychological disorders are caused by a disruption in our connection with our true soul. Its concern is not with the personal traumas of this life as an issue in themselves, but with the ongoing evolution of the soul.

The law of *karma*, tells us that we are responsible for our state in life, even the condition of our birth and childhood. We have created these situations, and we can transcend them as well. It is not necessary to look back upon them (they cannot be changed anyway, nor is there anyone to blame for them). We should rather act in the present moment in such a way that creates an improved condition for ourselves and for all life for the future.

If we want to change anything in our lives, it is invariably one of the two things: either how we are feeling or our behaviours. Certainly, we can learn how to change our emotions or feelings within a context. For example, if you feel fearful of being rejected as an actor, you can condition yourself so that you no longer feel fearful. Or, we can make second kind of change: the change of outlook. A metaphor for this might be that if we want to change the way our computer is processing data, you change the software that you are using so that when you hit the keys what shows up on the screen is formatted differently. Or, if you make a change that will not only affect this type of file, but multiple environments, you can change the computer's operating system. By changing the 'system', we can change as how to interact in a variety of circumstances.

> Nothing splendid has ever been achieved except by those who dared to believe that something inside of them was superior to circumstances. — Bruce Barton

By the Yogic view, true knowledge, perception and happiness is only achieved when the mind is silent, when it is emptied of its burden of emotion, thought and knowledge. This requires emptying the mind of its contents, not sorting out or categorizing them. The practice of yoga itself is traditionally defined "as the negation of the thought patterns of the mindstuff." According to the system of yoga, the intellect can never give us perception of truth. It can only organize ideas. Hence, intellectual understanding has no real value to change our lives, though it can make us function more smoothly or efficiently. Yoga emphasizes not intellectual knowledge but consciousness — moment by moment awareness — as the facts of true understanding.

The Vedic psychology is impersonal and aims at the non-ego. It tells us that we are all different combinations of the same cosmic forces coming through the planets and stars. The ego, our sense of personal identity, is a fiction, an illusion which does not really exist. We all have the same basic nature, both superficial and deep, and must all go through the basic life experiences good and bad, for the growth of our consciousness. No soul gets any special treatment, good or bad, in this regard. Our differences come from being at different stages of this process, not because we are really different or separate, better or worse than one another.

As souls, we all have the same potential and the same basic problems to work out in our destiny. The spiritual goal is to go beyond outer influences — primarily the need to be somebody in the external world. The present body is structure we have created, though not entirely in this life, and one we can change in time by changing our daily action.

The Vedic psychology thus has a spiritual orientation and a focus on the destiny of the soul — its movement from ignorance to knowledge, from bondage to the cycle of rebirth, to liberation into the Divine.

The basis of Vedic psychology, therefore, is in directing us to the spiritual life. This means we must first become conscious of our soul within us. This is awakening to our own sun, the light of truth within us, which is the real light of the world. It is to begin to see the universe within us, and ourself behind the universe. This is to take a longer look into the outer world for our definition as to who we are, but by going back to our internal light, our eternal nature. It is to question our identification with the body, senses, and mind, and to come to rest in our true nature as a conscious being, not as an object or a person in the world. It is to reconnect with our soul's will in incarnation to grow in consciousness and unite with eternal life.

From this basic insight into our true nature and purpose, we must reorient our faculties and the domains of our life. We need the utmost refinement of insight to pierce through the veil of time and illusion and come to rest in the eternal light. We must follow the process of negation to the ultimate point of pure affirmation, seeing our self in all beings and all beings in our self.

It is the deep human insight and admirable penetrating psychology that is at the basis of the Hell and Retribution ideas in the Puranic Hindu Religion. They knew that sweet whistling will not make the buffalo move, whereas whipping will. We know how on the eve of building the great bridge to Lanka, when requests failed to make the ocean-king behave suitably, Rama took out an arrow in anger. The very next instant was the Sagara-Raja pleading with folded hands before Rama. Likewise, to good man of noble deeds, high aspirations and righteous conduct, the Puranic sages held out before him bright prospects and extolled the untold benefits and blessings of good life. Here they tried to appeal to man's human side. But when he indulged in extreme sin and bestial acts of gross sensuality, they knew that it was not the occasion for mincing matters. The beast could only be chastened through a true and vivid description of the inevitable results of his actions. Here we must note that they did not exaggerate or utter any falsehood, but gave a special importance to emphasize the matter by dilating upon it in graphic detail and spared no pains in doing this. They therefore confronted the man with a terrific array of dire consequences that would inevitably accrue to the sinner for his evil actions. They gave graphic descriptions of the various punishments awaiting the wanton transgressor of moral and spiritual laws. This has given rise to modern terminology:

> Without the cane the monkey will not dance.
> — Tamil Proverb

> The cobbler's deity worship is by shoes.
> — Marathi Proverb

A Marathi (Maharashtrian) poet-saint and visionary of experience, Tukaram Maharaj, (CE 1608-1650) says: "God belongs to me and I belong to God." This is the doctrine of Vedanta, and it is soul-sleuthing as well as 'soul-tracking.'

The Buddhist psychology discusses the five *skandhas* — the aggregates that compose our whole mental and physical existence. They are the constituents of our experience, the support for grasping of ego, and also the basis for the suffering of living. Thery are: form, feeling, perception, intellect, and consciousness, also translated as form, sensation, recognition, formation and consciousness. The five *skandhas* represent the constant structure of human psychology as well as its pattern of evolution and the pattern of evolution of the world. The *skandhas* are also related to the blockages of different types — spiritual ones, material ones, and emotional ones.

All of these components will dissovle when we die. And each stage of the dissolution has its physical and psychological effect on the dying person, and is reflected by external physical signs as well as inner experiences.

According to functional psychology, the mental processes of sense-perception, emotion, volition, and thought are the functions of the biological organism and its adaptation to and control of its environment. Functionalism was developed as an alternative to structuralist psychology, according to which the task of psychology is to analyse and describe the nature of consciousness.

The sleuthing ability depends on psycho-physiological make-up. This means, first, that the various kinds of beings, human beings consititute only one; and second, the nature and limits of human knowledge is governed by the physiological and psychological constitution of the human being. This is the same as saying that had human being been of different psycho-physiological make-up than their present one, the nature and limits of knowledge they produce would be different (from that which they now, as a matter of fact, produce). There should be nothing surprising about this claim; for simply imagine our optic nerve being arranged differently; then it is only to be expected that our experience of colours would have been different from our present experience of them. Similar is the case with regard to our other sense organs. It is obvious, then, that our perceptions are ineluctably bound up with the constitution of our perceptual apparatus. To take another example, we are kind of beings who cannot see the back of an object simultaneously with its front. That is, if you hold up an object, say a book, in front of yourself, you can only see its front and not its back. There is nothing mysterious about this observation; on the contrary, it is a correct report about our ways of perceiving. We also know that changes in our biochemical make-up result in changes in our perceptions. It is a fact, then, that our perceptions are a function of our physiological constitution. Our claims as to what sort of things make up the world and what properties they possess, and what relations are obtained among them is a function of our physiological make-up.

But, in addition to our physiological make-up, our psychological constituion determines the nature of knowledge we produce. The term 'psychological' here is to be understood as encompassing the mental and emotional. In short, the psychological consists of the sentient and the sapient, the emotional and the mental respectively. What comes to us through our sense organs is ordered and organized — categorized — according to our psychological constitution. It goes without saying that beings endowed with a different psychological constitution than we are, will organize and categorize differently what they receive through their sense organs, thereby resulting in knowledge claims different from ours. It is to be noted that our psychological make-up allows for variety of ways of organizing and categorizing, each way being appropriate to a certain end and purpose. All the possible different ways of ordering, organizing and categorizing that which comes through our sensory channels and equipment define the 'range of our psychological make-up.'

It should be clear from the above that as human beings we are capable of perceptions and conceptions, actual and potential, lying within a certain range determined by our psycho-physiological constitution.

Psychologists are well aware that wisdom is a real phenomenon. If you pose a battery of problems to subjects who span a range of ages, the older ones will probably give wiser answers than the younger. The posed problem could be anything: deciding on whether you've been cheated in a business deal, or how to settle an international incident that could lead to war. A wiser answer might be to wait and see before acting on impulse, to ask for advice from several sources, or not to take any assumptions for granted. It does not matter really what the problem is. Wisdom is a perspective applied to any situation.

To a psychologist, wisdom is correlated with age and experience, but something much deeper is involved. Spiritual masters speak of a mysterious faculty known as a "second attention." First attention is concerned with the task at hand, with the data being brought in by five senses. It expresses itself as thoughts and feelings. Second attention is different. It looks beyond the task at hand and organizes the deeper levels of ordinary thinking. Intuition and wisdom both grow out of second attention.

Above all things, be not impatient in the pursuit of the knowledge; you will not learn a language in a day, neither must you expect to learn sleuthing in a day, nor must you expect to learn it in an hour. Consider psychometry, clairvoyance, telepathy as soul-psychic sleuthing tools earnestly — not in the light of an amusement, but as a work entailing depth of the thought, patience of research, and one worthy of the highest talents that you can give. If we study it right, we hold within our hands the keys of the mysteries of life. In it are hereditary laws, the sins of the society, the *karmas* of the past, the effect of the cause, the balance of things that have been, the shadow of things to be.

Let us be careful, then, that this knowledge be used aright. Let us be earnest in work and practice, humble if success may crown our work. Let us examine self before we examine others. If we see crime let us consider the temptation of the criminal. If we see faults let us remember we are not perfect.

Mind uncontrolled and unguided will drag us down, down for ever, rend us, kill us; and the mind controlled and guided will save us, free us. So it must be controlled, and psychology will teach us how to do it.

It is the science of psychology that teaches us to hold in check the wild gyrations of the mind, place it under the control of the will, and thus free ourselves from its tyrannous mandate. Psychology is therefore the science of sciences without which all sciences and all other knowledge are worthless.

Lt. Gen (Retd.) Surinder Kochar[5] writes: "The inner shattering of the psychological personality in man is projected out so vividly in the characterization of Arjuna that in the *Bhagavad Gita*, the Pandava prince represents the confused person of the world — the disillusioned youth of all times. The case-history of Arjuna is recorded with scientific precision in the opening chapter of the *Gita*. He is represented as an enthusiastic soldier who had reached this benumbing state of utter dejection. In such a state of dejection, an intelligent man-of-action discovers in himself many a logical arguments each one apparently righteous, to convince himself that he should run away from the field of his duty and positive action. This sense of escapism is detrimental to any great achievement. The exhortation given by Krishna to Arjuna, which is also the eternal *mantra* given by the *Gita* to anyone facing a challenge, is this: One must stand by one's convictions."

---

5. Lt. Gen (Retd.) Surinder Kochar, *Bhagavad Gita: Timelessly Pertinent*, Himalayan Books, 2005, p. xxxv.

Dr. John Gray,[6] a renowned psychologist, says: "Every man knows that when his wife is appreciating him for the little things that he does, what does he want to do? He wants to do more. It's always about the appreciation. It pulls things in. It attracts support."

The famous Amercian psychologist and philosopher William James, who was wont to record the personal testimonies of those who had experienced mental renewal, recommends yoga, meditation . . . for control of the gyrating mind.

Deep, deep within, is the soul, the essential man, the self. Turn the mind inward and become united to that, and from that standpoint of stability, the gyration of mind can be watched and facts observed . . .. Such facts, such data, are to be found by those who go deep enough and only by such.

Thus, by way of psychology we may switch over from the outer 'psychic tracking' to our 'inner-psychic-tracking', i.e. the tracking of enemies (emotions, feeling. thoughts, belief . . ..) on the path of the human evolution.

Now having developed the abilites of telepathy, clairvoyance, psychometry and having gleaned psychology of man, you really have already within your grasp the key to those mysteries of human body, mind and soul, you are bent upon probing.

---

6. Dr. John Gray, *Men are from Mars, Women are from Venus*, website: www.marsvenus.com

6

Sleuthing Oracle

THE word "oracle" is of the Greek origin, and it carries five different senses, or meanings, which are: (1) The seat of worship of some ancient divinity, as of Apollo at Delphi, where prophecies were given out by the priests in answer to queries, (2) The prophecies thus given, (3) The deity whose prophecies were given, (4) A person of unquestioned wisdom or knowledge, or something regarded as of infallible authority, and (5) A wise saying.

The title 'sleuthing oracle' has been used here in the same context, but without the similar high-flown aura. Further, no particular religion, prophet, philosophy, place, professional person, poetry or proverb has been preferred and quoted. Thus, this chapter carries random ideas, concepts, thoughts and teensy-weensy guidelines limited by lurkingly and tangentially and crankily bounded knowledge of the author, in undulating form, similar to landscaping of the soul-psychic sleuthing terrain. Please read through:

> Those who understand me,
> I like them.
> Those who like me,
> I love them.
> Those who love me,
> I worship them.
> I never consider,
> Myself worthy of being remembered. — N. Vanvari

Soul-psychic sleuthing answer brings forth many questions. There is no end to a question/answer session. It can go on forever! if you answer one question, it will bring forth another ten questions. Questions and answers are the pair, the couple, but they have no family planning.

We know that every emotion has a sensation in the physiology. A specific part of the body resonates with definite emotions. When you observe the sensations, the emotions disappear and dissolve. When you observe the sensations, you see that the body and consciousness are separate. As you move on with the observation, you see you are simply linking the sensation with an event outside.

Wisdom lies in de-linking the event with the emotion, and de-linking the emotion with the sensation. Ignorance is linking any sensation, sadness, or other feeling to some event. That makes you more miserable, and it sets the cycle going on and on. Many people go for psychotherapy for years, fifteen years, twenty years, and nothing happens.

In this respect, a psychiatrist likes to say, "You will know a lot about human motivation once you realize one thing: ninety-nine per cent of humanity spends ninety-nine per cent of their time trying to avoid painful truths." Therefore, if you want to avoid the psychological suffering, try to live life within the four walls of (1) truth, (2) positive thinking of positive emotions, (3) logic (along with conscious and conscience) and (4) law of land; and avoid indulgence in superstitions, dream interpretations and omens. Then, people around you will gyrate.

Continue reading, there may be many more oracles and mysteries which have been unveilded by sages, savants and scientists.

The modern world, because of its divorce from the nature, its repudiation of universal laws of growth, its alienation from the Divine and its reliance on indulgence in the show and glitter as the end-all and be-all of life, carries with it the curse attached to luxury, loss of values, flippancy, dissipation and vice, is heading for self destruction.

The world we live in is sorrow's shrine. It echoes and re-echoes with the mocking laughter of transitoriness. The whole life is a ceaseless struggle to ward off misery and gain a bit of pleasure.

The tragedy is that the modern man has absolutely no inkling of the volcanic formations in the collective auric spectrum of the mankind. It is only possible for the clairvoyants or the divinely illuminated to have a glimpse of it. The ghastly fear of a nuclear holocaust or a natural catastrophe which forms an occasional or almost constant feature of the consciousness of millions of sensitive minds all over the earth today, is but a very faint reflection of the auric deterioration of the mankind. Increase in aggression, violence, lust, greed and other unsavoury traits of character are nothing but telltale symptoms of the same disaster. What means the nature would adopt to rescue mankind from this self-caused maelstorm of psychic forces remains to be seen.

Under the skin we are essentially the same; a great fraternity of fools. However, by nature Indians, perhaps more than any other group, tend to regard the unseen as more real than seen. This readiness of belief renders India receptive to every kind of superstitions and perversion, sorcery and sacrifice, diabolism, etc.

We are "worms of earth" because we cling with all our aspirations to earth. If we can enter upon a path of evolution, by which we become less material and more ethereal, a very different order of civilization would be established. Things which now appear indispensable and necessary would cease to be useful; if we could transfer our consciousness with the velocity of thought from one part of the globe to another, the present modes of communication would be no longer required (as it was in Lumeria — full of perfect telepathists). The deeper we sink into matter, the more material means for comfort will be needed; the essential and powerful god in man is not material, and independent of restrictions, laid upon matter. What are the real necessities of life? The answer to this question depends entirely on what we imagine to be necessary. Railways, steamers, airplanes, etc. are now a necessity to us and yet millions of people have lived long enough and happily, knowing nothing about them.

We are communities of cells interacting. Each cell is like a little individual which has its own function, its own *karma*. Whether you are a liver cell that has to digest poison, or a colon cell that has to deal with wind and feaces, or a heart cell facing the task of ramping endless litres of blood, it does not matter; you have your own function. A heart cell cannot want to be a colon cell, otherwise cancer would develop. Each cell must communicate with all the other cells. The colon communicates with the heart and brain. This communication can be experienced as a supreme intelligence, an overall appreciation of who we are. Intracellular communication creates an experience of our life.

You can consciously direct your life. You can live your life one of the two ways. You can be like Pavlov's dogs, responding to all the trends and messages that are sent your way. Or you can be romanced by war, lured by junk food, or captivated by every trend that pours through the TV tubes. Someone once described advertising as "the science of arresting the human intelligence long enough to get money from it." Some of us live in a world of perpetually arrested intelligence.

The alternative is to try something more elegant. You can learn to use your brain (with thoughtful soul-psychic sleuthing techniques), so that you choose the behaviours and internal representations that will make you a better person and this a better world. You can become aware of when you are being programmed and manipulated. You can determine your real values. And then you can act on the things that have real value and purpose.

The trials and ordeals you encounter in life are character-testing, and character-forming. You are not permitted to peek and see what the next test of your faith and understanding may be, any more than a good school teacher would supply the students with a list of the answers to the examination question before examination.

You must learn to live so that you merit easier examinations and this can be done only by mastering the techniques of soul-psychic sleuthing.

Just call a halt in the mad rush of the days, once a while, and ask yourself seriously if, after all, you are putting up the emphasis on the right things. See whether you are giving proper time and attention and interest to the things that are really worthwhile. When you face the realities of life through the vision of some great sorrow or the loss of those dearer to you than your own life, will the things that engross your attention seem as important as they do now?

When you live in harmony with the soul at the centre of your being, everything you do prospers. You may not become a moneyed tycoon for years, or possibly not in this lifetime. Or, being rich may be one of the tests you must go through, to see if you know how to wisely use what has been given to you.

We all need money. It is our medium of exchange for many of good things of life. But money and the honourable way of getting money can be made to serve the purpose of the finer senses, for, "It's the set of soul that decides the goal." The whole gamut of the lower senses may be used, if only one lives in the finer senses, in the upper realms of life. Some millionaires are splendid examples of the possibility of making and spending money in a way that will benefit all humanity.

The soul holds us inexorably to our accounting and carries out the final reckoning to the utmost farthing. We cannot escape the law. If we sacrifice the higher (values and ideals) to the lower, sooner or later we come to a final reckoning and we must pay the price.

There is latent, in each individual soul, the Divine Power sufficient to transform the entire life into perfection. That power is filtered through the human consciousness. There is no other way it can operate, for if God is to do anything for us He has to do it through us.

Right now, the mind is the master and we are the slaves. If the mind says, "Do this," we do it. If the mind says, "Do not do this," we do not do it. If the mind says, "Accept this," we accept it. If the mind says, "Do not accept this," we do not accept it. Most of our life is governed by the mind and the different manifestations of mind.

Coordinating the external faculty with the inner faculty in the mind is a continuous action which is being performed by the ego. For example, if we look in the mirror, what do we see? If we see ourselves, it means that we are observing our own ego only. If we were free of the ego, we would say, "I see the mirror." Although we know that we are seeing a reflection in the mirror, we do not acknowledge the existence of the mirror. What do we see? We see ourselves. That is the functioning of the ego. No one will say, "I see the mirror," but everyone will say, "I see myself." So in a simple situation like this we will see our own ego reflected. With this kind of mentality, how far we will go? We may try to go up, but we will always come back to square one.

Although we live in the world by coordinating the sensorial experiences with the rational mind, negative mental patterns build up unless this sensorial is properly controlled and regulated. To break these intellectual patterns is very difficult. If we think about how much we have to eat and sleep, then food and sleep become obsessions. Comfort and pleasure, name and prestige also become obsessions. When external things become obsessions they rule our lives. In this regard, we should remember the maxim: "Eat to live, not live to eat."

> He who knows both action and knowledge, with action overcomes fear of death and with knowledge reaches immortality.
>
> — *Isha Upanishad*

So long as the human mind functions as a storm-centre of passion, desire and lust there is no way to avoid this distortion and disorientation of the intellect. It needs constant cleansing and purification from within. All healthy religious disciplines are designed to effect this purgation to illumine the intellect with the infalliable 'light' aglow in the soul of man. This is the reason why Revelation was allotted such a high place of honour all through the past. Like the velocity of light — the invariant of Einstein — which is used as the standard of measurement for all other motions and speeds in the universe, there is an invariant hidden deep in the recesses of human consciousness. It sometimes reveals itself specially to gifted men and women in wakefulness, dream or the elevated state of mystical ecstasy. This has been happening now for thousands of years and shall continue for years to come, till all the mankind is established in this sublime dimension of consciousness. The mode of life and social orders of human beings need to be oriented time and again to harmonize them with this evolutionary trasformation in their consciousness. The crises occur when the intellect fails to adjust itself to the change, resulting in upheavals to domolish and reform a disharmonious social order. This is the situation we are facing today.

Mind is the prime cause of pleasure and sufferings, and the whole wheel of life turns and twirls because of mind. This mind is an Alladin's lamp that can conjure into existence comforts and luxuries galore, but it can also raise Frankensteinian monsters that make life a nightmare.

Mind is a terrible god, stronger than the strongest. He who has it under his control is verily the God of gods. Without subjugating this relentless foe, man falls foul of 'follow-me'. Identifying himself with the body which is nothing but a mental construct, he roams about deluded in this endless darkness.

Bertrand Russel[1] says:

> What the world needs is reasonableness, tolerance and realization of the interdependence of the parts of the human family. This interdependence has been enormously increased by modern inventions, and the purely mundane arguments for a kindly attitude to one's neighbour, are very much stronger than they were at any earlier time. It is to such consideration that we must look and not return to obscurantist myths. Intelligence, it might be said, has caused our troubles, but it is not unintelligence that will cure them. Only more and wiser intelligence can make a happier world. . . .

We must realize, intellectual bankruptcy may sometimes be genuine, but may not always be the cause for callous decisions. These may be the conscious decisions made at the bidding of the ultimate master — God.

There's a saying in the computer world, "GIGO: Garbage In – Garbage Out." It means that the quality you get out of a system

1. Bertrand Russel, *Why I am Not a Christian*, Allen and Unwin Ltd, London, 1957.

depends entirely on what you put into it. If you put in bad, faulty, or incomplete information, you'll get the same kind of results. Many people in our culture today give little or no conscious thought to the quality of information and experience as being the daily input.

The knowledge that we have today, Stone Age man did not have. The knowledge which our future generations will have, we do not possess at this moment. Even science tells us that our brain is not fully active, not fully awake. Out of the total capacity of the brain, only about ten per cent is active and the remaining ninety percent is dormant.

After controlling our mind, the task is to start awakening the dormant ninety per cent of our brain. This awakening is self-realization. Finding God is not self-realization. Awakening the remaining dormant brain and removing the barriers which divide the consciousness is realization. This leads to the perfect expression of the precisely tuned instrument which we know as the human being.

If the ultimate aim of knowledge is to illumine the mind, to instil noble virtues and to create an environment of peace and happiness for the greatest number of human beings, then it can be said, without fear of contradiction, the modern knowledge instead of this purpose has created a situation, on account of its ignorance about the aim of life and the forces of evolution, which threatens the very survival of the mankind.

The present-day science and technology with its whole emphasis on the study of the physical world, by its own short-sightedness, denies to itself the glorious vision of emancipated consciousness. The denial of the glorious vision that is the *summum bonum* of human life, leaves no other outlet for the exuberant energy in human beings except to expend it on the gratification of lust or in the pursuit of boundless wealth and power. It is this wrongly directed energy that has been instrumental in creating the present explosive situation of the world.

We have become so divided in our ways that we have forgotten the underlying unity of the quest that unites science and religion. Unified field theory — the quest of Albert Einstein in later years — has returned us to the awareness that science too has its 'god' term. Hence, once again we have the possibility of a synergistic convergence between science and religion — reinforcing rather than demeaning each other's goals.

Rama and Krishna were followed by five leading lights of sixth century BCE — Zarathustra, Confucius, Lao Tse, Mahavira and Buddha. Then came Christ and Mohammed and Guru Nanak. Every human being has to strive to be what they were — an ideal son, ideal father, ideal friend, ideal lover, ideal husband, ideal warrior, ideal statesman and ideal guide.

It must be clearly understood that all the religious movements are shaped by the times and tides in which they rise. God lives and dies as ideas in the minds of men, functioning to man's current needs and desires; the godmen worshiped are more often than not, reflections of himself and his conception of socio-political environment.

This thought has been aptly and delicately explained by William James in his description of Christianity in the Middle Ages: "The monarchial type of sovereignty was . . . so ineradicably planted in the mind of our own forefathers that a dose of cruelty and arbitrariness in their deity seems positively to have been required by their imagination. They called the cruelty 'retributive justice', and God without it would certainly have struck them as not 'sovereign enough'."

The majority of us are still in the hold of the great ship — Humanity, looking out of the portholes. Mystics are the exceptions who climb to the upper decks and vision the wide horizon of a higher world. It is only here and there that some rare soul ascends to the lookout spot of the huge ship, senses the truth and beauty away and above the reach of the physical senses and ESP, and inhabits a spiritual realm more real to him than the physical universe is to the average man or woman.

The last century saw two mystic souls among many other great souls — Suzuki and Krishnamurti.

Dr. D.T. Suzuki (CE 1870-1960), the world's foremost authority on Zen, has explained that the aim of Zen was enlightenment, an immediate, unreflected insight into reality without rationalization or intellectualization, the relation of oneself to the Universe.

Dr. Suzuki emphasized that rational knowledge plays an important role in life and science has contributed greatly to man's benefit; however it has dulled his access to intuitive wealth. He says: "Man does not become free from the intricacies of life by withdrawing into the seclusion of a temple or 'dropping out'. He must be both spectator and participant. A scientist possesses much background knowledge gained from assiduous application to his subject but this knowledge blooms into creativity during moments of silence (tranquil mind)."

Dr. Suzuki made the point that lying dormant in all of us are latent creative and benevolent powers. Because of ignorance we are generally unaware of these powers. Zen could dispel this ignorance and open doors to an infinitely blessed life.

A world roaming philosopher, J. Krishnamurti[2] (1897-1986), says "When there is pleasure there is pain." He asks: "When there is no pleasure and no pain what do you have?" Watch that, watch that very carefully and see what there is — the transcendental state. Krishnamurti's message is that one must look to oneself for the truth, for enlightenment — look inward at yourself.

Few people ever get anything more than a mere glimpse of the true glory of life. Many of us do not sense any real sentiment in our days or see anything above the animal existence, the animal pleasure. We look upon our daily occupation as a disagreeable necessity that somehow or the other might have been and ought to have been avoided, whereas, if our finer perceptions were more keen, we would see the underlying beauty, the infusing spirituality that makes the most common place work or circumstances a means of growth. We settle down to the treadmill of workaday existence and let the routine of

2. Jiddu Krishnamurti, (i) *The First and Last Freedom*, (ii) *Commentaries on Living*, KFI, India.

work run furrows in our souls. Most of us do not really live. We merely exist like a jelly-fish, or a clam, in the lower functionings, while our finer senses dwarf for lack of use.

Why do some people adjust easily and some people find it difficult? Everyone is experiencing the same environment, the same situations, so why is it easy for some and difficult for others? We can say that it is the programming of the mental computer. Yoga philosophy says that it is the body and mind which create the environment in order to experience the outside world. In family situations we create an environment, and when there is a disruption of harmony in that environment, there is tension and fighting. When we cannot cope with that situation, we begin to bottle up and then there is suppression. All this is due to the environment which is self-created by the body and mind. There are certain methods to awaken a different kind of experience. Developing the ability to adjust to the prevailing environment is one method, cultivating naturalness through sleuthing practices is another.

Instinctive urge and transcendental potential reside together in human awareness. When man, fascinated by immediate pleasure, ignores his transcendental potential, he befriends the instinctive urge and fails to assert his humanness. This makes him feel restless. The instinctive urge is neither good nor evil; it is a natural necessity. This urge, which man shares with other creatures, needs moderation and not forceful repression or removal. A balance is required between the two, for together they prepare man for evolution into higher realms of consciousness.

There is an urge in everyone of us to find happiness, tranquility and harmony. We would like to attain psychological balance and avoid the tensions and conflicts of daily life.

Tensions arise from bipolarity of attributes and problems. However, Zen looks upon the dualistic distinctions as useless human inventions. Good and evil, flesh and spirit, truth and falsehood, finite and infinite, positive and negative, material and spiritual, eternal and temporal, subject and object, are illusory distinctions.

And, the inner conflicts — the anxiety, the fear and the guilt — which form a distressful feature of many minds occur because ascent towards higher regions of thought entails the need for greater care of the body and healthier discipline of the mind.

In order to get rid of problems, psychologists have advised to analyse its causes through introspection and self-analysis. These causes may be physical, mental, economic, political or social or of any other type. If a man remembers that essentially he is the eternal self who has come to this world to reap fruits of his past actions, and that his body, sense organs, organs of action, mind and intellect are not he himself but only his instruments, he will never be frustrated, as we are not frustrated by the failures of others. Thus, the basic cause of frustration is not failure but the concept of 'I' and 'mine' which are false, acquired, changing and can be changed. Then the essential remedy to all frustration and in fact to all mental afflictions is to know thyself. This is the remedy supported by all the great religions, their saints and scriptures.

"All the problems of human life", Sri Aurobindo[3] rightly said, "Arise from the complexity of our existence, the obscurity of its essential principles and the secrecy of the inmost power that makes out its determinations, and governs its purposes and its processes." The investigation of the facts of human problems, is the task of sleuthing. However, the enquiry into human problems as a whole cannot be attempted by any single technique exclusively, since man's complex personality cannot be comprehended by any one method. Man is a complex of physical, mental and psychical levels together with a spiritual essence.

Today, in our world, we find that we need two virtues to make our lives a complete success. The first virtue which we lack is vitality, which is not physical strength, but inner strength, will-power, clarity of mind and ability to perform every action with perfection. The second

---

3. Sri Aurobindo, *Essays on the Gita*, Arya Publishing House, Calcutta, 1949, p. 380.

virtue we lack is tranquillity. We are so engrossed in our day-to-day activities, in our intellectual and emotional tensions, that we have lost contact with our inner nature.

The soul-psychic sleuthing, hopefully, addresses both of the above aspects adequately, and enlivens you. Now, and here you start soul-psychic sleuthing . . ..

It seems, the whole world is sick, it is flooded with patients; we know it, we even realize it; the soul-psychic sleuthing is a placebo — a harmless substance to be taken by the patients.

The first objective of the sleuthing is to find out the "truth", the most powerful instrument of the nature. I assure you, if you are "right" (closer to the truth with uncertainties incorporated), your opponents' "millions, mischief and might shall melt before you as snow melts before the sun." Any way:

> Remain seekers, cultivate in the garden of your soul that plant of curiosity that will yield satisfying fruit. — J. Dible

> God spare me sclerosis of the curiosity, for the curiosity which craves to keep us informed about the small things no less than the large is the mainspring, the dynamo, the jet propulsion of all complete living. — John Mason Brown

The second objective of the sleuthing is to watch, observe and accept ourselves. There is a beautiful poem by St. Francis, which reads:

> "God grant me the serenity to accept the things I cannot change,
> The courage to change the things I can,
> And the wisdom to know the difference."

The final purpose of soul-psychic sleuthing is to evolve the true understanding of life, and achieve the sense of fulfilment — awaken yourself — activate your *kundalini* — have self-realization. And, transform the whole system into living experience:

1. Practice relaxation and meditation by removing attention from an effect.

2. Have a fervent desire to entertain only constructive ideas.
3. Have a complete emancipation from discord of any kind if you will be diligent about never hurting others, not even with a wrong thought about them.
4. Search within your mind for a new idea. Do this, by holding your thoughts, emotions, and consciousness still. The idea is already there, and will come to conscious thought — truth always surfaces.
5. Stop looking for results. As long as you keep looking for them you are subtley obstructing evolution.
6. Always concentrate on "Aum/Amen/Amin/Amon/Arhint. . .."

Open your (*chakras*) petals of power and beauty and fling out the fragrance (awakened *kundalini*) of your life in the place that has been assigned to you (by the macrocosmic creator).

Napoleon said: "God is always on the side of the strongest battalions." In the moral sense that is true. He is always on the side of the best prepared, the most vigilant, the pluckiest, and the most determined. However, a codicil can be added to this under the soul-psychic sleuthing philosophy: "God is always on the side of the Truth."

In order to have different realizations and understandings and to have a complete picture, various sleuthing practices and yoga have been prescribed. *Karma yoga* is the yoga of being aware of our actions in the world, and also being aware of the *karmas* and their influence on our personality. *Jnana yoga* is a means to develop awareness and interaction in the world of objects as well as to have the knowledge of the experiences possible in the unknown dimension. *Hatha yoga* is a means to purify the elements of the body and mind. *Raja yoga* is practised to enter the realm of psychic awareness. *Mantra yoga* cuts the bondage of ignorance, and finally *Laya yoga* allows our consciousness to dissolve in the higher identity.

Sleuthing always stresses being positive, creative and constructive. Do not identify with any ideas which are negative or detrimental in nature towards anyone or anything, not even in dreams. This also includes negativity towards oneself, because if there is no negative thought about the self, then there will be no guilt either. Positive thought will create positive desire, positive motivation and positive action whereas negative thought will create negative desire, negative motivation and negative action, and then there will be problems. We face these kinds of problems in our life invariably because of our own volition.

The characteristics such as detachment, faith in divinity, greater introversion, liking for a simple life, austere habits, love of truth, charity, self-conquest and desire for perfection are considered to be the hallmarks of a truly enlightened personality.

The soul-psychic sleuthing has to grow slowly from stage to stage until a new being emerges, in tune with cosmic consciousness, ennobled both in the heart and head, filled with deep humanity and sublime knowledge of the eternal truths. Transformed by the inherent processes active in the normal frame of man, every human being has the potentiality, sooner or later, to be a participant of Life Divine, always acting a noble part, assigned by fate, to make the Earth an Elysium of happiness, plenty and peace.

The evolutionary target in front of mankind will be attained in any case and at any cost. The alternatives before the mankind are either to conform to the laws and canons of this evolutionary thrust or to face devastating hammer-blows of nature for violations, time after time, till the insurgence is quelled and she forges ahead, like a broken horse, made responsive to the rein.

It is not only that human being is evolving, but also the spiritual and ethical laws and understanding are evolving. Not only materialstic thinking has become high-tech but also the soul-psychic sleuthing is becoming hi-tech; for example the death event can be presaged precisely by picturising 'genome'. Spiritual (meditative/Yogic) centres equipped with Faraday cage, high-tech biofeedback equipment and brain-electrical-activity-mapping (BEAM) instruments have mushroomed all over U.S.A and Japan.

Although every human being who has a strong will and an ability to persevere can reach the quiet and peaceful state required for sleuthing, the devotion and practice, all takes time. And, time is a commodity most people are short of these days.

The trial and error, the frustration which arises from initial failure, the constant going back to square one, all make serious inroads into the amount of spare time an average individual can spend on doing something that isn't directly concerned with his work or his home life. Because of social or family duties, economical or professional commitments, it's difficult for most average men and women to give the necessary time to a soul-psychic search.

The result is that most people will do nothing about it. They put up with strains because they don't see any immediate way out; it is part of living and they just accept it.

Is the modern young man really too busy to give an hour a day to self-improvement, self-enlargement, soul-psychic sleuthing? One hour a day for a short time profitably employed would enable men of ordinary capacity to master a complete science. One hour a day in ten years would make an ignorant man a well-informed man. In an hour a day boy or girl could read twenty pages thoughtfully — more than seven thousand pages in a year. An hour a day might make — nay — has made — an unknown man famous, a useless man a benefactor to his race. Think of the mighty possibilities of two, four, yes, even six hours a day that are often thrown away by young men and women in frivolous amusement.

The challenge is to live a deliberate, studied, self-disciplined life, always considerate of others, always concerned for the common good; a life grounded in various good habits that form a strong character.

Once the path of life's journey is known, a lot of work goes into maintaining the orientation and developing inner capacities — telepathy, clairvoyance, psychometry, ESP, intuition and strong will.

This comes out of living in awareness and digesting experience *vis-à-vis* one's self. Abraham Lincoln and Nelson Mandela spent years on this type of journey.

Soul-psychic sleuthing would bring into the orbit of man's observation a world more extended and amazing than the sidereal universe. Unprecedented progress in material science has brought mankind to a point in its evolutionary career where it must either extend the frontiers of its knowledge to know more about the working of intelligence forces of nature or pay for its short-sightedness and ignorance with its sanity and life.

Soul-psychic sleuthing may give you glimpses of your strength and weaknesses. It clears the way for your opportunities to be seen by you. It makes you alert and full of energy to face the threats hanging around you. It fully covers SWOT analysis. Besides, it turns your thought away from wrong beliefs and causes you to see that whatever God wants you to do is what you want to do.

A lofty aim and a firm purpose to adhere to soul-psychic sleuthing is to strengthen character and add dignity and beauty to life, while an ambition that grovels, that looks down, weakens the character and then demoralizes the whole being. Sometimes we try to hide, even from ourselves our real aims and motives, but this cannot be done. Everyone who knows us sees which way we are going, whether upward or downward, whether we are aspiring or wallowing. No pretence can deceive the world as to the road we have elected to travel, and the aspiring soul, the one who is struggling to get up as well as to get on, but who will not allow allurements to draw him from the straight path of his highest ideal, wins the respect and admiration of all.

When we practise sleuthing, we need to practise it for attaining balance, harmony and equilibrium in all aspects of our personality and expression. We do not believe that by inducing certain states of consciousness, we can improve the quality of our life. We believe that by experiencing life as it is, and by discovering and knowing our limitations, we can evolve mentally, intellectually and physically.

Remember that the intention of the vision during soul-psychic sleuthing is to warn the lower-self of the approach of some calamity, either in order that it may be prevented or, if that be not possible, that the shock may be minimized by preparation.

The fruits of soul-psychic sleuthing, when it is truly achieved, give one a new lease on life, redouble an individual's capacity for vigorous and creative action by eliminating all obsession with the pursuit of pleasure or the evasion of pain, and indeed promote the full enjoyment of life with all its good and bad, its beauty and ugliness. It permits one to act instead of constantly reacting. It frees the mind from the eternal conflict of the opposites, increases the joy of living and the ability to cope effectively with life's problems. Even more, it enhances one's feelings of compassion so that mind's freedom cannot be used to the detriment of others and that alone is no small virtue in today's environment.

It is an excellent thing to acquire sleuthing ability, to cultivate the faculty to turn possibilities into realities — the genius who does things, brings about great material results. We protest only against the false estimate of the sleuthing techniques, against their being placed above the higher and nobler qualities of brain and heart. They can and frequently do exist side by side, and when the lower is made to serve the higher we have one of the highest, the finest and the most useful types of mankind.

Hope the objectives of soul-psychic sleuthing philosophy were possible to blazen in the sky, where they would burn into consciousness of every life, the marvellous results of even one hour a day spent in persistent, concentrated, earnest self-culture.

Yet if you are one of the wayward few who wish to break off from the multitudes, who grope the straight and narrow path towards Heaven, and want to follow the more alluring shortcuts to Hell, the soul-psychic sleuthing is no solution.

Verily, it is easier for a camel to pass through the eye of a needle than for a sleuthing person to pass through a door. And whether the door be a barn door or a temple door it might be wiser that he should consent to be an ordinary man and walk in rather than wait till all the difficulties involved in a sleuthingness are resloved.

> To be nobody-but-myself — in a world which is doing its best, night and day, to make you everybody else — means to fight the hardest battle which any human being can fight, and never stop fighting.
>
> — E.E. Cummings

The moment we realize that we have command over a psychic talent, there will be tendency to use it according to the nature of our personality. Then the power play begins on the psychic level and the grandiose idea of, "I'm, great!" develops. The idea, "I am superior", "I know what is happening" comes and then after some time depression sets in.

Depression sets in because when psychic experiences of this kind come in contact with our external nature, which overshadow the psychic manifestation and after some time it stops. By the time manifestations have stopped, you may have already advertized your qualities and abilities to the extent that you are giving demonstrations of your powers in front of people, when there is a short circuit and no results. Then a psychic depression begins, which is the worst kind, as there is no cure for such depressions. Even your psychic readings may result in harm for your sitter. Except such situations, soul-psychic sleuthing is a placebo.

> Do not blame God for having created the tiger, but thank him for not having given it wings.
>
> — Indian Proverb

God does everything for our good. But God is not a man we can wheedle into doing some thing for us, as we seem to think. God balances accounts, offered in temples, churches, and all sorts of religious congregations. Some persons will lay a little more than they feel they can afford in the basket/hundi. Others will first look to see what the average offering is, and do likewise. Some will surreptitiously drop in a dime or a quarter, and there are those who forget all about it. Demand and supply are two ends of the same stick, and niggardly givers know it.

It is sometimes objected that the possession of the faculties of telepathic readings, clairvoyance, and psychometric investigation destroys all privacy, and confers a limitless ability to explore the secrets of others. No doubt, it does confer such an ability, but it is quite inconceivable that any one, having before him the splendid fields for investigation which telepathy, clairvoyance and psychometry open up, could ever have the slightest wish to pry into the trumpery little secrets of any individual man. Well for us that these grand faculties will not be possessed by winged tigers — all humanity until it has evolved to a far higher level in morality as well as in wisdom.

Adopting philosophies of "favours" and "forgiveness" will make you fly free in the space of superconsciousness. Those, who would use you only for favour of sleuthing guidance you might grant, stand in awe of you. Others can say all manner of things against you, slander you, revile you, defame you, and persecute you, but everything they attempt to do will somehow turn into an advantage for you.

You must make an effort to remain in soul-psychic awareness, it can expand so that you are always alert to get the guidance from sleuthing excursions. The veil is lifted for you; you have a job to do. The virtues, or values worth expressing are yours to express.

There are people who are very earnest about pursuing the path of self-perfection to such an extent that they are free from lust, anger, and greed. They are definitely not the demonic type, but their knowledge of scriptural ordinances is very meagre though they are not antipathic to it. Circumstances do not permit their acquiring accurate and elaborate knowledge of the scriptures. They pursue the right path, being prompted by their pure motive. Their earnestness is bound to take them upward on the ladder of evolution — soul-psychic sleuthing or no sleuthing.

Cultural and social values keep changing. There was a time when card-playing and even dancing were considered to be infractions of God's laws. In order to account for this and other similar value drifts, the doctrine of human evolution is not enough, soul-psychic march is the answer.

Soul — the higher-self — is the avenue through which to express joy, peace, serenity and intelligence; the mind feels these pleasures and activates them into correct thoughts and manifestations.

Our own nature is so base, proud, ambitious, and so full of its own appetites, judgements, and opinions, that if temptation is not restrained, it would be undone without remedy; therefore, are we tempted to the end that we may know overselves and be humble. Know that the greatest temptation is to be without temptation, wherefore be glad when it assaults thee, and with resignation, peace and constancy resist it.

Life is a great teacher: it is a great manifestation of soul, and soul manifests the Supreme. Hence, all methods are good and all are but parts of the great aim, which is devotion. "Devotion is success in action," says the *Bhagavad Gita*. The psychic powers, as they come, must also be used, for they reveal laws. But their value must not be exaggerated, nor must their danger be ignored. He who relies on them is like a man who gives way to pride and triumph, because he has reached the first wayside station on the peaks he has set out to climb.

One may see that just about everything is an obstacle of one kind or another, and feel dejected as if there was no solution to the problem. Definitely, there is a solution, but it requires determination and will-power to work out one's perfection with absolute faith in the ever–presence of Divine Grace. Success is certain as it is the law of nature that one's deepest wish will be granted if intense devotion and yearning is there.

"If this life is not a real fight in which something is eternally gained for the universe," says Professor William James, "It is no better than a game of private theatricals. But it feels like a real fight, as if there were something really wild in the universe, which we with our idealities and faithfulness are needed to reform."

There is no more real fight than that which is being waged perpetually between man's higher and lower nature — the natures being identified and detected by sleuthing techniques. If this lower nature triumphs; if one elects to live only in his coarser animal nature, in his lower senses, he pays for his choice in coin of his finer nature, in the gradual atrophy of his noblest qualities.

Some would say that metaphysical and soul-psychic pursuits have nothing to offer; that to dabble in them is to repudiate reason and true science; that a belief in magic and the supernatural is to regress to the age of superstition or to a childish mentality which uncritically accepts all marvels just because they are marvellous.

Let the reason be your prudent minister, a loyal guide and a wise counsellor. The reason is light in darkness, as anger is darkness amidst light.

Savants and many others around the globe believe that the future is immutable, which means that you have seen the effects even before the causes have come into action. According to quantum physics this is possible. However, research has shown that the 'precognated future' is perhaps the 'strongest possible outcome', based on the present trend of events, if it continues to be so. If by the application of free will or otherwise, the present trend of events can be changed, the real happenings in the future may differ from the predicted future. Nevertheless, our habits have become so hardened over the years, that we cannot change our ways of living, even if we try. And that is why we are predictable. Even so, in quantum physics, an electron on being disturbed from its path of rotation has the free will to choose a new path of rotation; but invariably it chooses the same old path because it is familiar and easy. This explains how or why precognition and hence soul-psychic sleuthing works.

Technological inventions will promote certain changes and will help improve the standard of living. Reforms may accelerate the changes and will humanize the system. Perhaps the standard of living will improve, but along with it, the dehumanizing process is getting strengthened. We are creating wars.

Each war, however deadly, would but provide the base for a still deadlier one. The only remedy lies in changing the direction of the human mind from the temporal to spiritual objectives. This has to be done one day to conform to the evolutionary change in the human brain. But it would be a blessing, indeed, if this could be done before the hanging sword falls. Let us learn from history. Let us avoid mistakes that the others have made. Let us create a new civilization.

The goal for sober-minded thinkers is to cast another look on the prevalent values and norms to find where the error lies. If this is done, the need for the reorientation of our thinking and planning will at once become apparent. The aim of nature is to lift Man to another dimension of consciousness, to be a superman in his own right possessed of amazing powers of body and mind.

Future man would not be an ascetic wedded to monastic vows, but a warm-blooded human being, with all his instincts intact yet well under control, living in a strife-free, harmonious world, in perennial communication with universal consciousness. The biological variations in his system will be observable, but not the variations in his illuminated mind.

The holistic exercise of soul-psychic sleuthing is to see that your spiritual vision opens up and it does not remain opaque, for it might have hobbled you in all ways. Your spiritual vision becomes clear, with your perservering practice, even "Beyond the Visual Range," as it is called BVR for a radar — a vision of Reality.

Soul-psychic sleuthing control and monitor switch has to be 'ON' always; and not intermittently showering a glimpse of goodness now and then, when you have merely been playing a peek-a-boo!

Man, working in variety of civilizational environments, collected empirical data and elaborated crafts of considerable ingenuity. This is the story of 5000 years of life in the river valleys on Nile, the Euphrates and the Indus. It covers "the history of clothes, textile, jewellery, cities, houses, temples, arms and armours, vehicles, domestic animals, crafts, writings, scriptures, and pottery." Every man was bound by the status into which he was born. Neither freedom of untramelled inquiry nor man as an individual, had yet emerged. Popes, prelates and kings ruled by the Divine Right. And questions could not be raised when the Bible or the Vedas gave all answers.

Such is the panorama of man's history on this Earth, of his knowledge both of the external world which surrounded him and of his inner-self. Science did enhance man's seeming wisdom; but neither science nor technology answers the fundamental questions: Has life any meaning? What is man's destiny? What am I? Where am I going?

"Unless a breed of modern inquisitors take possession of us all, we will continue to uphold the scientific truths that the Earth goes round the Sun and that man along with the lizard, the chimpanzee, the hippopotamus or just fungus, is a product of long evolution by natural selection and that the story of our being and becoming what we are is, genetically speaking, about 3000 million years old. Measured on this scale of time, man's social and cultural evolution represents a small segment of time of barely 10,000 years. Before that for another 10,000 years or more, man had lived precariously, gathering fruit and hunting," said Haksar.[4] Man can seek truth through soul-psychic sleuthing.

Reality is not an exhibit for man's inspection, labelled 'Do not touch'. There are no appearances to be photographed, no experiences to be copied, in which we do not take part. We re-make nature by the act of discovery, in a poem or in a theorem. And the great poem and the deep theorem are new to every reader, and yet are his own experiences, because he himself re-creates them. They are the marks of unity in variety; and the instant when the mind seizes this for itself, in the art of telepathic thought or in the science of clairvoyant vision, or in the technology of psychometry, the heart misses a beat.

We must catch up with the advanced level of long-lived spirituality. . . . Only by mastering the soul-psychic sleuthing can we ensure ourselves of an impregnable moral defence, a powerful and up-to-date economy and adequate means to join the awakened souls of the past in defeating the corrupt and perverted thoughts of greed, lust, prejudice, hatred and war. Soul-psychic sleuthing promises and

---

4. P.N. Haksar, *Premonitions*, Interpress Ltd, Bombay.

epitomizes man's inherent ability for transcendence from relativity to Reality.

It is said that in his later years when Einstein was trying to develop the 'Unified Theory of Relativity' he rejected many of his hypotheses and perceptions saying that the Good Lord could not have created the world in such a complex manner! Anyway, soul-psychic sleuthing is a complicated task, but so is the living a life in this complex world.

The preceding discussion on various parameters and factors, it is hoped, has given you an idea of the complexity as well as interlinkages of various factors of modern living on the one hand and the development of the techniques for better life and the future evolved life on the other. Live on. . . .

Where there is no vision, people perish. There is an urgent need to create a vision for mankind drawing its sources of inspiration from the long march of Man in search of knowledge, both of himself and of Nature. Bernard Shaw once said: "The fact that a believer is happier than a sceptic is no more to the point than the fact that a drunken man is happier than a sober one. The happiness of credulity is a cheap and equally dangerous quality."

Hope, from the Future Man of the world, one can expect a high level of intellectual attainment, sense of responsibility, social consciousness and rational attitude, etc.

But carping critics are always around. Every other savant with an opinion will be asking, "Why think of the soul-psychic sleuthing when millions are going to bed hungry? And maybe equally large numbers are prospering and enjoying riches through fraudulent means?" That debate may rage on like it has for centuries since the earliest civilization, but it is verily surprising to note that as you practice soul-psychic sleuthing, you yourself shall experience peace and prosperity.

It is a fact of life that, "love begets love." These words are so hackneyed that captain F.D. Colabavala,[5] blushed to type them, yet

5. Captian F.D. Colabavala, *Tantra the Erotic Cult,* Orient Paperbacks, New Delhi, 1976, p. 141.

only the most sagacious put them into practice. "I don't know why. I am convinced that what is more than anything else lacking in life of an average well-intentioned person of today is being able to give and receive love and affection." A wise man will avoid improper speech, bullying and braggart boldness.

Our energy is increased by adopting a more refined or sensitive existence, by taking a more appreciative and affectionate mode in life. It is important to be more creative or artistic, and to strive to improve our expression in life, both with our speech and our hands. It is helpful to have more beauty and colour around onself and in one's environment. One should increase one's feminine attributes if one is woman. If one is man, it helps to give more respect to the women in one's life, particularly as the beloved, or the muse on an intellectual plane.

We are the only beings on the planet who lead such rich internal lives that it is not the events that matter most to us, but rather, it is how we interpret those events that will determine how we think about ourselves and how we will act in the future. One of the things that makes us so special is our marvellous ability to adapt, to transform, to manipulate objects or ideas to produce something more pleasing or useful. And foremost among our adaptive talents is the ability to take the raw experience of our lives, relate it to other experience and create from it a Kaleidoscopic tapestry of meaning that is different from everyone else's in the world. Only human beings can, for example, change their associations so that physical pain will result in pleasure, or vice versa.

Albert Einstein says, "The important thing is not to stop questioning. Curiosity has its own reason for existing. One cannot help but be in awe when he contemplates the mysteries of Eternity, of Life, of the marvellous structure of Reality. It is enough if one tries merely to comprehend a little of this mystery everyday. . . ."

According to Cheiro, a well-known occultist, "To know is power — let us then be wise, and use our brains with every good intent, that at the end we come with tired eyes, and give to Nature more than what she lent."

Let your conscience be the benchmark for you. Soul-psychic sleuthing shall certainly lead to peace, joy and finally to ecstatic and heavenly life.

The soul-psychic sleuthing makes you understand paradigm establishing humanity's relationship to the universe: human as a microcosm. Each person is a miniature of the macrocosm. All the forces that make up the universe (cosmos) are also functioning within us all.

The world moves in a predetermined direction according to well-established principles. There are no exceptions to rule. If we follow those rules we can say so many things. The divine arithmetic is so exact and precise that we can in advance say where a particular planet (sun, moon, mars, mercury, ...) will be and under what condition *vis-à-vis* the other planets at a particular point of time. Such exactitude of time and movement can only be studied and not questioned.

So is the case with the mighty ocean of star-clusters, composed of galaxies within a galaxy, a lone star (God) amidst yet another giant star system is wheeling in the depths of space. The stars, the star-groups, the star-systems maintain their own axial and orbital flights, tiny and mighty, resembling interwoven galactic wheels. It is a galactic tapestry in motion. This motion is yet to be unveiled.

> Who knows now and who can declare which are the paths that lead to the gods. Only their lower habitations are visible, who dwell in regions of supreme mystery. — *Rigveda* III.54.5

Act . . . begin soul-psychic sleuthing. . . . May be you will experience all the fun, adventure, magic, and mystery of life along with the exhilaration, the exultation and the evolution of your own spirit.

Bibliography

Atkinson, William Walker, *Practical Psychometry and Crystal Gazing*, U.S.A.

Bedi, Ashok, *Path to the Soul*, New Age Book, New Delhi, 2005.

Blavatsky, H.P., *Practical Occultisim*, Theosopical Publishing House, Madras, India, 1967.

Blavatsky, H.P., *The Voice of Silence,* Theosophical Publishing House, Madras, India, 1968.

Blitz Editons, *The Unexplained Mysteries of Mind, Space and Time*, Orbis Publishing, Hungary, 1992.

Cavendish, Richard, *The Black Arts*, Picacor, London, 1977.

Chopra, Deepak, *The Seven Spiritual Laws of Success*, Excel Books, New Delhi, 2000.

Denning, Melita and Osborne Philips, *Psychic Power A Practal Guide*, New Age Books, New Delhi, 2002.

Farvington, Kaven, *The History of Supernatural, Chancellor Press*, Octopus Publishing, London, 2000.

Frieolander, John, Gloria Hemsher, *Basic psychic Development*, New Age Books, New Delhi, 2000.

Gillchrest, Muriel Noyes, *The Power of Mind*, Crest Publishing House, New Delhi, 1999.

Kaw, M.K., *The Science of Spirituality*, Full Circle Publishing, Delhi, 2000.

Kinsman, Francis, *The Future Tense*, Pendulaum Publishing, England, 1980.

Leadbeater, C.W., *Clairvoyance*, Theosophical Publishing House, Madras, India, 1965.

Ostranders, S., and Schroeder, L., *Psychic Discoveries Behind the Iron Curtain*, Prentice–Hall, New Jersy, 1970, also Abacus, England, 1973.

Puharich, Andrija, *Beyond Telepathy*, Picador, London, 1973.

Rampa, Lobsang T., *The Third Eye*, Corgi Books, London, 1967.

Rawcliffe, D.H., *Illusion and Dellusions of the Supernatural and Occult*, Wehman, New York.

Ravindra Kumar, *Psychic Development: All You Wanted to Know About*, New Dawn, Sterling Publishers (P) Ltd, New Delhi, 2001.

Vanvari, Nandlal, *Understanding Mysteries of Mind*, D.K. Printworld, New Delhi, 2004.

Vanvari, Nandlal, *Dreams: As foreshadows of the future, mirrored in fantasies of the present and fixations of the past*, D.K. Printworld, New Delhi, 2009.

Verner, Alexr; *How to Converse with Spirit Friends*, U.S.A.

Ward, Tara, *Discover Your Psychic Powers*, Academic Publishers, New Delhi, 2000.

Index

absence of conscious mind, 68
absolute faith, 259
act of,
    communal awareness, 163
    visual concentration, 180
adaptive talents, 264
Advaita, 173, 207
advent of CT scans and MRIs, 106
Agrippa, Cornelius, 148
akashic records, 80, 210
Aladdin's lamp, 1
all-knowing nature, 204
Analysis of memory, 29
ancient philosophers, 83
ancient seers of India, 204
anthropology, 148
application of thought transference, 22
Arigo, Jose, 132
Aristotle, 84, 188
arrested intelligence, 242
art of,
    problem-solving, 19
    psychometry, 209
Articulate Knowledge (*sruta-jnana*), 166-67
aspects of contemporary physics, 207
astral aura, 170
astral clairvoyance, 170
astral projections, 200
Astral sight, 169
astral travel(s) (AT), 159, 227
astral vibrations, 210
Astral vision, 170
astral-projection, 190
astrology, 221
Asuras, 202
Atlantis, civilization of, 206
Atman, the Universal Consciousness, 25
Atman-Parmatman, 26
Atri, 202
attachment of satisfaction, 158
attitude of science, 2
AUM, 143
auric showers, 212
Aurobindo, Sri, 183, 250
automatism, 190
autonomic nervous system, 126
availability of clairaudience faculty, 186
Avalokiteshvara,
    incarnation of, 206
awakeness,
    experiences of, 203

awareness,
subtle field of, 161
awareness of non-duality, 71
Ayurveda, 186
backward time-travel, 165
Bacon, Francis, 77
Badarayana, 88
Bandler, Richard, 66
Barrett, Sir William, 93
barrier of space, 150
basic truths, 203
basis of telepathy, 109
Bates Technique, 176
beginning of world, 8
behaviourism, 24
belief system of ancient world, 193
Bell, Sir Charles, 85
Bender, Hans, 210
Benham, G. William, 84
Berger, Hans, 93
Bermuda Triangle, 140
bestial acts of gross sensuality, 233
Bhagavad Gita, 259
Bharadvaja, 202
Bharata, 204
Bhavani, 61
Big-Bang proposers, 49
bigger fields of influence, 164
biological processes, 108
bipolarity of attributes, 249
birth of Christ, 82
blank unconsciousness, 171
body language changes, 55
Brahma, 202
Brahman, 3, 54
concept of, 3-4
idea of, 3
brain-electrical-activity-mapping (BEAM), 254
brainwave divisions, 111
brainwaves, 103, 111, 137, 160
branches of science, 171
Buchanan, Joseph Rhodes, 210
Buddha (Lord), 20, 49
Buddhist faith, 82
Buddhist mystic, 83
Buddhist psychology, 234
Buddhists, 206-07
calirvoyant ability, 184
Calligaris (Prof.), 55, 114, 168
candle technique, 179
Cannon, late Walter B., 117
carnal eyes, 182
carnal mind, 111
Carrel, Alexis (Dr), 59
Cassandra, 193
causation, 223
cause of,
pleasure, 245
sufferings, 245
Cayce, Edgar, 132
centre of consciousness, 82, 126
cerebrospinal fluid, 175
chakra(s), 25, 180-81, 252
technique, 180
Chanakya, 204
character-forming, 242
character-testing, 242
Cheiro, 264
chemical processes, 108
Chinese culture, 31

Chirognomy, science of, 84
Chopra, Deepak, 162
Christ, 247
  birth of, 82
Christianity, 247
Christians, 207
Churchill, Winston, 131
civilization of Atlantis, 206
clairaudience, 30, 169, 185, 187, 206, 225
  faculties of, 167
clairaudience faculty,
  availability of, 186
clairaudient information, 186
clairaudient prophecy, 185
clairaudient sound-bits, 222
Claire, Prophet Elizabeth, 205
clairsentience, 187, 206, 225
  capability, 189
clairsentient excursion, 189
clairvoyance (*avadhi-jnana*), 30-31, 36-37, 49-52, 95, 98, 165-66, 167-69, 176, 180-81, 186, 206-07, 218, 224-25, 227, 236, 238, 254, 258
  ability, 182, 201
  definition of, 168
  development of, 166, 174
  eyes to, 189
  faculties of, 167
  investigations, 112
  learner, 179
  meaning of, 165
  powers of, 200
  prevision type of, 171
  Simple, 169
  talent, 179
clairvoyance in space, 169
clairvoyance in time, 169
clairvoyant(s), 183-84, 202, 205, 241
  ability, 174
  exercise, 176
  experiences, 182
  eye, 170
  readings, 212
  sight(s), 178, 222
  view, 175
  vision, 135
  witches, 202
clairvoyant/telepathic manifestations, 207
clarity of mind, 250
clear sensing, 187
closed society, 166
Colabavala, F.D., 263
collective consciousness,
  energy of, 164
collective unconsciousness, 35
colossal epochs of time, 187
commanded wisdom, 191
common sense, 50
commonplace of existence, 171
communal awareness,
  act of, 163
communication system(s), 91, 145
complete science, 254
complex capability of mind, 98
complexities of telepathy, 153
compulsive thinking, 36
concentration of mind, 44
concentration practice, 181
concept of (psychological) time, 205
concept of,
  Brahman, 3-4

self, 111
spiritual being, 159
conception of socio-political environment, 247
conflicts of daily life, 249
Confucian texts, 31
Confucius, 34, 90, 155, 247
conscience, 50
conscious mind, 67
absence of, 68
purification of, 125
conscious states,
scrutiny of, 24
conscious thought, 252
consciousness,
centre of, 82, 126
different levels of, 76
dimension of, 245
higher realms of, 249
mobile centre of, 65, 167
nature of, 56, 234
radual unfolding of, 165
rays of, 56
state of, 56, 73, 131
transhuman state of, 225
unfolding of, 165
unification of, 183
constant structure of human psychology, 234
constructive ideas, 252
contemporary physics,
aspects of, 207
continuity of soul, 58
continuous telepathic contact, 164
contradictory thoughts, 123
control of mind, 182
cosmic consciousness, 87, 116, 222, 253
representation of, 97
cosmic energies, 196
cosmic law, 89
cosmic mind, 71, 73, 196
Crance, George, 9
creation,
plan of, 8
creative energy, 164
creative scientific discoveries, 94
Croiset, Gerard, a Dutch clairvoyant, 184
Crookes, Sir William (British physicist), 129
cross-cultural problems, 156
crystal gazers, 202
crystal-gazing, 190, 225
Curiosity, 264
cycle of human civilization, 204
cycle of rebirth, 232
Dalai Lama (His Holiness), 206-07
Darwin, 15
David-Neel, Madame, a prolific writer on Tibetan mysteries, 41
deep dreamless sleep,
phase of, 197
deeper unconscious,
language of, 196
deep-memory process, 150
definition of clairvoyance, 168
degree of,
detachment, 21-22
distance, 21
emotional charge, 21
intensity, 22
will-power, 126
democracy,
dream of, 199

Demonic entities, 135
Depression, 257
depth of thought, 236
depth psychology, 148
Descartes, 64-65
desciplines of Tibetan Buddhism, 143
detachment,
  degree of, 21-22
Devas, 202
development of,
  clairvoyance, 166
  instrumentation, 161
different levels of,
  consciousness, 76
  mind, 76
different manifestations of mind, 243
different spiritual traditions, 76
dimension(s) of,
  breadth, 159
  consciousness, 245
  height, 159
  length, 159
  problems, 53
Disembodied Mind, 65
distance influence, 133
Divine Grace, ever–presence of, 259
Divine Intelligence, 16
Divine Mind, 10, 173
Divine Power, 243
divine realization, 205
Divine Right, 262
Divine scheme of things, 86
Divine will, 87
Divinisation of individual, 45
Dixon, Jean (1918-1997), 184
doctrine of human evolution, 258
doctrine of Vedanta, 234
dogs of war, 39
domain of senses, 68
doubt-waves, 184
Dream Clairvoyance, 192
dream images, 196
dream of democracy, 199
dream visionaries, 202
Dreams of prophetic, 194
Drummond, Henry, 92, 156
dualistic distinctions, 249
Durov, Vladimir, 134
Dzogchen,
  practitioners, 200, 202
  view, 201
ears to clairaudience, 189
earth-bound spirits, 132
earthly thoughts, 218
East Euopean researchers, 134
easy-to-use mechanism, 164
Eccless, Sir John, 139
ectoplasma, 136
ectoplasma sprays, 212
Edison, Thomas Alva, 147
EEG,
  Use of, 93
effectiveness of soul-psychic sleuthing, 222
ego,
  plays of, 21
Einstein('s), Albert, 55, 98, 106, 246, 263
  ESPs, 99
  relativity darshan, 208
  theory of relativity, 169
electro-encephalo-graphic waves (EEGs), 108

elements of human behaviour, 229
Elysium of happiness, 253
emotional charge,
  degree of, 21
emotional sensations, 108
emotional tensions, 251
emotional–instinctual nature, 214
emotion-field, 114
Emotions, 100
Empirical Knowledge (*mati-jnana*), 166-67
endocrine system, 137
energy field, 164
energy of collective consciousness, 164
enlightened personality, 253
enlightenment,
  occurrence of, 198
EQ (emotional quotient), 156
esoteric love, 213
ESP(s), 25, 30-31, 44, 73, 77, 96, 99-101, 109, 115, 118, 161, 168, 208, 211, 222, 227-28, 247, 254
  cards, 127
  centres, 100
  cognition, 99, 178, 184
  existence of, 102
  games, 50
  heightened sense of, 204
  offshoots of, 98
  phenomenon of, 102
  power(s) of, 109
  rudiments of, 224
  recipients of, 174
eternal distribution of energy, 164
Eternal knowledge, 65
eternal nature, 233
eternal truths, 253
eternal values,
  realization of, 25
eternal Vedas, 204
etheric double, 170
Etheric sight, 169
ever–presence of Divine Grace, 259
evil spirits, 132, 200
evolution of life, 120
evolution,
  forces of, 246
  ladder of, 258
  Law of, 15
  path of, 114
evolutionary movement, 188
evolutionary trasformation, 245
exchange of physical energy, 209
existence of,
  ESP, 102
  worlds, 146
expansion of creativity, 25
experience of,
  outer senses, 96
  awakeness, 203
expression of individuality, 205
external mind, 74
external physical signs, 234
extrasensorial centres, 175
extrasensory powers, 144, 168
eye of mind, 1
eyes to clairvoyance, 189
faculty(ies) of,
  clairaudience, 167
  clairvoyance, 167
  psychometry, 218
  telegnosis, 223
  telepathy, 227

Fakhri, Yusif El, 12
fakirs (Muslim ascetics), 52
false knowledge, 59, 62
family problems, 53
Father Jertullin (A Christian), 194
feeling,
  psychic sense of, 187
field(s) of,
  human-consciousness, 45
  intelligence, 160
  psychic domain, 43
final purpose of soul-psychic sleuthing, 251
First attention, 236
five pure lights, 201
five senses, 58
  sensual feeling of, 159
flow of electricity, 197
forces of,
  evolution, 246
  nature, 43
foresight,
  types of, 94
form of,
  dream, 196
  hypertension, 39
  Shastras, 204
  Shrutis, 204
Fo-shu-hing-tsan-king, 189
foundation of telepathy, 113
Francis, St., 251
Frankensteinian monsters, 245
free-soul life, 49
Freud, 69
function of soul, 8
functional psychology, 234
functioning of ego, 244
Functions of mind, 8
Gandha Baba, 143
Gandhi, Mahatma, 129, 131
Ganzfield stimulation, 189
gardens of Heaven, 1
Gardner, John, 5
Garga, 204
Garuda, 202
Generations of Tibetan lamas, 207
Gibran, Kahlil, 80
God,
  mind of, 173
  Power of, 8
  telepathic command of, 153
  vision of, 202
God-realized persons, 48
Goethe, 51
Gogh, Van, 51
Gogh, Vincet Van, 129
goniometer, 148
Gotama, 202
gradual unfolding of consciousness, 165
gratification of lust, 246
Gravitational fields, 155
Gray, 11
great knowledge of,
  light, 201
  space, 201
Greek thought, 188
Grinder, John, (a linguist), 66
Gropius, Walter, 5
growth of knowledge, 53
Gurdjief, George Iranovich, 81
Guru Nanak, 247

Gypsies, 205
gyrating mind, 238
Hagelin, John (Dr), 47
hallucinations, 190
hallucinatory clairaudience, 187
Hanuman (Lord), the monkey-god, 87
happiness, 232
Hart, Ben (professor of Animal Physiology), 101
harvest of insight, 22
Hatha yoga, 252
healthy religious disciplines, 244
hearing voices,
  psychic ability of, 185
heart *Chakra* (centre), 61, 182
heightened sense of ESP, 204
Helena Petrovna Blavatsky, Madame, 206
helper-soul, 129
Hermetic exercise, 176
high telepathic ratings, 154
high tension wire,
  vibration of, 185
high-class living, 39
higher consciousness, 196
higher realms of consciousness, 249
higher-self, 194, 259
highest spiritual ideal, 218
high-flown aura, 239
highly sensitive psychics, 226
high-sea warfare, 134
Hildegard (1098-1149), female hermit of Benger, 35
Hindu(s), 148
  faith, 82
  lore, 204
  mystic, 83
  mythology, 82
  philosophy, 80
  Religion, 233
holy angels, 194
Home, Daniel Dunglas, 130, 132
Howitzer, 123
human awareness, 249
human behaviour, 230
  elements of, 229
  process of, 229
human beings,
  teleportation of, 140
human civilization,
  cycle of, 204
human communication, 186
human consciousness, 36, 98, 243
  recesses of, 244
human ego, 177
human evolution, 238
  doctrine of, 258
human insight, 233
human intelligence, 242
human knowledge,
  limits of, 234
human limitations, 45
Human Mind, 66, 125
human motivation, 240
human psychology,
  constant structure of, 234
human soul, 79
human-consciousness,
  field of, 45
hyperspace darshan, 208
hypertension,
  form of, 39

hypnogogic half-dreams, 112
hypno-meditation, 186
I-Ching, 31-32
ida-nadi, 118-19, 181
idea of,
    Brahman, 3
    growth, 188
    meditation, 21
ideation of thoughts, 91
ignorance,
    world of, 45
illuminated mind, 261
illusory distinctions, 249
images of nature, 64
immediate pleasure, 249
incarnation of Avalokiteshvara, 206
Indian occultism, 143
Indian Rope Trick hallucination, 153
Indian(s), 241
Indian sages, 151
individual,
    psychological states of, 24
individual,
    actors, 159
    experiences, 75
    mind, 71
individuality,
    expression of, 205
infinite potencies of vibrations, 143
infinite space-time continuum, 166
information transfer, 150
inner capacities, 254
inner consciousness, 29
inner experiences, 234
inner or spiritual sciences, 28
inner sense, 24
inner-mind, 75, 77, 222
inner-psychic-tracking, 238
insight,
    refinement of, 233
instances of repetition, 195
instinctive knowledge, 96
Instinctive urge, 249
instrumentation,
    development of, 161
integrative intelligence, 83
intellectual function, 141
intellectual knowledge, 20, 96
intellectual tensions, 251
intellectualization, 248
intellectual-mental energy, 118
intelligence transmission, 152
intention of vision, 256
internal communication, 95
internal light, 233
internal representations, 242
interpretations and omens, 240
Intracellular communication, 242
intrinsic sense of logic, 228
introspection, 250
Intuition, 51, 96, 161, 236, 254
intuitive apprehensions, 98
intuitive awareness of self, 97
intuitive knowledge, 96
Investigation Technique, 218
invisible energy field, 107
inward realization, 97
Italian witches, 199
Jaimini, 204
Jaina way of thinking, 166
Jamadagni, 202

James, William, 23, 51, 238, 259
Jews, 207
jivanmukti, 72
Jnana yoga, 252
Johnson, Raynor, 210
journey of discovery, 54
Jung, C.G., 32
Jungian psychology, 196
Kabir, Saint, 53
Kalam, APJ Abdul, 10
Kaleidoscopic tapestry of meaning, 264
karma(s), 49, 86, 151, 207, 237, 241
Karma yoga, 252
Karmic Cycle, 196
Karmic Law, 36
Kashyapa, 202
Kaw, M.K., 114
Kennedy, F. John, 185
Kennedy, Robert, 185
kinds of thoughts, 121
kinesthetic (feeling) sensitivity, 189
kinesthetic people, 189
kinesthetic systems, 56
King, Martin Luther, 51, 129, 185
knowledge of,
  Lord, 23
  past lives, 29
  psychology, 230
  rishis, 204
  truth, 28
known dynamics, 227
Kodikal, Deepa, 61
Koestler, Arther, 138
Krishna, 247
Krishnamurti, J., 23, 247-48
Kritya Shakti (creative power), 143
Krush (Professor), 199
kundalini, 83, 227, 251-52
Kundalini-awakening, 224
kundalini system, 118
laboratory experimentation, 47
lack of energy, 123
ladder of evolution, 258
Lakshmi, 61
language of,
  deeper unconscious, 196
  dreams, 196
  sleuthing, 15
  symbols, 196
Lao Tse, 247
laughter of transitoriness, 240
Law(s) of,
  Evolution, 15
  karma, 231
  life, 54
  Nature, 8, 134, 156
  truth, 54
Laya yoga, 252
Leadbeater (British occultist), 211
Leibniz, 162
less-than-perfect childhoods, 109
level(s) of,
  ordinary thinking, 236
  psyche, 190
  soul-psychic sleuthing, 116
  superconsciousness, 52
  transparency, 205
levitation, 206, 227
Lewis techniques, 177
Lewis, H. Spencer (Dr), 177-78

liberation of soul, 73
Life Divine, 253
life-energy, 80
life-force, 131
life-producing,
 storehouse of, 118
light of truth, 232
light reflection,
 physical process of, 227
limitation of time, 29
limits of human knowledge, 234
Lincoln, Abraham, 255
list of speculums, 190
lives of seers, 203
logic,
 intrinsic sense of, 228
logical reason, 24
low-class living, 39
lucid dreaming, 227
Lucrelius, 188
luminosity of self, 61
Lutzenberger, 13
Macintosh, 104
macrocosm, 115
macrocosmic creator, 252
magic key, 1
magnetic waves,
 vibrations of, 137
Mahabharata, 90, 204
Mahabharata times, 204
Maharsi, Shri Ramana, 11
Mahashay, Lahiri, 206
Mahavira, 247
malevolent spirits, 135
Mandela, Nelson, 255
manifestations of *prana*, 111
man-made machines, 113
manomania, 40
Mantra yoga, 252
mantras, 87
mantrika remedies, 87
Manu, 202
mass psychotic images, 146
material universe, 102
materializations of mundane vibrations, 143
matter of experience, 201
Max, Heindel (occult scientist), 83
Mayan culture, 206
meaning of clairvoyance, 165
mechanism of visual organ, 60
meditating monk(s), 52, 202
meditation, 238
 idea of, 21
meditative suspension, 195
medium for telepathy, 161
medium of communication, 130
mediumistic monk(s), 52, 202-03
mediumship, 206
MEG (magneto-encephalo-graphic), 113
memory centres of brain, 105
mental body, 212
Mental experimentation, 47
mental healing,
 various schools of, 193
mental health, 132
mental impression, 96
mental kingdom, 40
mental manipulation, process of, 133

mental processes of sense-perception, 234
mental stream of associations, 179
mental weaknesses, 40
mental-suggestion, 133
messages of,
  prophecies, 185
  soul, 22
metaphysical pursuits, 260
metaphysical things, 213
method(s) of,
  physical perception, 225
  modern psychology, 231
Michio Kaku's superstring theory *darshan*, 208
microcosm, 115
Middle Ages, 205, 247
Milton, 38
mind of God, 173
mind,
  movement of, 24
Mind-reading (*manah paryaya-jnana*), 166
Mipham (Himalayan Leonardo da Vinci), 37
Mirror magic, 190-91
mirror magic conjurers, 202
mobile centre of consciousness, 65, 167
mode of communication, 92
modern communication technology, 27
modern computer technology, 104
modern knowledge, 2
modern psychology experts, 156
modern psychology, 231
modern psychology,
  Methods of, 231
modern scientific researchers, 147
modern terminology, 234
modes of,
  communication, 186
  transmission, 186
Mohammed, 247
moments of crisis, 91
monastic vows, 261
Moore, George, 41
moral imperatives, 46
moral laws,
  transgressor of, 234
moralistic traditions, 39
motor impulses,
  transfer of, 133
movement of mind, 24
M-theory, 163
Muktananda (Swami), 46
multi-cultural societies, 156
multi-ethnic societies, 156
multiple-personality syndrome, 197
mundane vibrations,
  materializations of, 143
mutual telepathy, 158
Mutual understanding of thoughts, 159
Myers, F.W.H., 92
mysteries of,
  life, 98
  nature, 8
mysterious force, 139
Mystic Clairvoyance, 173
mystic experiences, 192
Mystics, 202-03, 207, 47
Mystique Cross, 205

Nagarjuna, 203
Narada, 204
Narada Purana, 202
natural disasters, 102
natural healing powers, 205
natural necessity, 249
nature of,
    consciousness, 56, 234
    knowledge, 235
    mind, 201
    physical universe, 28
    tulpa, 141
Near-Death-Experiences (NDEs), 128, 155, 159
negative thought, 253
nervous system, 170
neurobiology, 207
Neuro-Linguistic Programming (NLP), 66
neurotransmitter line, 118
neuro-transmitters, 105
New Age, 2, 133
Newton, 162
Newton's gravity *darshan*, 208
Nietzsche, 7, 51
nirvana, 49
Nisargadatta Maharaj, 9
non-duality,
    awareness of, 71
non-ego, 232
non-perception of stimuli, 59
non-violence, 207
normal range of perception, 200
Nostradamus, 206
numerology, 221
objective mind, 81
objective predictions, 221
objective senses, 74
objective(s) of sleuthing, 18, 251
occular Fatigue technique, 176
occult scientists, 183
occurrence of enlightenment, 198
ocular evidence, 32
odic forces, 212
offshoots of ESP, 98
Omniscience (*kevala-jnana*), 166, 190
oral traditions, 204
ordinary consciousness, 77
ordinary thinking,
    levels of, 236
organisms,
    species of, 55
organs of action, 250
orthochromatic process film, 145
outer sciences, 28
outer senses,
    experience of, 96
outer-mind (conscious mind), 68, 124
Out-of-Body Experiences (OBEs), 25, 128, 196
painful austerities, 34
palmistry, 221
paralysing patterns, 151
paranormal faculties, 2
    prevalence of, 1
paranormal phenomena, 204
para-psychologists, 83, 146
parapsychology, 134, 148
Parashara Shakti, 204
parasympathetic activation, 119

parasympathetic nervous system, 118
paroptic vision, 165
part of telegnosis, 223
past life regression phenomenon, 150
past lives,
  knowledge of, 29
Patanjali, 204
path of,
  evolution, 114
  soul-psychic march, 26
  time-travel, 165
patience of research, 236
Penfield, Wilder, 106-07
pent-up electric potentials, 197
perception,
  normal range of, 200
  reception of, 189
  type of, 103
perception(s) of, 71, 100, 232
  mind, 165
  movement, 59
  truth, 232
perceptive abilities, 166
perennial state of superconsciousness, 83
perfect clairvoyant, 205
perfection of purity, 217
period of Rahu, 87
periphery of visual perception, 62
personality tracts, 221
perspective of telepathy, 118
PET (Positron Emission Tomography), 119
phase of deep dreamless sleep, 197
phenomenal powers, 205
phenomenological approach, 158
phenomenon of ESP, 102
Philo, Jewish philospher, 174
philosophers,
  spirit-centric belief of, 208
philosophical reason, 24
philosophies of,
  favours, 258
  forgiveness, 258
phobias, 151
Phoenix, Susan (Dr), an acknowledged aura photographer, 133
photonic energy, 227
physical affliction, 184
physical ailments, 53
Physical dreams, 194
physical energy,
  exchange of, 209
physical perception,
  method of, 225
physical process of light reflection, 227
physical science,
  realm of, 77
physical senses, 75, 91, 247
physical universe,
  nature of, 28
physio-electrical aspect of *prana*, 111
physiological make-up, 235
physiological speciality, 224
physiology, 240
Picaso, 129
picturesque-thoughts, 144
pingala-nadi, 118, 120, 181
plan of creation, 8
Plato, 174
plays of ego, 21

Plutarch, 5
Poe, Edgar Allan, 130
Positive thought, 253
possession of psychic powers, 25
possibility of,
 communion, 92
 error, 183
 understanding, 22
power(s) of,
 concentration, 179, 191
 cosmos, 160
 ESP, 109
 God, 8
 psyche, 95
 self-control, 131
 telepathy, 108-09
 thought, 111
Powerful Intelligence, 16
powers of clairvoyance, 200
practice of psychometry, 216
practitioners of psycho-kinesis (PK), 138
prana, 77
 manifestations of, 111
 physio-electrical aspect of, 111
Pranabananda (Swami), 160
precognition, 260
prediction(s), 51
 ten sets of, 221
Predictive Psychometry, 221
premonitary dreams, 224
present modes of communication, 241
present-day science, 246
prevalence of paranormal faculties, 1
previous life, 149
Prevision, 169
prevision type of clairvoyance, 171
Price, H.H. (Oxford Philosopher), 158
primary inductor of intelligence, 212
procedure in psychometry, 216
process of,
 human behaviour, 229
 mental manipulation, 133
 psychometry, 216
processes for sleuthing, 34
production of meaning, 158
prophecies,
 messages of, 185
Prophetic vision(s), 169, 171, 222, 224
Providential Design, 88
pscho-physical activities, 154
pseudo-self, 10
Psi-plasma, 145, 155
 fields, 212
psychiatric symptoms, 22
psychic ability of hearing voices, 185
Psychic(s), 168
 artists, 132
 atmosphere, 142
 attacks, 134
 awareness, 182
 domain, fields of, 43
 energies, 219
 forces, 241
 function, 33
 investigation, 219
 investigations, 89
 phenomenon, 117
 potentials, 37
 practice, 181
 readers, 200, 202, 225, 227
 reading(s), 89, 225

seeing, 177
sense of feeling, 187
sensitivity, 142
sight, 178
talent(s), 42, 257
violence, 134
psychic powers,
possession of, 25
psychic powers of *tejaleshya*, 134
psychical levels, 250
psychical phenomenon, 211
psychic-reading, 224
psychic-trackers, 230
psychic-tracking, 229-30
psychism, 51
psychoanalysis, 76
psycho-kinesis (PK),
practitioners of, 138
psycho-kinesis, 136, 139
psychokinetic activity, 135
psycho-kinetic force, 138
psychokinetic push, 192
psychological balance, 249
psychological disorders, 231
psychological make-up, 236
psychological pressure, 197
psychological states of individual, 24
psychology of man, 238
Psychology, 76, 207
knowledge of, 230
science of, 237
task of, 234
psychometric impressions, 47
psychometric investigation, 218, 221, 258
psychometric reader, 179
psychometric reading(s), 47, 213
psychometric vibrations, 219
psychometrist(s)/psychometer, 218-19
psychometry, 30-31, 36-37, 49-50, 52, 84, 166, 209-11, 212, 214, 216, 218, 221-22, 224-25, 227, 230, 236, 238, 254, 258
art of, 209
faculty of, 218
practice of, 216
procedure in, 216
process of, 216
realm of, 209
technique of, 145
technology of, 262
Psychometry Talent Development, 212
psychopath, 128
psycho-physical activities, 112
psycho-physiological constitution, 236
psycho-physiological make-up, 234-35
psycho-physiological relaxation, 126
psychotherapy, 76, 240
psychotic's hallucinations, 112
Psychotronics, 133
Puharich, Andrija, 65, 178, 225
puharich technique, 178
Puranic sages, 233
pure clairvoyance, 226
pure consciousness,
state(s) of, 28, 111
purification of,
conscious mind, 125
subconscious mind, 125
unconscious mind, 125

quality of intention, 116
quantum of energy, 161
Quantum physics, 106, 163, 260
Quinine, 187
Radhakrishnan, S., 19, 78, 98
radio-broadcasting station, 157
radio-frequency spectroscope, 157
Rahu,
    period of, 87
Raja yoga, 224, 252
Rajdak, Dr Zdenek (Czechoslovakian researcher), 134
Rama (Lord), 04, 233, 247
Rama (Swami), 198
Ravi Shankar, Sri Sri (an enlightened master), 149
rays of consciousness, 56
Reality,
    structure of, 264
realization of eternal values, 25
realm of,
    physical science, 77
    psychometry, 209
real-Self, 10
rebirth,
    cycle of, 232
re-birth cases, 150
Rebirth phenomenon, 149-50, 152
recalls, 149
reception of perception, 189
recesses of,
    human consciousness, 244
    mind, 45
recipients of ESPs, 174
refinement of insight, 233
regular geometrical figures, 179
reincarnation, 151
relationships, 151
Relativity,
    Unified Theory of, 263
Rene, French philosopher, 64
repetition,
    instances of, 195
representation of cosmic consciousness, 97
Rhine E. Louisa, 102
Rhine, J.B., 102
Rhine, Joseph Banks, 76
Rigveda, 104
Rimbaud, 51
rishis,
    knowledge of, 204
ritual process, 192
Robbins, Anthony, 229
Royal College of Science, 93
RSPK (Recurrent Spontaneous Psycho-Kinesis), 138-39
rudiments of ESP, 224
Russel, Bertrand, 245
Rutherford's atomic *darshan*, 208
sacred scriptures, 167
Sagara-Raja, 233
Saiid, Abu (Persian mystic), 52
samadhi,
    state of, 203
samskaras, 77
Sanders, Alex, 199-200
Sanskrit language, 62
Sapta Rishis, 202
Saraswati, 61
Schlitz, Marilyn (paranormal investigator), 172-73

Schutz, Alfred, 158
Science fiction, 173
science of,
  Chirognomy, 84
  psychology, 237
scientific reason, 24
scrutiny of conscious states, 24
seat of soul, 58
second attention, 236
second objective of sleuthing, 251
second-hand prayer book, 215
second-sight, 171
seership, 204
self,
  intuitive awareness of, 97
  luminosity of, 61
Self-acceptance, 39, 42
self-analysis, 250
self-awareness, 188
self-contained computer, 104
self-control, 38-39, 42
  power of, 131
self-deception, 176
self-discipline, 43
self-disciplined life, 254
self-discovery, 151
self-dominion, 37-38, 41-42, 44, 46-48, 50
self-effulgent, 24
self-enlargement, 17, 254
Self-expression, 17
self-growth, 17
self-hypnotization, 56
self-image, 48
self-improvement, 254
selfishness, 170
Self-knowledge, 28-29
self-love, 54
Self-mastery, 38
Self-mortification, 46
self-realization, 131, 246, 251
  state of, 73
self-torture, 202
self-training, 215
self-unfoldment, 28
sense energy changes, 212
sense of sin, 34
sense organs, 59, 250
sense perception(s), 57, 78
sense-perception,
  mental processes of, 234
sensitive person, 212
sensory modality of touch, 212
sensual feeling of five senses, 159
sensuality, 170
serial X-ray of soul, 32
sexual intercourse, 200
Shankara, 203
Shastras,
  form of, 204
Shaw, Bernard, 263
sheetaleshya, 134
Shiva (Lord), 82
Shivananda, Swami (Hindu mystic), 89, 149
short-sightedness, 255
Shrutis,
  form of, 204
shut-out sense impressions, 41
Simple clairvoyance, 169
sins of society, 237
Sixth Sense, 98, 101

skandhas, 234
Sleuthing, 12, 23, 29-30, 37, 41, 50, 252, 255
  ability, 24, 234, 256
  exercises, 224
  guidance, 258
  methodology, 21
  oracle, 239
  practices, 249
  techniques, 19, 42, 44, 259
sleuthing,
  language of, 15
  objective(s) of, 18, 251
  processes for, 34
  second objective of, 251
  task of, 250
sleuthingness, 257
sober-minded thinkers, 261
socio-political environment,
  conception of, 247
Socrates, 185
soma-rasa, 100
somnambulence,
  state of, 93
soul,
  liberation of, 73
  messages of, 22
  serial X-ray of, 32
soul energy, 84
soul signals, 33
soul-God, 26
soul-inspiration, 27
soul-psychic,
  abilities, 34
  attributes, 18
  awareness, 258
  illumination, 5
  investigation, 51, 63
  march, 149, 258
  pursuits, 260
  search, 254
soul-psychic march,
  path of, 26
soul-psychic sleuthing, 1, 5, 8, 12, 16, 25-29, 36, 41, 49, 52, 54, 75, 115, 120, 156, 193-94, 199, 207, 228, 236, 239, 242, 251, 253-58, 260-63, 265
  effectiveness of, 222
  final purpose of, 251
  levels of, 116
  practices, 83
  system of, 3
  techniques, 53, 224
  terrain, 239
soul-psychic techniques of telepathy, 52
soul-tracking, 234
space-time continuum, 25
species of organisms, 55
Speculum(s), 190
  list of, 190
Spinoza, 175
spirit voices, 148
spirit-centric belief of philosophers, 208
spirit-guides, 131
spiritual aspiration, 171
spiritual awakening, 156
spiritual being,
  concept of, 159
spiritual dreams, 194
spiritual excellence, 124
spiritual humanity, 204

spiritual laws,
transgressor of, 234
spiritual masters, 174, 236
spiritual objectives, 261
spiritual realization, 203-04
spiritual strength, 156
spiritual teachers of humanity, 36
spiritual traditions, 82
Spiritual vision, 165, 169, 171
spiritualism, 154, 156
split personality, 76
SQ (spiritual quotient), 156
SQUID (Semiconducting Quantum Interference Device), 113
Stalin, Joseph (Russian dictator), 206
standard of living, 260
state of Cholinergia (approaching alpha brainwaves), 153
state(s) of,
consciousness, 56, 73, 131
mind, 24-25, 41
pure consciousness, 28, 111
samadhi, 203
self-realization, 73
somnambulence, 93
witness-consciousness, 46
Stone Age, 246
storehouse of life-producing, 118
strength of telepathic communication, 127
stress,
symbols of, 197
Stromberg, Gustar, 78
strong will, 254
structure of,
energies, 29
Reality, 264
subconscious mind,
purification of, 125
sublime knowledge, 253
Subtle energy, 47
subtle field of awareness, 161
subtle vibrational energies, 217
suffering of living, 234
sugar-coated personality, 42
superconscious energy, 78
Superconscious mind, 73, 203
superconsciousness,
level of, 52
perennial state of, 83
super-ego, 69
supernatural phenomena, 120
super-natural power, 78
supersensitive clairvoyants, 201
supersensitive perception, 195
supersensorial impressions, 168
Supreme-Self, 71
Surya tradition, 182
Surya-tradition techinque, 182
Sushruta, 204
sushumna, 181
Suzuki (Dr), 247-48
SWOT analysis (Strength, Weakness, Opportunity, Threats), 42, 255
symbols of stress, 197
synchronistic events, 22, 84
system of,
soul-psychic sleuthing, 3
yoga, 232
Tabor meditation, 186
tantra, 87
Tantric yogis, 143
Taoist wisdom texts, 31

TAROT (Trend Analysis by Relative Opinion Testing), 86, 155
TAROT analysis,
  use of, 89
task of,
  psychology, 234
  sleuthing, 250
Tauler, 11
technique of psychometry, 145
Technological inventions, 260
technology of psychometry, 262
tejaleshya,
  psychic powers of, 134
telegnosis, 222-23
  faculty of, 223
telekinesis, 139
telekinetic energy, 139
teleological causation, 223-224
telepathic command of God, 153
telepathic communication(s), 95, 114, 123, 159-60
  strength of, 127
telepathic conversations, 155
telepathic dialling, 106
telepathic interaction, 126, 153
telepathic nature, 194
telepathic network, 152
telepathic poaching, 225
telepathic practices, 127
telepathic process, 113
telepathic readings, 212
telepathic receiver, 126, 179
telepathic receptivity, 155
telepathic senders, 153
telepathic sense enhancement, 154
Telepathic sense, 153, 155-56
telepathic sensitivity, 155
telepathic signal(s), 123, 152, 158, 161, 223
telepathic situation, 153
Telepathic talent demonstration, 127
telepathic thought-impressions, 146
telepathic thoughts, 222
telepathic thought-targeting, 123
telepathic transmission, 121
telepathic transmitter, 223
telepathic TV, 190
telepathists, 164
telepathy, 30-31, 36-37, 49-51, 91-92, 94-95, 98, 112, 127, 144, 150-52, 162, 223-24, 227, 236, 238, 254, 258
  basis of, 109
  complexities of, 153
  faculties of, 227
  foundation of, 113
  medium for, 161
  perspective of, 118
  power(s) of, 108-09
  soul-psychic techniques of, 52
Tele-picturesque-spots, 144
teleportation of human beings, 140
Teleportation, 63, 139-40
ten sets of predictions, 221
termiantion-tendency of visual perception, 62
terror-stricken emotions, 142
theological problems, 21
thermo-nuclear power reactor, 141
third sensitive centre, 209
third-eye or eyebrow *chakra*, 82, 180, 182
third-eye sight, 165

thought command, 113
Thought impressions, 212
thought ripple, 141
thought transference, 91, 98, 214, 222-23
  application of, 22
thoughtograph, 145
Thoughtography, 144-45
thoughtons, 152
thoughts,
  kinds of, 121
thought-wave influences, 111
thought-waves, 103, 109, 113-14, 152
Tibetan Buddhism,
  desciplines of, 143
Tibetan Buddhists, 141-42
Tibetan deity, 141
Tibetan lamas,
  Generations of, 207
time-concept, 63
time-travel,
  path of, 165
Tolstoy, 51
tradition of *tulpa*, 141
transcendental meditation, 186
transcendental potential, 249
transfer of motor impulses, 133
transgressor of,
  moral laws, 234
  spiritual laws, 234
transhuman state of consciousness, 225
transitoriness,
  laughter of, 240
transmigration of soul, 149
transmission of thoughts, 122
true knowledge, 232
truth of unity, 29
truth,
  knowledge of, 28
Tsu Tse, 34
Tukaram Maharaj, 234
tulpa(s), 140-42
  nature of, 141
  tradition of, 141
type(s) of,
  foresight, 94
  perception, 103
UFO(s) mysteries, 146
unbounded possibilities, 47
unconscious mind, 68-69
  purification of, 125
unconscious tuning mechanism, 152
unfolding of consciousness, 165
Unidentified Flying Objects (UFOs), 145
unification of consciousness, 183
Unified Theory of Relativity, 263
Universal Consciousness, 26, 204
Universal Intelligence, 18
universal knowledge, 28
Universal Mind, 74, 119
unknown information, 191
unnecessary thinking, 197
Unprecedented progress, 255
unspoken thoughts, 121
Upanishadic seers, 203
Upanishads, 11
Use of EEG, 93
use of TAROT analysis, 89
utterances of,
  beliefs, 128

ideas, 128
vagaries of nature, 156
validity of laws, 168
variety(ies) of,
circumstances, 231
knowledge, 166
various kinds of beings, 234
various meditations, 186
various schools of mental healing, 193
Vasiliev, I. Leonid (Dr), soviet para, 133
Vasishtha (Rishi), 202, 204
Veda(s), 28, 206-07
Vedanta, 72
doctrine of, 234
Vedanta *darshan*, 208
Vedantic philosophy, 56
Vedantic view, 131
Vedic era, 28
Vedic knowledge, 204
Vedic psychology, 231-32
Vedic rishis, 204
Vedic times, 82, 188
Vedic tradition, 28
Vedvyasa, son of Parashara, 204
velocity of light, 244
vibration(s) of,
high tension wire, 185
magnetic waves, 137
infinite potencies of, 143
Victoria, Queen, 131
violent emotional forces, 135
Vishnu, 202
Vishuddhananda (Swami), 143
Vishvamitra, 202
vision of God, 202
visual concentration,
act of, 180
visual hallucinations, 100
visual organ,
mechanism of, 60
visual perception,
periphery of, 62
visual perception,
termiantion-tendency of, 62
visualization, 190
vital energy, 198
Vivekananda (Swami), 94, 158
Walsch, Neale Donald, 33
warm-blooded human being, 261
wave-like patterns of motion, 121
weapons of mass destruction (WMD), 13
Wells , H.G., 66
Western cultures, 155
wheel of,
life, 245
Time, 53
Wilde, Oscar, 131
will-power,
degree of, 126
wireless stations, 50
wisdom-energy, 61
Witchcraft Clairvoyance, 199
witness-consciousness,
state of, 46
Wittgenstein, Ludwig, 5
women's intuition, 97
Worf, L. Benjamin, 58
world(s) of,
ignorance, 45

knowledge, 212
wow factor, 125
Yoga, 232, 238
system of, 232
yoga *darshan*, 208
Yoga Nidra, 126, 128
Yoga philosophy, 249
Yoga psychology, 231
Yogananda, Paramahamsa, 3, 4, 152
Yogavasishtha, 204
Yogic techinque, 181
Yogic view, 232
York, Donald (Neuro-physiologist), 113
Zarathustra, 247